FLORIDA'S
LIVING BEACHES

A Guide for the Curious Beachcomber

FLORIDA'S
LIVING BEACHES
A Guide for the Curious Beachcomber

Blair and Dawn Witherington

Pineapple Press, Inc.
Sarasota, Florida

To our parents

Front Cover Photographs
St. Joseph Peninsula beach
Hatchling loggerhead sea turtle
    (Caretta caretta)
Rough scallops *(Lindapecten muscosus)*
Royal tern *(Sterna maxima)*
Blue button *(Porpita porpita)*
Lined sea star *(Luidia clathrata)*
Pelagic sargassum *(Sargassum fluitans)*

Hamburger beans *(Mucuna* spp.)
Railroad vine *(Ipmoea pes-caprae)*
Seaglass

Back Cover
Great blue heron *(Ardea herodias)*

Front Flap
Common purple sea snail *(Janthina janthina)*

Text, photographs, and illustrations copyright © 2007, 2010 by Blair and Dawn Witherington
unless otherwise noted

Inquiries should be addressed to:

Pineapple Press, Inc.
P.O. Box 3889
Sarasota, Florida 34230

www.pineapplepress.com

Library of Congress Cataloging-in-Publication Data

Witherington, Blair E., 1962-
  Florida's living beaches : a guide for the curious beachcomber / Blair and Dawn Witherington.
-- 1st ed.
      p. cm.
   Includes index.
   ISBN 978-1-56164-386-8 (pbk. : alk. paper)
  1. Seashore animals--Florida--Identification. 2. Seashore plants--Florida--Identification. 3.
Beaches--Florida. 4. Beachcombing--Florida. I. Witherington, Dawn. II. Title.
   QL169.W58 2007
   591.769'9--dc22
                         2006100378

First Edition
13 12 11 10 9 8 7 6

Design by Blair and Dawn Witheringon
Printed in China

Contents

Acknowledgments and Photo Credits

For their contributions, reviews, and advice we are greatly indebted to Dean Bagley, Alice Bard, Mike Blanchard, Michael Bresette, Paul Choate, Meghan Conti, Carrie Crady, Terry Doonan, Curtis Ebbesmeyer, Kevin Edwards, the Florida Fish and Wildlife Conservation Commission, Bill Frank, Mac Hatcher, Laura Herren, Shigetomo Hirama, Karen Holloway-Adkins, Inwater Research Group, Ron Johns, Steve Johnson, Suzanne Kennedy (www.floravista.com), Maura Kraus, Stacy Kubis, Adam Lambert, Kevin Lilly, J.B. Miller, Ray Mojica, Ed Perry, Tom Pitchford, Anne Rudloe, Jack Rudloe, Thomas Scott, Megan Stolen, and Ricardo Zambrano.

Photographs are © Blair Witherington and Dawn Witherington unless listed below:

Page 21 top, © Collier County Property Appraiser
Page 23 bottom, © Shutterstock, Inc.
Page 24 bottom, © Shutterstock, Inc.
Page 25 top, courtesy of NOAA
Page 25 center, courtesy of USGS
Page 26 top, © Photodisc, Inc.
Page 26 top, © Photodisc, Inc.
Page 26 bottom, courtesy of NASA
Page 28 bottom, © Sebastian Inlet SP
Page 29 top, © Collier County Property Appraiser
Page 29 bottom, © Environmentally Endangered Lands Program, Brevard
Page 43 top, © Bill Frank
Page 43 bottom, © Dave Norris
Page 152 center, © Stacy Kubis
Page 157 top, © Shigetomo Hirama

Page 159 bottom, © Shutterstock Inc.
Page 165 bottom, © Kevin Edwards
Page 171 center, © Kevin Edwards
Page 172 center, © Kevin Edwards
Page 172 bottom, © Kevin Edwards
Page 191 bottom, © Kevin Edwards
Page 192 bottom, © Ricardo Zambrano
Page 195 top, © Kevin Edwards
Page 195 center, © Kevin Edwards
Page 196 bottom, © Shutterstock Inc.
Page 197 © Florida FWC and Florida DEP
Page 198 top, © Steve Johnson
Page 198 center, © Shutterstock Inc.
Page 200 top, © Shutterstock Inc.
Page 200 center, © Tom Pitchford
Page 200 bottom, © Tom Pitchford
Page 201 bottom, © Hubbs SeaWorld
Page 301 bottom, courtesy of NOAA

Florida's Top Fifty Living Beaches

Every Florida beach has life, but some beaches stand out as vibrant examples of natural processes free to run their course. These are not beaches devoid of humans (many are among the most visited shores in the state). But they are beaches where our influence has been more casual than insistent. In geographic order the list includes:

1. Santa Rosa Island
2. Topsail Hill to Grayton Beach
3. St. Andrews Beach and Shell Island
4. Crooked Island
5. St. Joseph Peninsula
6. St. Vincent Island
7. St. George Island
8. Dog Island
9. Alligator Point
10. Anclote Keys
11. Honeymoon Island
12. Caladesi Island
13. Mullet & Shell Keys
14. Egmont Key
15. Midnight Pass Beach, Casey Key
16. Caspersen Beach, Manasota Key
17. Stump Pass and Don Pedro Is. (Little Gasparilla)
18. Cayo Costa
19. Captiva Island
20. Sanibel Island
21. Lovers Key
22. Barefoot Beach
23. Keewadin, Rookery Bay
24. Tigertail Beach, Marco Is.
25. Cape Romano
26. Cape Sabal
27. Dry Tortugas
28. Boca Grande Key
29. Bahia Honda Key
30. Long Key
31. Elliott Key
32. Cape Florida
33. Lloyd Beach
34. Spanish River to South Beach Parks, Boca Raton
35. MacArthur Beach
36. Blowing Rocks Preserve
37. Hobe Sound Refuge
38. Walton Rocks to Ft. Pierce, Hutchinson Is.
39. Archie Carr Refuge
40. Cape Canaveral
41. Canaveral Seashore
42. Smyrna Dunes
43. North Peninsula Beach
44. Washington Oaks Beach
45. Ft. Matanzas Beach
46. Anastasia Island
47. Guana River Beach
48. Little Talbot Island
49. Southern Amelia Island
50. Fort Clinch

The Beaches are Alive!

Yes, Florida's beaches are alive. Some of this beach-life is obvious. Stroll onto the beach, sink your toes in the sand, and look around you. On the dune-front, gulls glide above flagging sea oats. On the open beach, crabs toss sand from their burrows. And at the tide line, shorebirds busily poke and turn the clumps of seaweed.

Look closer and you'll see even greater evidence of life. The seashore is vibrant with dozens of dune-plant species; a diverse array of seashells; birds that dive, run, wade and soar; and the wrack—that ever-changing line of formerly floating drift-stuff from faraway.

Clearly, beaches attract, foster, and collect life . . . and the testament of life. But in an important way, beaches are also alive themselves. Beaches and dunes grow, diminish, evolve over years, and shift with the seasons. To pulsate with change is the very nature of a sandy sea coastline. Such change is the essence of what makes beaches so fascinating.

In the long term, beaches are tumultuous, even dangerous places. Yet, a short-term visit allows a pleasant acquaintance with the beauty generated by all that turmoil. Beaches are the easily accessible margins of a spectacular wilderness—the sea. To visit a beach is to peer into that wilderness and even examine it closely, for much of the sea's mysterious nature ends up on its beaches.

We hope that this book will provide some helpful interpretation for the curious seashore visitor. In part, it is a guide to critters, plants, formations, and stuff that might be puzzling enough to go nameless without a little assistance. But an additional aspect of this book is to share the mystery and intrigue of many things that are easily identified but little known. From the elegant to the plain, from the provocative to the mundane, everything on a beach has a story to tell.

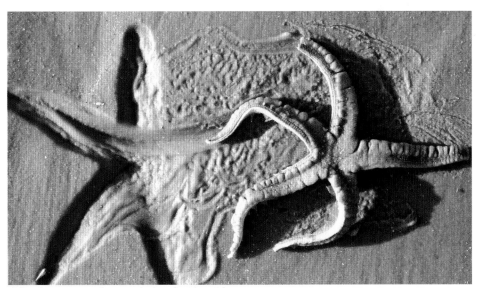

A lined sea star awakens on the beach at low tide

How the Story Unfolds

This book is organized into sections dividing major groups of beach stuff—Beach Features, Beach Animals, Beach Plants, Beach Minerals, and Hand of Man. Within each section, groups of related items are presented together and share an identifying icon at the top corner of the page.

Most items have a map showing where and when one might find it on a Florida beach. These ranges pertain specifically to an item's beach distribution, which may be different from the places it occupies when not on a beach. For instance, many of the plants that produce drifting seeds known as seabeans live far away within inland tropical rainforests. Few of these plants live in Florida, but their attractive floating seeds show up on Florida beaches at particular places and times (due to rivers, ocean currents, and weather). Coastal lines on the maps are **red** if they describe a warm-season distribution and **blue** if they describe a range during cooler months. **Purple** lines pertain to all seasons. Each line is solid where an item is relatively common, and is dotted where relatively uncommon. Because the range maps are not absolute, a gap may indicate either rarity or uncertainty. All maps show a gap along Florida's Big Bend, where the marshy, submerged coastline has little or no sandy beach.

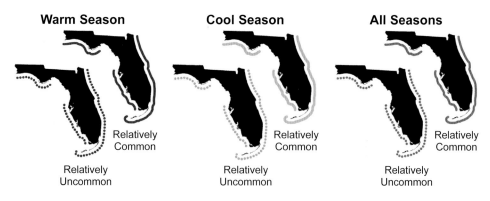

Because this is a guide to beach-found things, all the depictions are of things found on a beach. That is, some are likely to show a beach-worn look. Although we've tried to represent the living elegance of creatures, some are merely deceased lumps and blobs by the time they reach a beach.

Note that where an item's size is given, the measure refers to maximum length or height unless otherwise indicated. Also note that a few featured items hold the potential for an unpleasant encounter. These will have a hands-off symbol 🚫, which we hope you will see before you put one of these items in your pocket.

Rather than simply set the scene, introduce a cast of characters, and leave you hanging, we've tried to end with the motivation for an endeavor, or as we refer to them, quests. These target a selection of rare, beautiful, or otherwise compelling hope-to-finds that can provide a blanket excuse for beach adventure.

Blair and Dawn Witherington

BEACH FEATURES

What is a Beach Feature?

Beach features are life-signs of the beach itself. These signs reveal a beach's relationships, growth, withdrawal, and restless movement (yes, beaches move). Although much of this book describes beach things, this *Beach Features* section deals mostly with processes and the evidence they leave.

Beach features help describe the relationship between land and sea. Some may see this relationship as a battle, but another view sees an association with mutual exchange. However harsh or congenial it is, one of the most important elements in the land-sea relationship is sand. The land stakes claim to former seabottom blown into mounds (the dune) and covers its claim with pioneering greenery. But the sand is just a loan. In the economy of sand, this currency shifts between land and sea, between undersea features, between beach elevations, and between adjacent beaches. The fluid dynamics of this bustling economy can be read in a beach's features. To an educated eye, beach features are both telling evidence of history and indicators for prediction.

The give-and-take between land and sea also involves energy. As you'll see, beach features include exchanges of heat, wind, waves, and biological material that further define the beach economy.

To a true beach aficionado, an otherwise pedestrian pile of sand offers a host of signs exclaiming a beach's beating pulse. Sensing that pulse is basic to understanding what beaches are all about and can add wonder and intrigue to a coastal visit.

Good fishermen can read the features of a beach and surf to find their catch

Beach Anatomy

Each visit to a Florida beach is unique. No two beaches are exactly alike, and at any given beach, every day is different. But despite their dynamic forms, beaches tend to share a common anatomy that is predictable based on location and season.

You may have noticed that Florida beaches have a lot of sand. Most of this sand is quartz (once part of the Appalachian Mountains), although Florida Keys beaches are largely carbonate grit from the crushed skeletons of coralline algae and crusty critters. Shell bits make up most of the rest of our beach sands, which also have variable amounts of heavy sediments like metal oxides. Sand character varies between beaches, seasons, and the parts of a beach's anatomy. Finer grains are found on beaches fronting calm seas (like the Gulf of Mexico), during calm summer months, and in dunes. Coarser grains are found on steep, rough beaches, during winter, and on the lower beach.

Within each beach, anatomy is laid out relative to elevation above the sea. These beach zones range from high, dry, and occasionally wave-washed (the **dune**), to frequently wave-washed (the **backshore**), to constantly wave-washed (the **foreshore**). Further seaward are two zones critical to the beach (and formerly beach themselves): the **nearshore** and **offshore** zones.

Within each zone are the lumps, bumps, dips, waves, and wave-washed stuff that further describe a beach's structure. The **dune scarp**, if present, marks the elevation

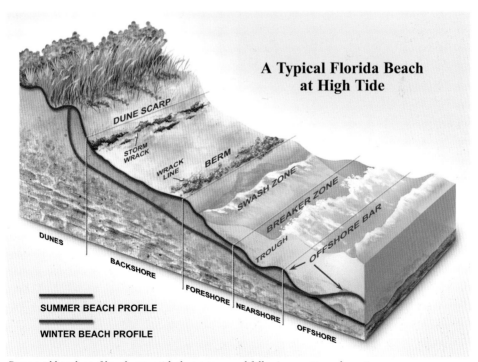

Dune and beach profiles change with the seasons and following events such as storms

where recent storms have swept away dune sands. Between the dune base and the daily high-tide mark lie one or more **wrack lines**, the piles of marine organisms (mostly seaweed) that in their death bring life to the beach. The highest average tide generally reaches the **berm**, a sandy platform between the flat backshore and the sloped foreshore. Beach meets sea at the **swash zone**, where waves rush the sandy incline and wash back into the following breaker. Often, this final pounding of wave energy creates a step-down into a **trough** landward of the **breaker zone**. The breakers begin where the **offshore bar** presents a rise shallow enough to trip incoming waves.

All of this anatomy changes between winter and summer, storm and calm. Compared to a summer beach fronting calm seas, winter and storm beaches tend to be steeper with little or no berm and a distant offshore bar. Artificially nourished (man-made) beaches begin with an engineered anatomy but equilibrate over a period of years as the sea sculpts the foreshore, then backshore, then dune.

Florida's beaches vary according to how they dissipate or reflect waves. Dissipating beaches are flat with fine sands, variable width, and have most of their sand in long offshore bars. Northeast Florida has predominantly dissipating beach types. Reflective beaches are steep with coarse sands, consistently narrow width, and have most of their sands within the upper beach and foredune. Reflective beaches make up most of Florida's central Atlantic coast. Beaches that are intermediate between these two types are common along the Gulf coast.

An Atlantic beach in a winter profile

A beachcomber who knows a little beach anatomy and coastal weather often finds the best beach stuff. The ocean scatters its varied treasures in different beach zones depending on its mood (sea conditions).

Combing the swash zone (**A**) at low tide is the best way to find small and delicate seashells. When a stiff onshore wind is blowing, this is also the place to find blue animals (oceanic drifters). The recent high-tide line at mid-beach (**B**) is normally the best place to find large or fluttery shells, buoyant items like seabeans, and invertebrates like sponges and soft corals. Keep in mind that the high-tide wrack from previous days may have been higher up the beach (**C**), where drift treasures can be found if they have not been covered with sand. The largest waves during the highest tides sweep up the beach to the storm wrack (**D**), which is often at the base of the dune. Although wrack-hunting is fruitful for almost anything immediately after a storm, even months-old storm wrack yields persistent, storm-stranded items like big shells, seabeans, driftwood, and lost cargo. Storm wrack on infrequently combed beaches is filled with rare finds.

Lettered areas show where to find beach treasures

Beach anatomy becomes less esoteric and more real to visitors who experience features forming before their eyes. **Aeolian** (wind-driven) **transport** of sand is but one of these watchable developmental processes. To experience sand flowing over a beach on a breezy day is to witness the origins and pulsation of many beach features. As sand rolls across the beach, some features are exposed, others are buried, sand ripples march with the wind, and the growth of a dune from seed begins at a seaweed clump that had drifted at sea for hundreds of miles.

Old storm-wrack provides the seed for a new dune

Aeolian transport of sand

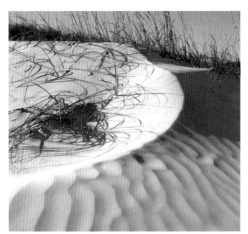

Central Atlantic coast

Southern Gulf coast

The Panhandle has some of Florida's largest dunes

Dunes

WHAT ARE THEY? Dunes are piles of wind-blown sand stabilized by fast-growing, salt-tolerant "pioneer" plants. Although the primary (most seaward) dune may be swept by storm tides every few years, the more stable back dunes often support semi-permanent woody vegetation between severe storms. Dunes are part of a sand "banking" system in which the beach makes continuous deposits and withdrawals.

SIZE: Small mounds to promontories more than 40 ft (12 m) high.

HOW COME? Dunes form when onshore winds blow beach sand into wind shadows behind old wrack lines and vegetation. Pioneer plants colonize these sand spits, their roots keep the sand from migrating windward, and the dune grows into a shore-parallel dune ridge.

FOUND: All beaches. Keys dunes tend to be small. Larger dunes form where there is a strong sea breeze, extensive sand supply, and unfettered plant growth. Beachfront development often levels the dune and prevents reformation.

SEASONS: All year. Rapid erosion and formation can occur during hurricanes.

DID YOU KNOW? Dune formation has made much of the Florida we see today. Dig a hole into the peninsula and you will likely find sand that was blown from a beach into an ancient dune.

Salt Pruning

WHAT IS IT? Salt pruning describes the trimming effects of salt spray. This process creates dune shrubs and trees with a sloping-hedge appearance.

SIZE: Salt spray can sculpt century-old live oaks into wavelike forms that are knee-high on their seaward side and well overhead on their protected side.

Sea grape

HOW COME? Salt spray from breaking waves settles on the outer leaves of dune plants. Evaporation of this spray leaves behind concentrated salt that can enter leaves through abrasions caused by wind-whipping. The salt gradually kills the most exposed, windward leaves. This trimming stimulates extensive branching, which produces dense, windward canopies. Salt pruning results in bonsai-looking shrubs that lean away from the sea. Like bonsai, the beautiful forms of salt-pruned dune shrubs are acquired over decades.

Sand live oak

FOUND: Beaches with mature dunes and woody vegetation. Northeast Florida and the Panhandle have some of the most picturesque examples of salt pruning.

SEASONS: All seasons, although most of the actual pruning occurs during the driest months when there is little rain to wash salt from exposed leaves.

DID YOU KNOW? Salt-spray resistance dictates which plants exist on the dune. Survivors of this torture benefit by having few plant-competitors.

Yaupon holly

Seagrass wrack in the Florida Keys

Sargassum wrack on the mid-Atlantic coast

A ruddy turnstone forages in the wrack

Wrack Lines

WHAT ARE THEY? Wrack lines, or strand lines, are lengthy piles of floating marine stuff that has washed in with the tide. Wrack tends to be composed mostly of the alga sargassum, uprooted sea-grasses, and reedy marsh plants. Much of this book contains descriptions of the varied animals, plants, and debris that occur in the wrack.

SIZE: Although knee-high piles are common following rough weather, under calm conditions a beach may be starved of wrack for weeks.

HOW COME? Everything that goes around comes around. This is especially true for organisms floating at sea. After years of roundabout travel in surface currents, these plants and animals often end up on a beach somewhere.

FOUND: All beaches, although the components of the wrack vary by region. There may be many wrack lines on a beach indicating where the tides have reached. Old wrack may remain high on the beach for weeks before disappearing under sand.

SEASONS: Wrack lines can be extensive in fall and spring following storms.

DID YOU KNOW? At the end of their life's journey, the plants and animals that wash onto beaches provide the base of an important beach food web. Many of the beach's most appealing animals would be absent were it not for the lowly wrack.

Beach Cusps and Scarps

Beach Cusps

Beach Scarps

WHAT ARE THEY? Cusps are waves in the sand on the lower beach, cresting and dipping at regular intervals. **Scarps** are cliffs in the beach marking the recent line where erosion has taken sand.

SIZE: Cusps and scarps are generally 1–6 ft (0.3–2 m) high. Scarps following hurricanes can be 12 ft (3.5 m) or more.

HOW COME? Cusps form when persistent winds blow at an oblique angle to the beach. These winds drive the longshore current and the "edge wave" in the surf, which create a series of circulations that crest sand into cusps. Scarps form due to rapid erosion, often within a single tidal cycle. They form following storms or after periods of sand buildup (accretion). Scarps form when there are stiff winds and a strong longshore current.

FOUND: All beaches. Steep beaches with coarse-grained sands have the most pronounced cusps. Many artificial (nourished) beaches have persistent scarps because of the cementing nature of artificially pumped sands.

SEASONS: Cusps are common in summer as beaches are building and scarps are common in the stormier fall, winter, and spring.

DID YOU KNOW? Cusps move slowly in wave-like fashion down the beach. Large scarps in the dune can persist for years.

Partially scarped beach cusps

A collapsing beach scarp

9

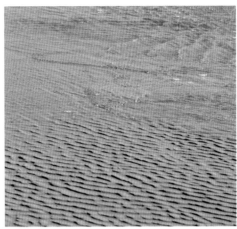

Tide runnel with current ripples

Wind ripples; arrow shows wind direction

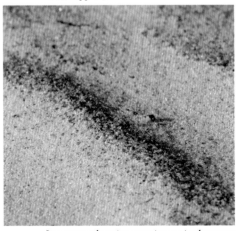

Larger sand grains remain on ripple crests

Sand Ripples

WHAT ARE THEY? Sand ripples are elongate miniature dunes arranged perpendicular to the swift wind or current that formed them.

SIZE: Remarkably, sand ripples are almost always about 3 in (7.5 cm) from crest to crest.

HOW COME? There is much debate. A widely accepted explanation is that ripples are formed and spaced by how far a sand grain can leap. Wind and water move sand by saltation: sand grains leaping, bouncing, and jostling other grains that further leap, bounce, and jostle others. The horizontally leaping grains are more likely to land where there is a slight rise, and these rises gain sand. The "wavelength" between rises is about how far grains can leap over the wind/current shadows between crests. As crests get too high, their exposed grains leap to the next ripple. Ripples move slowly downwind or down current.

FOUND: All medium- to fine-grained beaches, in dry sand, and in runnels (mid-beach, water-filled troughs).

SEASONS: Ripples form during winds greater than 15 mph (24 kph) and when runnels flow on falling tides.

DID YOU KNOW? Ripple crests tend to have larger grains, which occasionally shades crests and troughs with contrasting colors.

Dark Sands and Shell Hash

WHAT ARE THEY? **Dark sands** are thin layers of the heaviest (densest) mineral grains on the beach. **Shell hash** describes surface patches of mollusk shell-shards.

SIZE: Dark sand layers are typically less than 1/4 in (6.5 mm) thick. Shell hash may be a foot (30 cm) or more thick and cover thousands of square feet.

HOW COME? Dark sands appear following storm erosion. Sands appear "dirty," but are perfectly "clean" minerals that make up a tiny fraction of the beach's sand grains. The mineral grains are mostly iron and titanium oxides, the heaviest on the beach. They tend to settle together in sheets and are last to suspend in wave-wash. Shell hash forms from mollusk shells broken into shards. Rounded, polished pieces of all sizes exist on the beach. After a period of rough surf, the largest shell shards settle out first in patches that are often concentrated in the upper swash zone at low tide.

FOUND: Dark sands and shell hash are common on steep beaches. Coarse sands on the southwest coast speckled with dark grains contain fossil bits blackened by iron compounds.

SEASONS: All seasons, but most common during calm periods after storms.

DID YOU KNOW? Dark sands contain tiny grains of semi-precious gemstones. Shell hash often contains seaglass.

Dark mineral sands in layers following erosion

A patch of shell hash

11

Shorebirds feeding in the swash zone

Swash marks studded with fluttery shells

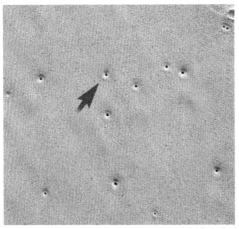
Bubble holes

Swash and Backwash

WHAT IS IT? Swash and **backwash** are the sweeps of water from spent waves. Swash rushes up onto the beach and backwash flows down into the next wave. This wave-lapping moves sand, creates lines and bubble holes, and defines an important home for critters in the sand.

SIZE: From a few feet (about 1 m) to over 100 ft (30 m) wide.

HOW COME? The distant energy that produced a wave is finally spent in the swash zone. Sand in this zone can have air trapped within a mushy matrix. As the backwash recedes, air bubbling out makes nail-sized **bubble holes**. The most landward travel of each swash also leaves tiny, ridgeline **swash marks** from swept-in sand. Swash sands have unique properties. Seawater soaking into the porous beach transforms the sand into a liquidlike medium giving animals like mole crabs and coquina clams a momentary opportunity to sand-swim.

FOUND: All beaches. Larger waves mean a wider swash zone.

SEASONS: All seasons.

DID YOU KNOW? The swash zone is not quite beach and not quite sea. It is probably the liveliest part of the beach, being home to crabs, clams, and worms that feed a host of birds, fishes, and other animals. See the *Beach Animals* section for tracks, burrows, and other evidence of these swash-zone critters.

Sea Foam

Particularly sudsy sea foam

WHAT IS IT? Sea foam is the white, greenish, or brownish froth brought to the beach by breaking waves.

SIZE: Most sea foam probably comes from diatoms, which are microscopic single-celled plants in glasslike capsules. The foam they generate in the wave wash is generally the consistency of a good stout beer, but airy sea foam can occasionally roll from the swash in thick suds rivaling any bubble bath.

HOW COME? Sea foam originates from a wide range of mostly planktonic (small and drifting) plants and animals. Wind and surface currents bring billions of these tiny critters to the surf where their cells are pulverized and their fat is whipped into suds.

FOUND: All beaches.

Sanderlings forage near brownish sea foam

SEASONS: Sea foam is generated when there are nearby "blooms" of plankton and when local sea conditions are rough enough to whip the plankton into froth. Spring and summer tend to have the foamiest surf.

DID YOU KNOW? Most sea foam is harmless. However, bursting sea-foam bubbles during a red-tide event can release algal toxins that severely irritate the nose and throat.

Sea foam comes from pulverized plankton

13

Former dune downdrift from an inlet jetty

A dune becomes beach

Post-storm erosion

Sand Erosion

WHAT IS IT? Erosion is beach-sand loss. Of course, the sand isn't really lost. It just goes someplace else. The term "critical erosion" is used to describe sand loss that threatens buildings on the dune.

SIZE: It is common to lose 1–2 ft (30–60 cm) of sand depth after a moderate storm. During hurricanes, 10 ft (3 m) of sand can disappear in a matter of hours.

HOW COME? Erosion comes from waves and currents. Waves suspend the sand and currents carry it away. Erosion is constant, even on beaches that seem to be growing. When accretion (sand build-up) is out-paced by erosion, beaches become steeper and shorter. This net erosion can occur rapidly during storms that drive rough surf and strong longshore currents. Chronic erosion can occur where updrift inlets and jetties intercept the longshore flow of replacement sands.

FOUND: All beaches. Occasionally, net erosion can "sink" beaches at the ends of barrier islands. Where dunes are replaced by coastal armoring, short, eroded beaches become nonexistent beaches.

SEASONS: Most erosion occurs late fall through winter. Profound erosion can occur during intense storms.

DID YOU KNOW? Sand that erodes from beaches generally goes no farther than the offshore bar. After severe storms, this bar widens to become exposed beach at low tide.

Sand Accretion

WHAT IS IT? **Accretion** is beach sand build-up. Accretion and erosion (sand loss) are the yin and yang of Florida's beaches. Their dynamic balance maintains beaches as open and sandy places.

SIZE: Beach accretion is noticeable when things on the upper beach get covered with sand. Logs and other large items on the lower beach may be buried in sand within a single tidal cycle.

HOW COME? Accreting sand comes from eroding updrift beaches (up the longshore current stream) and from the eroding offshore sand bar. Accretion is typically more gradual than erosion. During calm periods, breakers suspend sand and carry it up the beach-face where the sand falls out of suspension. To understand the perpetual nature of a beach's dynamic sand balance, watch your footprint disappear after a single wave wash.

FOUND: All beaches. Some beaches, such as those updrift from inlets and passes, may experience years of net accretion (more accretion than erosion).

SEASONS: Most accretion occurs gradually during summer. Rapid accretion can occur during or after intense storms.

DID YOU KNOW? Although beach erosion makes headlines, beach accretion takes place in obscurity. Judging only by news reports, there should be nothing left of Florida.

A post-hurricane beach, Brevard County

The beach in the top photo after one accretion season

A sign of accretion

15

An exposed sandbar on New Smyrna Beach

Sandbars are favored loafing spots for seabirds

A brownish sandbar and greenish trough

Sandbars

WHAT IS IT? A beach's **sandbar** (also called the longshore bar) is a long, narrow shoal just off the beach and parallel to the coast. A trough separates the sandbar from the beach.

SIZE: From 50 ft (15 m) to more than 1000 ft (300 m) off the beach, and in 3–20 ft (1–6 m) of water. The shallowest bars are often exposed at the lowest tides.

HOW COME? The sandbar is part of the beach's sand exchange system, which also includes the dune, updrift and downdrift beaches, and offshore shoals. The sandbar typically has the most sand when the beach has the least, and vice-versa. A bar that is removed will re-form at the expense of the beach.

FOUND: Nearly all beaches. Beaches with gentle slopes have the most pronounced sandbars.

SEASONS: The summer bar is typically smaller and closer to the beach than the winter bar.

DID YOU KNOW? After a severe hurricane, sandbars swell with the sand eroded from the beach and dune. Extensive beach-sand loss can be mirrored by a similar increase in sandbar elevation. Much of this sand returns quickly (in weeks) to nearby beaches. The sandbar is home to a varied array of small animals living within its shifting sands.

Ridges and Runnels (Lagoons)

WHAT ARE THEY? Beach **ridges** are exposed sandbars or berms that have been breached by high tides. **Runnels** are mid-beach troughs that are filled with water at high tide and may linger as **"beach lagoons"** at low tide.

SIZE: Ridges may be up to hundreds of feet wide at low water. Runnels may be equally wide and up to 6 ft (2 m) deep.

HOW COME? Ridges and runnels indicate a beach in transition. Offshore sand bars become beach ridges when they have swelled with sand from the eroded beach. Runnels are troughs formerly carved by longshore currents or by water-flow after flooding tides. Ridges often trap water from the high-tide swash. This water may persist when muddy sediment slows drainage through the sand. Some ridges grow into barrier islands, and some runnels grow into persistent lagoons.

FOUND: Most common on the fine-grained, intermediate-sloped beaches of northeastern Florida and the Gulf.

SEASONS: All seasons. Ridges and runnels often form following storm erosion and on accreting beaches during very high and low tides.

DID YOU KNOW? Runnels that persist as lagoons become important areas for beach life. Receding waters concentrate trapped invertebrates and small fishes, which in turn attract shorebirds and wading birds.

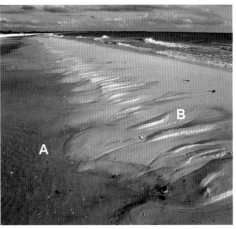

A beach runnel (A) and ridge (B) at low tide

An egret haunts a beach lagoon

A Panhandle beach lagoon at dusk

17

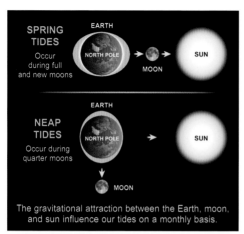

SPRING TIDES

Occur during full and new moons

EARTH
NORTH POLE
MOON → SUN

NEAP TIDES

Occur during quarter moons

EARTH
NORTH POLE → SUN
MOON

The gravitational attraction between the Earth, moon, and sun influence our tides on a monthly basis.

The highest tides occur when sun and moon align

Phases of the Moon

NEW — FIRST QUARTER

FULL — LAST QUARTER

Tidal amplitude is related to moon phase.
A lunar month is 27 1/2 days.

Tidal cycles are linked to moon phase

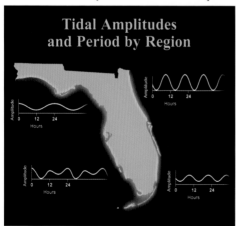

Tidal Amplitudes and Period by Region

Florida tides vary between diurnal and semidiurnal

Tides

WHAT ARE THEY? Tides are periodic changes in local sea level.

SIZE: Average amplitudes between high and low tide vary: 5 ft (1.5 m) in northeast Florida, 1.5 ft (45 cm) in the Keys, and 1 ft (30 cm) in the Panhandle.

HOW COME? Tides can be predicted from the Earth's position relative to the sun and moon. Their celestial gravity pulls a water bulge around the planet's oceans and sets the Gulf into rhythmic sloshing between its middle and margin.

FOUND: Atlantic beach tides are **semidiurnal**, meaning that every 24 hours sees two sets of high and low tides. Northern Gulf beaches have **diurnal** tides, with only one low and one high each day. In southwest Florida the tides are mixed, having two sets of tides per day with one low and one high being dominant.

SEASONS: Spring tides, when highs are highest and lows are lowest, generally occur near full- and new-moon periods. **Neap tides** have the smallest amplitude and typically occur during quarter-moon periods. Spring and neap effects are small in the northern Gulf where these tides are offset several days from the lunar cycle.

DID YOU KNOW? High and low tides occur about 48 minutes later each day. Low barometric pressure, onshore winds, and big waves can create storm tides much higher than normal.

Waves and Surf

WHAT ARE THEY? Waves bring energy to the beach from far away. Waves that enter shallow water trip into breakers and become **surf**.

SIZE: From 1–12 ft (0.3–3.5 m) in height (measured base to crest). A typical 3-ft (1-m) wave offshore with a 10-second swell-period will evolve into about a 4-ft (1.2-m) breaker.

HOW COME? As a wave enters shallow water, it drags the bottom and slows down. This drag causes waves from many directions to gradually turn parallel to shore (to refract). At a water depth of about 1.3 times wave height, a wave breaks. Breaking occurs when the entire length of a wave piles into the shallows. Waves slow down, and become higher and steeper before breaking. The wave crest slows last and pushes ahead of the breaker. Wave crests identify three kinds of breakers: **spilling**, **plunging**, and **surging**. Spilling breakers have frothy crests flowing down the wave-front and occur when waves advance on a gentle nearshore slope. Plunging breakers have crests that curl over to crash before the wave-base and occur when large waves enter shallows with a moderate nearshore slope. Surging breakers have crests that just begin to spill when the leading wave-base slides rapidly up the beach. Surging breakers occur when the beach approach is very steep relative to wave height.

Spilling wave (crumbling wave)

Plunging wave (barreling wave)

Surging wave

19

Anatomy of a wave

A left-peeling wave puts a surfer in the green room

A grom gets boosted

FOUND: All beaches have some surf from time to time. Steep Atlantic beaches tend to have the highest surf. Reef-protected and shallow-approach beaches have the lowest surf.

SEASONS: Summer has calmer surf than the other seasons, but nearby or distant storms can bring high surf at any time.

DID YOU KNOW? Wavelength (distance crest-to-crest) greatly determines surf height. A long wavelength as indicated by a 20-second swell-period can mean that hip-high offshore waves become surf as tall as a single-story house.

SURFSPEAK: To fully appreciate surf, it helps to speak the language. Parts of the awesome wave in the top photo include the **face**, the **lip**, and the **curl**. In the middle photo, a dude gets tubed by a clean wave that peels left. In the bottom photo, a grom (grommet, or young surfer) gets boosted into a floater as the wave closes out into soup (whitewater). Other surf descriptions include **blown out** (windy-choppy conditions not good for surfing), **clean** (waves with smooth, glassy faces), **gnarly** (intimidating), **ground swell** (long swell-period waves from distant sources producing big surf), **mushy** (slow, low-power waves), **set** (an approaching group of rideable waves), **shore break** (waves that close out on the beach), **peak** (tallest wave-point where a breaker forms and peels in both directions), and **rippin'** (to shred, to make the most of available surf, including but not limited to cutbacks, slashes, airs, tailslides, 360s, chop-hops, and floaters).

Nearshore Currents

WHAT ARE THEY? Nearshore currents include the **longshore current**, which flows parallel to the beach, and **rip currents**, which flow perpendicular to the beach.

SIZE: The longshore current runs for many miles along a beach. Rip currents run only a few hundred feet (about 100 m) into a plumelike head just outside the breakers. Each current can flow at a swift walking pace.

HOW COME? The longshore current runs inside the surf and is driven by waves striking the beach at oblique angles. Longshore currents tend to run north-to-south on the Atlantic coast and east-to-west on the northern Gulf coast. Rip currents come from waves driving water into the trough between the beach and the offshore bar. This water rushes away from the beach along short-lived rip channels through the bar. Rip currents are strongest when large swells arrive near low tide.

FOUND: All beaches. Nearshore currents are strongest on beaches with high surf.

SEASONS: Nearshore currents are strongest fall through spring.

DANGERS: Rip currents and the panic they induce cause many drowning deaths. To save your life, do not swim into a rip back toward shore. Swim parallel to the beach until you exit the rip or until it subsides outside the surf.

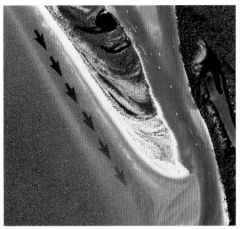

Longshore current path off Keewadin Island

A small rip in a shallow bar

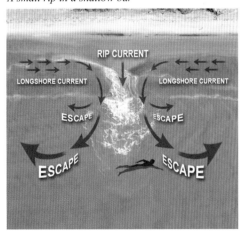

Escaping a rip current

21

Offshore Currents

Many will be surprised to learn of links between Florida beaches and faraway events. The state juts out into the Atlantic Ocean basin at the margin of the **North Atlantic Gyre**, a clockwise swirl of surface currents spanning the New and Old Worlds. These currents are pushed by easterly tropical tradewinds and include a continuous flood into the Gulf of Mexico between Yucatan and Cuba. This head of water drives the **Loop Current**, which makes a U-turn short of the Florida Panhandle. The Loop Current connects with eastward flows to squirt out of the Gulf as the **Florida Current**. After veering left and rushing due north past Florida, this ocean river evolves into the **Gulf Stream**. Examples abound showing how these ocean currents link Florida beaches with distant places and processes:

A) Warm Gulf Stream eddies spin into the cold Labrador Current to create upwellings. These conditions bring jellyfish, which feed the leatherback sea turtles that lay their eggs on Florida's Atlantic beaches.

B) Buoyant, stone-hard seabeans from Central American vines plop into rivers, float to the Caribbean, and eventually strand on Florida's coasts.

C) Airy pumice rocks blown from volcanoes in the Windward Islands bob at sea for months or years before making a Florida landfall.

D) Blisterpod fruits, palm nuts, and porcupine seeds exhaled by the Amazon rainforest are swept into ocean currents that allow an arrival in Florida after a long, circuitous journey.

E) Waters surrounding the Azores host nursery-age, current-riding, loggerhead sea turtles that first scampered to the surf as hatchlings off Florida beaches.

F) Nearly five million plastic LEGO-toy pieces spill off Land's End, England, in 1997, and begin a voyage that would end for many in the hand of a curious Florida beachcomber.

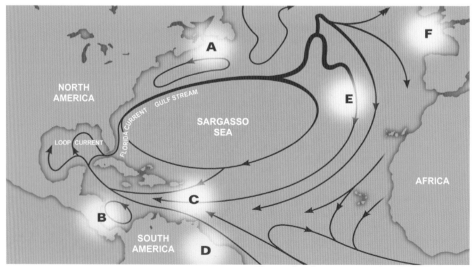

The North Atlantic Gyre and associated currents

Beach Weather

WHAT IS IT? Beach weather, described by temperature, humidity, wind, rain, and sunshine, is often different from inland weather because of a beach's closeness to the sea.

HOW COME? In warm months, inland surface air heats and begins to rise around midday. This rising air is replaced by cooler air rushing in from the coast. In summer, this pleasant **sea breeze** often makes beach air cooler than inland sites by 5° F (2° C). A strong sea breeze can postpone the arrival of inland afternoon thunderstorms to the beach by a few hours (or completely). At night, when the sea is warmer than the land, a weak land breeze (reverse sea breeze) can form, often just before dawn. In winter, the high heat capacity of the sea moderates beach temperatures, making beach areas less prone to freezes. In summer, **offshore winds** and wayward currents can drive out warm surface-waters, which are replaced by cold water from the depths. These upwellings bring a clammy chill to what would normally be sultry summer weather. **Salt spray** is unique to beaches and is a highly local-ized form of weather. A briny aerosol mist is formed during high humidity and rough surf. Sunshine really is brighter on the beach. Reflection from the sea and sand can intensify the ultraviolet light we receive. By the same token, **sunrises** and sunsets are more vivid at the beach. An open horizon and reflecting sea enhance the visual experience.

FOUND: Sea breezes, land breezes, salt spray, and sunshine occur on all beaches. Keys weather tends to have smaller sea-breeze effects, with more

Flagging sea oats show an afternoon sea breeze

Atlantic coast salt spray

An Atlantic coast sunrise

23

A pelican surfs a wave-updraft from offshore winds

A Gulf coast green flash

Beaches can be lightning hotspots

nocturnal showers in summer. The central Atlantic coast has frequent summer upwellings and occasionally dense salt spray.

SEASONS: Sea-breeze seasons are late spring through fall. Except for their moderated temperatures, beaches are most like the mainland in the winter. Passing cold fronts can make for spectacular sunsets (Gulf coast) and offshore winds perfect for surfing pelicans (Atlantic). Summer showers over the Gulf Stream either extinguish or enhance the beauty of dawn on the Atlantic coast.

DID YOU KNOW? Beachside plant species tend to be more tropical and salt-tolerant than their landward neighbors. Many species common in the Caribbean are at home on Florida's beaches. One of the most enigmatic and elusive features of a Gulf sunset is the **green flash**. It is real. The flash is visible immediately after the sun dips beneath a clear horizon under conditions without clouds or haze. The flash is the setting of the sun's spectral (rainbow) bands separated in prismlike fashion by the atmosphere. Only at sunset is the sun's intense light diminished enough to see the green flash. Red and yellow bands set before the sun does, and blue/violet bands (above the green) are scattered by blue sky. The only remaining spectral band is green.

DANGER: Sunburn increases skin-cancer risk and kills about 2000 Americans each year. Wear a hat and sunglasses and enjoy the beach at dawn and dusk. **Lightning** is a danger due to the electrical exposure of an open beach. Take shelter when thunder is heard.

Hurricanes and Other Storms

Hurricanes   Nor'easters

WHAT ARE THEY? Hurricanes and tropical storms are counterclockwise-spinning low-pressure systems with a cloud-free central eye. They come from warm seas between Africa and the Caribbean. Nor'easters are low-pressure cyclones often born in the northern Gulf Stream. Their strongest winds are not near the center as are a hurricane's.

SIZE: Disturbances from each of these storms can occupy an area larger than Florida itself. Usually a storm's greatest effects come from storm surge (elevated sea level). Florida's Gulf beaches with gradual offshore slopes have potential hurricane surges higher than 30 ft (9 m).

HOW COME? These intense storms are fueled by heat energy released from water vapor condensing and/or freezing.

FOUND: Hurricanes have affected all Florida beaches. Nor'easters have the greatest effect on Florida's north- and central-Atlantic coast.

SEASONS: Most hurricanes occur August to October. Nor'easters occur between late fall and early spring.

DID YOU KNOW? Occasional assaults by storms set back the advance of land plants, shift sands between land and sea, and foster some stunning, rugged scenery. Storms make beaches beautiful and wondrous places to visit, but scary places to live.

Hurricane Frances, 2004

A Vero Beach dune after Hurricane Frances

Captiva Island split by Hurricane Charley, 2004

25

A red tide fish-kill

Arrow shows area of red tide

Red Tide

WHAT IS IT? Red tide is a bloom (population explosion) of toxic dinoflagellates (single-celled, whip-tailed algae). In Florida, the dinoflagellate in most red tides is *Karenia brevis*. In high concentrations, a toxin made by this alga kills marine life and irritates breathing in humans. At peak bloom, red-tide algae color the water red, brown, or yellow.

SIZE: *Karenia brevis* is a fragile microscopic single cell. Its blooms can span hundreds of square miles.

HOW COME? It is unclear what triggers red-tide blooms, whether pollution plays a role, and whether these events have increased along with Florida's human population. Red-tide algae in the Gulf are common in low concentrations. Only the high-concentration blooms cause problems for humans and marine life. Respiratory troubles come from the red-tide toxin in salt-spray.

FOUND: Principally in southwest Florida. Blooms occasionally enter the northern Gulf and Atlantic coast.

SEASONS: Red tides in the Gulf occur almost every year. Red tides are least common in spring and early summer.

DID YOU KNOW? Red tides have been known from Florida's Gulf coast since the 1840s and their effects were mentioned in Spanish explorers' logs from the 1600s.

Water Color

WHAT IS IT? From the beach, seawater may appear blue, turquoise, emerald, mint-green, tea-colored, or gray-brown.

SIZE: Algae that tint seawater green are smaller than pinheads. Calcium carbonate particles are about the same size and include the bleached cells of dead algae.

Sky reflection can make any water appear blue

HOW COME? Pure shallow seawater is faint blue, but coastal water tends to have extra stuff in it. Some of this stuff includes algae, which color the water green. When turbidity is low, these algae give shallow waters over white sand an emerald color. On coasts with high waves, suspended particles reflect a pale gray into the mix, giving us turquoise hues ranging from pure to dirty. Where most of this suspension is calcium carbonate, water color ranges from powder blue (no algae) to "seafoam" (mint) green (with algae). The surf downstream from a lagoon inlet may receive tidal water stained by tannins from fallen leaves, giving the water a tea-like, red-brown color. Red-brown plus turbidity equals gray-brown water.

Turquoise water contains suspended particles

FOUND: Gulf waters are typically light-blue, emerald, or mint green. Keys waters are commonly turquoise. Atlantic waters are mint, or on calm days, blue-green. Rainy weather brings tea coloration to waters near inlets.

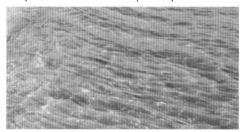

Algae and low turbidity give an emerald hue

SEASONS: The bluest waters are in spring and early summer. Rough winter waters tend to be mint-green or gray-brown.

DID YOU KNOW? Fish living in different water colors have different sensitivities to color.

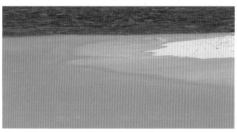

Densely suspended particles produce mint green

Tea-colored plus turbid equals gray-brown

27

Ponce de Leon Inlet

Wiggins Pass, the Gulf coast

Sebastian Inlet, Atlantic coast

Inlets and Passes

WHAT ARE THEY? Inlets (also called **passes**) are channels through barrier islands that allow the sea to flow into and out of the embayment behind the island.

SIZE: From 100 ft. (30 m) to about three miles wide. Natural inlets are 3–20 ft (1–6 m) deep, and dredged inlets may be over 40 ft (12 m) deep.

HOW COME? These passages are either cut by man or by natural events such as storms. They are maintained (kept open) by tidal currents or by dredging. Natural inlets can fill with sand when a newly formed inlet into a shared bay "steals" some of the local tidal current. There is a tendency for all inlets to fill in with sand swept down the coast by the longshore current. Because of this, many inlets that serve boat traffic have a sand-blocking jetty on either side of their opening to the sea.

FOUND: There are over 60 inlets through and between Florida's beaches.

SEASONS: All year.

DID YOU KNOW? Dredged inlets have jetties that block longshore sand transport and their channels allow deep currents that divert nearshore sand away from down-drift beaches. Inlets are the most important cause of rapid shoreline change (net erosion) in Florida. Temporary, natural inlets have played a critical role in the life history of marine species within coastal estuaries.

Barrier Islands

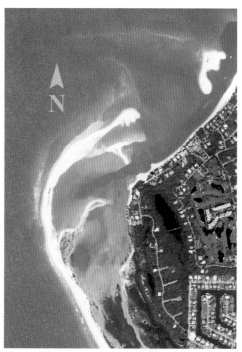

WHAT ARE THEY? These beach-islands are sinuous spits of sand parallel to the dry mainland and separated from it by lagoons, bays, or marshes. Most **barrier islands** have been dry long enough to support woody plants behind the dunes. This describes every Florida beach other than in the Keys.

SIZE: Santa Rosa Island is Florida's longest island at about 40 mi (65 km). Most Florida barrier islands are several miles long between inlets and passes.

HOW COME? Barrier islands were drowned dune ridges or exposed sand bars 2000–8000 years ago when sea levels were lower. The islands accreted above the waves as glaciers melted and seas rose. Footholds by dune plants helped sand retention and dune building. Barrier islands unimpeded by coastal development are believed to be increasing in height and migrating landward as our seas continue their rise.

Tigertail beach, Marco Island

FOUND: All sandy beaches outside the Keys.

SEASONS: Although occasionally divided by hurricanes, barrier islands persist over many hundreds of years.

DID YOU KNOW? Florida has more barrier-island beaches than any other state. The islands are barriers to wave energy and allow the formation of ecologically diverse lagoons and wetlands behind them.

An Atlantic barrier island, Brevard County

Our Milky Way galaxy

Perseid meteors give a mid-summer night's show

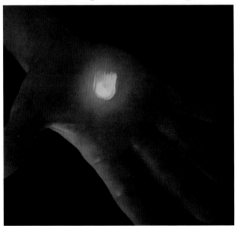

Glowing bacteria on a mole crab shell

Beaches at Night

WHAT HAPPENS AT NIGHT? Some beaches are splendid places to see nature's subtle glow. Nighttime glow-shows include the **stars** and **planets**, **meteor showers**, and **bioluminescence.**

SIZE: Glowing bacteria and dinofla-gellates are microscopic. Luminescent comb-jellies are walnut-sized. Brilliant as they are, most meteors are the size of sand grains. The Universe is infinite.

HOW COME? Many barrier-island and Keys beaches are distant from large, lighted cities. These beaches are some of the last convenient vantage points where Florida's urban glow has yet to bleach the heavens. Bioluminescence on dark-ened beaches is visible in the surf from dinoflagellates and comb-jellies that glow green when disturbed. In the swash zone, parts of mole crabs and other animals have a greenish glow from a coat-ing of luminescent bacteria.

FOUND: Beaches preserved as public land or backed by sparse development with glare-managed lighting.

SEASONS: Consult astronomical charts for seasonal night-sky features. Perseid meteors fly in mid-August, and Leonid meteors can be seen on clear nights in mid-November.

DID YOU KNOW? To protect nesting sea turtles, many beaches enforce light-control ordinances, which also enhance star-gazing.

BEACH ANIMALS

What are Beach Animals?

This section highlights animals whose paths lead to the beach. For some animals, this means living near, on, or inside the beach. For others, a beach visit is a brief stop during a grand life journey. And for many, the beach is reached only at life's end.

Figuring out what is and isn't an animal—or what used to be one—can be tricky. Although most folks could place a bird, crab, or fish into a general animal category, some of the lowlier critters can be a puzzle. A wide variety of beach animals seem to be plants, rocks, blobs, trivial specks, or visitors from space. Some of these mystery items are what they seem (and are featured in other sections of this book), but others may be animals, colonies of animals, or their lingering parts.

As a rule, live animals twitch when prodded, and dead ones smell worse than rocks or plants. But the sniff test may fail to identify an animal's mineral remnants, and among these there may be impostors. Sun-bleached, brittle, and branching things could be coral or bryozoans (both are animals), but also could be an alga (which is a plant). Fibrous tufts could be skeletons from bryozoan animals or sponges, or an alga. Quivering jelly, soft lumps, and gobs of goo are generally animal in nature but could be tunicates, jellyfish relatives, or a host of other invertebrates.

This section also includes tracks, burrows, and other evidence from some familiar but elusive beach animals. Beach sands can provide an elegant record of animals that are rare, nocturnal, or shy. Note that we've placed fossils from animals in the *Minerals* section and that human traces are in the *Hand of Man* section.

The chambered spiral shell of a ram's horn squid

Red Foram and Swash Meiofauna

Swash Meiofauna   Red Forams

RELATIVES: Forams are single-celled creatures (animal-like protozoa) in the class Sarcodina. The beach sand meiofauna include several animal groups.

IDENTIFYING FEATURES:

Red forams *(Homotrema rubrum),* 1/2 in (13 mm), are reddish, crusty splotches on rock, shell, or coral.

Swash meiofauna (MY-o-fawna) are tiny animals within beach sands and include **copepods** (small crustaceans) (**A**), **nematodes** (**B**), **water bears** (tardigrades, chubby critters with stubby arms and bearlike claws) (**C**), and **bristle worms** (polychaetes) (**D**).

HABITAT: Red forams attach to hard surfaces in shallow waters. Swash meiofauna live between the wet sand grains.

DID YOU KNOW? A foram is an amoeba with a shell. They feed like animals and photosynthesize with the aid of symbiotic algae. Other than bacteria, forams are the most common group of critters on Earth. Crushed red forams are the reason for Bermuda's famous pink beaches. The meiofauna have an important place in a living beach and the cleanest beaches have the most diverse array of these critters. They gather detritus and hunt each other while wiggling between wave-pounded sand grains. Water bears shrivel dry at low tide but reanimate when waves return.

Red forams on a beached lobster trap

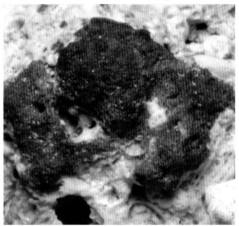

Close-up of red forams on coral

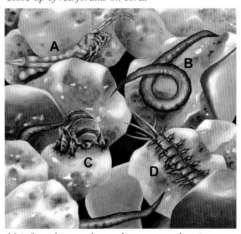

Meiofaunal invertebrates between sand grains

33

Tube sponge (A), vase sponge (B)

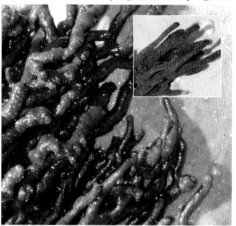
Dead-man's fingers, color variation (inset)

Beach-worn spongin skeleton

Sponges
(Vase, Tube, and Dead-man's Fingers)

Tube and Vase Sponges | Dead-man's Fingers

RELATIVES: Sponges are in the phylum Porifera. These commonly beached species are related to bath sponges (class Demospongiae).

IDENTIFYING FEATURES: Most sponges are difficult to tell apart using only shape and color, but these species have characteristic forms and are firm but flexible.

Tube sponges *(Callyspongia vaginalis)* have individual chimneylike tubes about 2 in (5 cm) wide.

Vase sponges *(Ircinia campana)*, 24 in (60 cm), are vase-shaped and smell really bad after being beached.

Dead-man's fingers *(Haliclona oculata)*, 24 in (60 cm), are spongy, finger-thick, branches attached at a thin wrist. Colors are gray, greenish, or orange.

HABITAT: Beached sponges have been torn free from shallow hardbottom or seagrass beds.

DID YOU KNOW? Sponges are simple animals without brains or other organs. They have persisted for about 500 million years and were probably Earth's first multi-celled animals. Sponges grow in place by filtering organic particles from the water. These bath-type sponges are "spongy" because of a plumbing network supported by **spongin**, a fibrous protein.

Sponges *(Loggerhead, White, Chicken Liver, and Purple Bleeding)*

Loggerhead and
White Sponges

Chicken Liver and
Purple Bleeding Sponges

IDENTIFYING FEATURES:

Loggerhead sponges *(Spheciospongia vesparium),* to 36 in (90 cm) across, are cake-shaped with numerous central holes (oscula).

White sponges *(Geodia gibberosa),* to 24 in (60 cm) across, are dirty-white lobed, masses with clusters of tiny pores.

Chicken liver sponges *(Chondrilla nucula),* 4 in (10 cm), look like their name when fresh, and are fibrous and tan when beach-worn.

Purple bleeding sponges *(Iotrochota birotulata),* to 18 in (50 cm) long, have green to purple-black rough fingers.

HABITAT: These sponges grow on hard-bottom and in seagrass beds.

DID YOU KNOW? Loggerhead sponges are among the largest sponges and provide habitat for many species of fishes and invertebrates. Chicken liver sponges are a favorite food of hawksbill sea turtles. Squeezing a fresh purple bleeding sponge releases a dark purple juice. Sponges filter an amazing amount of seawater through their bodies, up to ten thousand times their own volume each day.

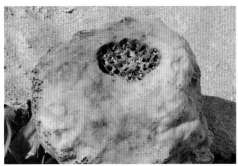

Loggerhead sponge

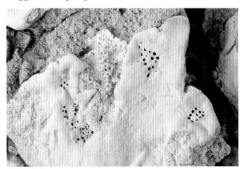

White sponge

Chicken liver sponges in various stages of decay

Purple bleeding sponge

35

Golfball sponge (A), red sponge (B)

Green sponge

Redbeard sponge

Sheepswool sponge

Sponges *(Golfball, Red, Green, Redbeard, and Sheepswool)*

IDENTIFYING FEATURES: Each of these sponges is relatively soft and squishable, even when dried. Their shape and color vary. Species identifications are certain only after a microscopic look at their sliverlike, skeletal spicules.

Golfball sponges *(Tethya diploderma),* 2 in (5 cm), are yellow to brown spheres with distinct pores.

Red sponges *(Haliclona rubens),* and **green sponges** *(H. viridis),* 6 in (15 cm), tend to be their indicated colors, or are brownish, and are beached as easily torn, encrusting lobes.

Redbeard sponges *(Microciona prolifera),* 8 in (20 cm), beach as bouquets of slim, velvety red branches.

Sheepswool sponges *(Hippospongia lachne),* 10 in (25 cm), are soft, brown, classic bath-sponge shapes.

HABITAT: These sponges grow on hardbottom and in seagrass beds.

DID YOU KNOW? Redbeard sponges are used in laboratories to study cellular reaggregation: the reassembly of disembodied cells back into a functional organism. After they are turned to soup in a blender, these sponges can eventually find themselves and rebuild their structure with correct cellular placement. Sheepswool sponges were once the focus of a large commercial sponge-diving effort in Florida.

Boring (Encrusting) Sponges

IDENTIFYING FEATURES:

Boring sponges *(Cliona* spp.) are given away by their habit of penetrating rock-hard substrates. Beached sponges are fist-size lobes, or are encrustations surrounding the item they washed in with, typically shells, rocks, or coral rubble.

Yellow boring sponges *(Cliona celata)* are generally bright yellow, and **red boring sponges** *(C. delitrix)* are orange-red. The largest part of these sponges is often within the shell, coral, or rock it has eroded. Exposed living sponge parts are soft and lumpy with one or more distinct pores (oscula). Detached lobes on beaches dry into smooth, hard, light, woodlike lumps covered by tiny pores.

Variable sponges *(Anthosigmella varians),* 12 in (30 cm), appear as woodlike orange lumps.

HABITAT: Shallow hardbottom.

DID YOU KNOW? Boring sponges are known to severely weaken concrete pilings that support bridges. Red boring sponges are also known to kill corals. These sponges are most common near dense human development where septic tanks leak sewage into nearby waters. The extra nitrates (fertilizer) grow algae on which the sponges thrive. Variable sponges bore into hardbottom and change their shape and spicule concentration in response to being nibbled on by sponge predators.

A freshly beached yellow boring sponge

Red boring sponge

Variable sponge

37

Cannonball jelly

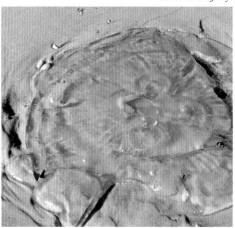

Moon jelly (male)

An upside-down view of a beached lion's mane

Jellyfishes
(Cannonball, Moon, and Lion's Mane)

RELATIVES: Jellyfishes are in the phylum Cnidaria, class Scyphozoa.

IDENTIFYING FEATURES:

Cannonball jellies *(Stomolophus meleagris)*, 8 in (20 cm), have a thick, rigid, dome-shaped bell with no marginal tentacles. The bell is a cloudy yellow in life, with brown around the margin.

Moon jellies *(Aurelia aurita)*, 12 in (30 cm), have a saucerlike bell that is clear except for four lobe-shaped gonads that are violet-pink (in males) or yellow (in females). Moon jellies have hundreds of short, marginal tentacles and four frilly, oral "arms."

Lion's mane jellyfish *(Cyanea capillata)*, 39 in (1 m), have an enormous bell with 16 marginal lobes.

HABITAT: Open ocean waters.

DID YOU KNOW? Cannonball jellies are a common food item in Asia. Their crunchy texture makes them suitable for "sea salads." Moon jellies have a detectable sting, which is a mild burning for most people. Lion's manes are the largest jellyfish, reaching more than six feet (2 m) across in northern latitudes. They can deliver severe blistering stings even after they are dead. Each of these species is an important predator of zooplankton. Their "swarms" can decimate populations of these drifting animals.

Sea Nettle, Comb Jellies, and **Mesoglea**

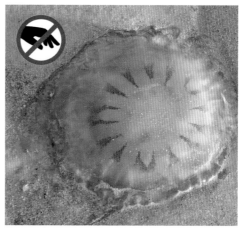
Sea nettle

RELATIVES: Sea nettles are jellyfish (Cnidaria, Scyphozoa), in a different phylum from comb jellies (Ctenophora). Mesoglea (mez-o-GLEE-a) is the "jelly" in jellyfish and comb jellies.

IDENTIFYING FEATURES:

Sea nettles *(Chrysaora quinquecirrha),* 10 in (25 cm), have red radiating stripes.

Ovate comb jellies *(Beroe ovata),* 4.5 in (11.2 cm), have pinkish egg-shaped bodies bearing eight rows of faint cilia.

Mesoglea, to 12 in or more (>30 cm), washes in as lumps of clear, nonsticky jelly. Comb jellies are often identifiable only as mesoglea.

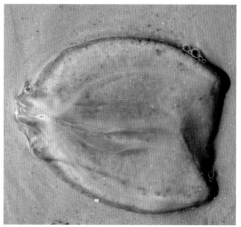
Ovate comb jelly

HABITAT: Sea nettles and ovate comb jellies live in coastal waters. Mesoglea is from jellies that lived in open waters before becoming stranded on the beach.

DID YOU KNOW? Ovate comb jellies feed on sea walnuts *(Mnemiopsis leidyi)*—smaller, lobed, comb jellies that are themselves voracious predators of fish larvae. Dense groups of comb jellies in the surf at night can be seen to pulse with brilliant luminescence. Mesoglea is the gelatinous, watery, scaffolding tissue used by jellies to anchor their swimming muscles. It is about 96% water, 3% salts, and only 1% organic. The organic part is a fibrous net of collagen. Mesoglea forms a jellyfish's "bell," which is the majority of its body.

Mesoglea beached, and in its former glory (inset)

39

Stinging tentacles trail on the beach

Man-o-war strand most commonly in winter

Portuguese Man-o-War

RELATIVES: These are hydralike animals, class Hydrozoa, in the phylum Cnidaria. They are siphonophores, which are distantly related to blue buttons and by-the-wind sailors.

IDENTIFYING FEATURES:

Portuguese man-o-war *(Physalia physalis)* look like a blue-tinged balloon with a pink-crested sail and trailing tentacles. The float-sail (pneumatophore) is 1–10 in (2.5–25 cm) long. Tentacles can be 6 ft (2 m) on the beach and reach 150 ft (46 m) when fully extended at sea.

HABITAT: The wide-open sea, except at the end of their voyage when they are found in the wave wash and wrack line.

CAUTION! Their tentacles sting and cling. If stung, remove tentacles without rubbing. Only after tentacle removal, treat skin with meat tenderizer or urine. For symptoms other than local pain and redness, seek medical attention.

DID YOU KNOW? These animals are only distantly related to jellyfish. Apparent individuals are actually colonies of many polyps (balloon, stinging, feeding, and breeding). Right- and left-sailing man-o-war travel in different directions. Their paralyzing tentacles capture small fish and shrimp for food. Beachings are most common December through May. April and May are peak months for abundance and individual size.

Blue Button and By-the-Wind Sailor

RELATIVES: These are hydralike animals, class Hydrozoa, in the phylum Cnidaria. They are chondrophorines, distantly related to siphonophores like the Portuguese man-o-war.

IDENTIFYING FEATURES:

Blue buttons *(Porpita porpita),* 1 in (2.5 cm), have a small disklike float, surrounded by blue-green tentacles.

By-the-wind sailors *(Velella velella),* 2 in (5 cm), have an oval float bearing a crestlike sail and deep blue tentacles beneath.

HABITAT: These animals float on the surface of the wide-open sea, except when beached. Their cellophane-like "floats" linger in the wrack for weeks.

DID YOU KNOW? Neither species is a jellyfish. Like the Portuguese man-o-war, they are colonies of many individual animals. Blue buttons and by-the-wind sailors feed on small animals captured by their tentacles (which are actually individual animals called zooids). By-the-wind sailors have mirror-image forms that are either right-sailing or left-sailing. Because of these directional tendencies, beaching events usually involve only one form.

Blue button

"Left-sailing" by-the-wind sailors

Newly beached and older (colorless) by-the-wind sailors

41

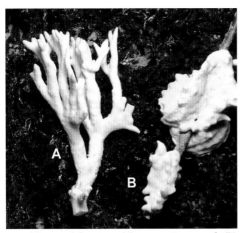

Fire coral fragment (A), encrusting growth (B)

Stinging hydroids on a trap rope

Sargassum hydroids on sargassum algae

Other Hydroids

*Fire Coral and
Stinging Hydroid*

Sargassum Hydroid

RELATIVES: These are colonial hydrozoans like the Portuguese man-o-war, blue button, and by-the-wind sailor.

IDENTIFYING FEATURES:

Fire coral *(Millepora* spp.), 12 in (30 cm), is brownish-orange with white tips when alive, and white when beached. It is smooth and grows in encrusting or fingered-blade shapes.

Stinging hydroids (family Sertulari-idae), 2 ft (60 cm), are plumes with wire-thin, dark branches growing on objects formerly on the sea bottom like coral rock or trap ropes.

Sargassum hydroids (order Hydroida), 1/4 in (6.3 mm), add a sparse tan fuzz to the varied drifting items they live on.

HABITAT: Fire coral and stinging hydroids grow on shallow reefs and in seagrass beds. Sargassum hydroids grow on ocean-drifting objects of all kinds, especially sargassum algae.

DID YOU KNOW? Fire coral is not a coral, but it does feel like its name. White fragments from the beach are harmless. Despite their name, stinging hydroids cause no more than a tingle in most folks. About 27 species of hydroids are known from drifting sargassum algae. These polyps trouble only the plankton they feed on and are themselves food for young sea turtles.

Sea Pansies

Common Sea Pansy   *Gulf Sea Pansy*

Common sea pansy

RELATIVES: Sea pansies are related to corals and anemones (phylum Cnidaria, class Anthozoa) and are in the order Pennatulacea, family Renillidae.

IDENTIFYING FEATURES:

Common sea pansies *(Renilla reniformis),* 2 in (5 cm), look like a purplish, thick, leaflike pad on a purple stalk called a peduncle.

Gulf sea pansies *(Renilla muelleri),* 2 in (5 cm), are similar to common sea pansies but have a wider pad and a shorter, thinner peduncle.

HABITAT: Sea pansies live on intertidal sands, especially on current-swept flats near inlets and passes.

DID YOU KNOW? Sea pansies are a collection of polyps, the largest of which is the peduncle that anchors them in the sand. Anemone-like feeding polyps cover the purplish pad, which also has specialized polyps for deflating at low tide and inflating when flooded at high tide. Sea pansies flash a green glow when disturbed. The light comes from a green fluorescent protein, which is currently being used as a tool in biochemical and medical research. Sea pansies feed on particle-size plants and animals and they are fed upon by striped sea slugs *(Armina tigrina)*.

Gulf sea pansy

Closeup of Gulf sea pansy polyps

43

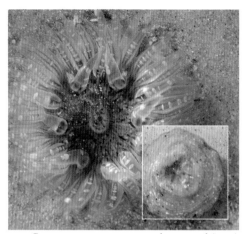

Gray warty anemone exposed, retracted (inset)

Onion anemone retracted, exposed (inset)

A retracted hermit crab anemone on a whelk shell

Sea Anemones

Gray Warty and Onion Anemones   *Hermit Crab Anemone*

RELATIVES: Sea anemones are related to corals and sea pansies, class Anthozoa.

IDENTIFYING FEATURES:

Gray warty anemones *(Anthopleura carneola),* 4 in (10 cm), appear in the surf as "flowers" made up of about 100 stubby tentacles that are translucent, striped, and flecked with white. When uncovered, these anemones pucker up into a warty gray ball.

Onion anemones *(Paranthus rapiformis),* 3 in (7.5 cm), have short, thin tentacles and anchor in the sand by a small disk at their base. When eroded from the sand they assume the shape and appearance of a cocktail onion.

Hermit crab anemones *(Calliactis tricolor),* 2 in (5 cm), have a fringe of fuzzy tentacles and a column tinted purple and yellow with basal dark spots.

HABITAT: Sandy bottom near beaches. Hermit crab anemones live on bottom debris and on gastropod shells occupied by hermit crabs.

DID YOU KNOW? Hermit crabs and their anemones have a cooperative agreement to trade travel for stinging protection. The hermit crabs are known to take their anemones with them when they upgrade to larger shells. This anemone can reproduce by dividing lengthwise, producing two new anemones.

44

Soft Corals *(Octocorals)*

Sea Fan and Sea Feather   *False Sea Fan and Sea Whip*

RELATIVES: These soft corals (class Anthozoa) are in the order Gorgonacea.

IDENTIFYING FEATURES: All may be found only as a core of tough, wood-like branches.

Purple sea fans *(Gorgonia flabellum),* 3 ft (1 m), are appropriately named purple fans.

Smooth sea feathers *(Pseudopterogorgia acerosa),* 6 ft (2 m), may be gray, purple, or yellow.

False sea fans *(Leptogorgia hebes),* 9 in (23 cm), have branched fans that are purple, red, or orange.

Sea whips *(Leptogorgia virgulata),* 3 ft (1 m), may have purple, red, orange, or yellow branches.

HABITAT: Reef and hardbottom less than 100 ft (30 m) deep

DID YOU KNOW? Soft corals are colonies of tiny polyps, each with 8 tentacles (hence their name: octocorals). Unlike stony corals, soft corals do not need symbiotic algae (zooxanthellae) to survive, so they can live in deeper more turbid areas with less light. Soft coral colonies are flexible, branched rods of hornlike protein (gorgonin) surrounded by tiny polyps bound to each other by a matrix of glasslike spicules. Color variation in sea whips is genetic; many areas may have more than one color growing.

Purple sea fan

Smooth sea feather

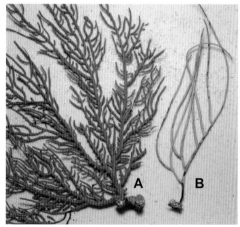

False sea fan (A), sea whip (B)

45

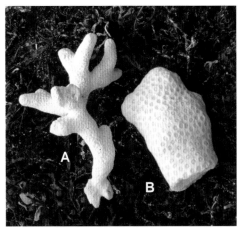

Thin finger coral (A), thick finger coral (B)

Staghorn coral (A), tube coral (B)

Golfball coral (A), starlet coral (B)

Stony Corals *(Reef Species)*

RELATIVES: Other stony corals in the order Scleractinia.

IDENTIFYING FEATURES: All are white when beached.

Thin finger coral *(Porites furcata)* has 1/2 in- (6.5 mm-) thick, forked branches covered by pinhead-size polyp cups.

Thick finger coral *(Porites porites)* is 1 in (2.5 cm) thick with lumpy ends.

Staghorn coral *(Acropora cervicornis)* has pointed branches with tubular cups.

Tube coral *(Cladocora arbuscula)* has thin branches ending in 1/8 in (3 mm) cups.

Golfball (star) coral *(Favia fragum)* forms 2-in (5-cm) knobs with irregularly rounded cups.

Starlet coral *(Siderastrea* spp.) covers shells and rocks, feels like coarse sandpaper, and forms boulders in deep water.

HABITAT: Shallow reef and hardbottom.

DID YOU KNOW? These corals are cemented colonies of tiny polyps that live with symbiotic micro-algae (zooxanthellae). Many reef invertebrates have a similar housing-for-food arrangement. South Florida beaches receive rubble from more than 50 species of stony corals. Identification of many of these is certain only with microscopic examination. Living coral is protected and should not be taken from the water.

Stony Corals
(Seagrass and Hardbottom Species)

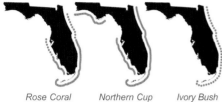

Rose Coral   Northern Cup   Ivory Bush
Coral   Coral

RELATIVES: Other stony corals in the order Scleractinia.

IDENTIFYING FEATURES: All are white when beached.

Rose coral *(Manicina areolata),* 4 in (10 cm), grows as a stalked, oval cone with undulating edges.

Northern cup coral *(Astrangia danae),* 2 in (5 cm), is a lone ball or encrusting dome with tight, deep, 3/16-in (5-mm) cups.

Ivory bush coral *(Oculina diffusa),* 12 in (30 cm), has pencil-thick branches with widely separated cups.

HABITAT: Hardbottom and seagrass.

DID YOU KNOW? These corals survive wave-washed, turbid, and dark conditions. Rose coral polyps can clean themselves of sediment. A wave-toppled rose coral rights itself when polyps cooperatively puff water into the seabottom until the erosion tips the colony upright. Cup and bush corals live without photosynthetic zooxanthellae and do well under low-light conditions. A species related to ivory bush coral, ivory tree coral *(Oculina varicosae),* forms important reefs in deep Gulf Stream waters between Ft. Pierce and Daytona Beach.

Rose coral

Northern cup coral

Ivory bush coral

47

Shelled Mollusk Anatomy

Seashells are the protective or supportive skeletons of mollusks (phylum Mollusca). The most common shells are from snails (with one coiled shell) and bivalves (with two hinged shells). Snails are gastropods, as are sea slugs and sea hares, which have an internal shell or none at all. Other shelled mollusks include tusk shells and some squids.

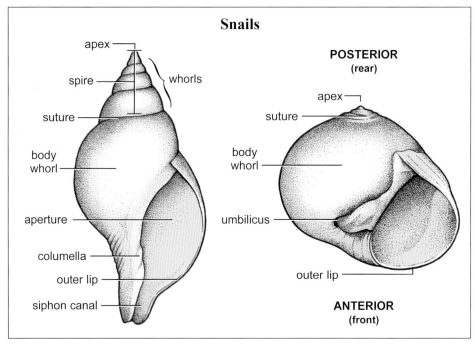

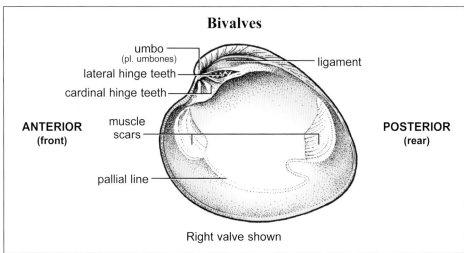

Limpets and Falselimpet

Cayenne
Keyhole Limpet

Meta
Keyhole
Limpet

Barbados and Rosy
Keyhole Limpets and
Striped Falselimpet

Cayenne keyhole limpet, max 2 in (5 cm)

RELATIVES: Keyhole limpets (family Fissurellidae) arc only distantly related to falselimpets (family Siphonariidae).

IDENTIFYING FEATURES: All are shaped like oval-based volcanoes.

Cayenne keyhole limpets *(Diodora cayenensis)* have a keyhole opening offset from center.

Meta keyhole limpet, max 1.5 in (3.8 cm)

Meta keyhole limpets *(Diodora meta)* are flattened with an oval top hole.

Barbados keyhole limpets *(Fissurella barbadensis)* have a nearly central, oval hole, and alternating small and large radiating ribs.

Barbados keyhole limpet, max 1 in (2.5 cm)

Rosy keyhole limpets *(Fissurella rosea)* have a broad oval top hole and pink or purple rays.

Striped falselimpets *(Siphonaria pectinata)* have a peak with no top hole.

HABITAT: On and under rocks. Falselimpets are frequently above water.

Rosy keyhole limpet, max 1.5 in (3.8 cm)

DID YOU KNOW? A limpet moves about by rippling its muscular foot and feeds on algae using a rasping, tongue-like radula. They anticipate low tide and return to resting spots before the water leaves their rock. Their top hole passes exhaust from their gills. Holeless falselimpets breathe air and can be found above the tide on jetty rocks.

Striped falselimpet, max 1 in (2.5 cm)

Scuptured topsnail, max 1 in (2.5 cm)

Jujube topsnail, max 1 in (2.5 cm)

Smooth Atlantic tegula, max 3/4 in (19 mm)

Topsnails and Tegula

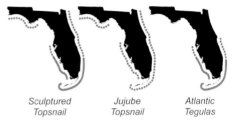

| Sculptured Topsnail | Jujube Topsnail | Atlantic Tegulas |

RELATIVES: Topsnails and tegulas are in the family Trochidae.

IDENTIFYING FEATURES:

Sculptured topsnails *(Calliostoma euglyptum)* have a dark-tipped apex and rounded whorls.

Jujube topsnails *(Calliostoma jujubinum)* are mottled red-brown or tan with a straight-sided, conelike shape.

Smooth (silky) Atlantic tegulas *(Tegula fasciata)* have a round-top turban shape.

HABITAT: Topsnails live on reefs and hardbottom. Smooth Atlantic tegulas prefer shallow seagrass beds.

DID YOU KNOW? An extensive commercial harvest of large, Indo-Pacific turban shells fuels a high-end market for shell buttons. The snails are also the typical substitute "escargot" for the region's tourists. Our Florida turban shells are too small for this enterprise. Most turbans feed on algae.

Star Shells and Chestnut Turban

Star Shell   Chestnut Turban

RELATIVES: Star and turban shells are in the family Turbinidae.

IDENTIFYING FEATURES: All are coarsely sculptured. Their colors are typically yellow to brown, but many beached shells are bleached white.

Long-spined star shell, max 1.75 in (4.5 cm)

Long-spined star shells *(Astralium phoebium)* have saw-toothed spines at the whorl sutures.

American star shells *(Lithopoma americanum)* have a conelike spire with lumps instead of spines.

Chestnut turbans *(Turbo castanea)* have rounded whorls like a beaded turban and have a circular aperture.

HABITAT: On and under rocks in shallow hardbottom areas.

DID YOU KNOW? Living American star shells are covered with a fluffy coat of algae that serves to camouflage them. Chestnut turbans are one of the most important grazers on algae in seagrass beds. The door to their aperture, their operculum, has a pearly sheen.

American star shell, max 1 in (2.5 cm)

Chestnut turban, max 1.5 in (4 cm)

51

Four-tooth nerite, max 1 in (2.5 cm)

Antillean nerite, max 1 in (2.5 cm)

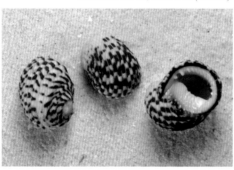

Checkered nerite, max 1 in (2.5 cm)

Virgin nerite, max 1/2 in (12.7 mm)

Nerites

Four-tooth, Antillean, and   *Virgin Nerite*
Checkered Nerites

RELATIVES: These "baby's tooth shells" are in the family Neritidae.

IDENTIFYING FEATURES: All have rounded spires and apertures that look like a toddler's smile.

Four-tooth nerites *(Nerita versicolor)* have thick spiral ridges with blurred markings of black, greenish-white, and maroon. They have four teeth on the inside lip.

Antillean nerites *(Nerita fulgurans)* are streaked and have spiral ridges separated by light sutures. They have two small central teeth on the inside lip.

Checkered nerites *(Nerita tessellata)* have alternating black and white markings and two tiny teeth on the inside lip.

Virgin nerites *(Vitta virginea)* are glossy and variably patterned with waves and swooshes.

HABITAT: Four-tooth, Antillean, and checkered nerites live on and under rocks in intertidal areas. Virgin nerites live in shallow waters of bay margins and seagrass beds.

DID YOU KNOW? Nerites have a thick, calcified operculum (aperture door) that keeps them locked up tight and protected from desiccating heat when exposed at low tide. They cluster in groups to graze at night on algae covering intertidal rocks.

Common Sundial and Wentletraps

Common Sundial

Angulate, Humphrey's, and
Brown-banded Wentletraps

Common sundial, max 2.5 in (6.4 cm)

RELATIVES: Sundials are in the family Architectonicidae. Wentletraps are in the family Epitoniidae.

IDENTIFYING FEATURES:

Common sundials *(Architectonica nobilis)* have a deep umbilicus and a spire like a flattened cone.

Angulate wentletraps *(Epitonium angulatum),* like most wentletraps, have a rounded, thick-lipped aperture and distinct, widely spaced ribs. The body whorl has 9–10 thin ribs that are angled at the whorl shoulders.

Angulate wentletrap, max 1 in (2.5 cm)

Humphrey's wentletraps *(Epitonium humphreysii)* have 8–9 thick, rounded ribs on the body whorl.

Brown-banded wentletraps *(Epitonium rupicola)* have rounded ribs of varying strengths and spiral bands of white, tan, and brown.

HABITAT: Sundials and wentletraps live in sandy areas to moderate depths.

Humphrey's wentletrap, max 1 in (2.5 cm)

DID YOU KNOW? Sundials spend their days buried spire-down in the sand and emerge at night to feed on sea pansies. Angulate wentletraps get away with chewing chunks off living anemones by soothing them with a purple anesthetic. More than 20 wentletrap species are known in Florida. "Wentletrap" comes from *wendeltreppe,* German for a winding staircase.

Brown-banded wentletrap, max 3/4 in (20 mm)

53

Interrupted periwinkle, max 1/2 in (13 mm)

Marsh periwinkle, max 1 in (2.5 cm)

Mangrove periwinkle, max 1 in (2.5 cm)

Beaded periwinkle, max 3/4 in (20 mm)

Periwinkles

| Interrupted Periwinkle | Mangrove and Beaded Periwinkles | Marsh Periwinkle |

RELATIVES: Periwinkles are in the family Littorinidae.

IDENTIFYING FEATURES: Periwinkles have rounded apertures and conical spires.

Interrupted periwinkles *(Nodilittorina interrupta)* have white and purple-brown wavy lines.

Marsh periwinkles *(Littoraria irrorata)* have thick aperture lips and are patterned with dashed streaks on their spiral ridges.

Mangrove periwinkles *(Littoraria angulifera)* have thin shells, sharp aperture lips, and a groove in their lower columella/inner aperture.

Beaded periwinkles *(Cenchritis muricatus)* are blue- or pink-gray and covered with white, beadlike knobs.

HABITAT: Periwinkles live just above the tide. Marsh periwinkles live on marsh reeds, mangrove periwinkles live on mangrove shorelines, and both interrupted and beaded periwinkles live on rocks near wave splash.

DID YOU KNOW? Periwinkles feed out of the water on algae that grows on plants and rocks, and their beached shells are most common near inlets. These snails are an important link in the food chain between estuarine plants and dozens of crab, fish, and bird species.

Worm Shells

Variable Worm Shell   Black Worm Shell and
                       Corroding Worm Shell

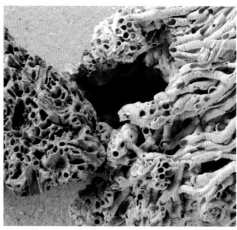

Variable worm shell

RELATIVES: Worm shells are in the family Vermetidae and are distantly related to ceriths and worm snails.

IDENTIFYING FEATURES: Worm shells are snails that grow in irregular patterns.

Variable worm shells *(Petaloconchus varians)* have an aperture to 1/16 in (1.6 mm) and grow in compact, rock-like, colonies of tangled tubes. Chunks of colonies are orange, brownish-purple, or whitish.

Black worm shells *(Petaloconchus nigricans)* have apertures to 3/16 in (5 mm) with horizontally wrinkled, purple-black shells. They grow in masses on hard surfaces between the tide lines.

Corroding worm shells *(Dendropoma corrodens)* have apertures to 1/4 in (6 mm) and are lumpy and white outside, shiny brown inside. They attach as individuals or groups to rocks and shells.

Black worm shell

HABITAT: Shallow reefs, hardbottom, and exposed rock.

DID YOU KNOW? These snails let their surroundings dictate their worm-like form. Some anchor to the bottom and form reefs. Worm-shell gastropods feed in place by gill-filtering plankton. Some south Florida mangrove islands owe their origins to reef-building variable worm shells.

Corroding worm shell

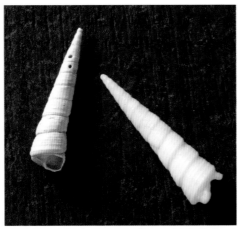

Boring turretsnail, max 1.5 in (3.8 cm)

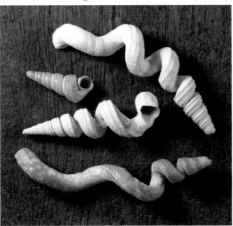

West Indian wormsnail

Florida wormsnail

Turretsnail and Wormsnails

Boring Turretsnail and   West Indian Wormsnail
Florida Wormsnail

RELATIVES: Turrets and wormsnails are in the family Turritellidae.

IDENTIFYING FEATURES:

Boring turretsnails *(Turritella acropora)* have pale, sharp spirals with rounder whorls than the similar-shaped auger shells. Turret apertures have no siphon canal.

West Indian wormsnails *(Vermicularia fargoi)* are more loosely coiled than turrets and have three spiral cords leading to a squarish aperture. Older West Indian wormsnails abandon the coil theme after reaching 1 in (2.5 cm) long and begin growing freestyle.

Florida wormsnails *(V. knorrii)* grow wormlike after reaching about 1/2 in (1.25 cm). Both wormsnails are brownish, but the Florida wormsnail often has a white spiral tip.

HABITAT: Boring turrets live in shallow sandy bottom. Wormsnails grow with sponges on reefs and hardbottom.

DID YOU KNOW? Wormsnails live life attached to the bottom or to other wormsnails and feed on suspended plankton and detritus. Their immediate environment dictates their uncoiled growth. Some wormsnails literally tie themselves together in knots.

Ceriths

Florida Cerith

Stocky, Fly-specked, and Dwarf Ceriths

Florida cerith, max 1.5 in (3.5 cm)

Stocky cerith, max 1 in (2.5 cm)

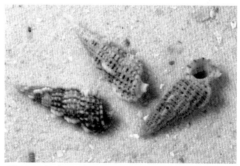

Fly-specked cerith, max 1 in (2.5 cm)

Dwarf cerith, max 3/4 in (20 mm)

RELATIVES: Ceriths are in the family Cerithiidae and are distantly related to worm shells and turretsnails.

IDENTIFYING FEATURES: Ceriths (*Cerithium* spp.) are bead-sculptured, slender snails with many whorls and distinct siphon canals opposite their pointed spires.

Florida ceriths *(C. atratum)*, 1.5 in (3.5 cm), have 18–20 beaded ridges per whorl and occasional larger lumps. Their beached shells are light to dark, often spiraled with brown and white.

Stocky ceriths *(C. litteratum)* are compact and compared to Florida ceriths have fewer but larger beads in their sculpture.

Fly-specked ceriths *(C. muscarum)* have 9–11 ridges per whorl that are crossed by spiral lines. New shells are "fly-specked" with spiral rows of brown dots.

Dwarf Atlantic ceriths *(C. lutosum)* are brown with a light apex and a thick aperture lip.

HABITAT: All live on subtidal sandy bottom or seagrass.

DID YOU KNOW? Ceriths feed on algae and detritus. The Florida cerith is the most common beached species, but all can be abundant near inlets.

57

West Indian false cerith, max 3/4 in (20 mm)

Ladder horn snail, max 1.2 in (3 cm)

Button snail, max 1/2 in (12.7 mm)

False Cerith, Ladder Horn Snail, and **Button Snail**

West Indian False Cerith and Ladder Horn Snail

Button Snail

RELATIVES: False ceriths (family Batillariidae), hornsnails (Potamididae), and button snails (family Modulidae) are all distantly related to ceriths.

IDENTIFYING FEATURES:

West Indian false ceriths *(Batillaria minima)* are gray to black with light spiral bands. Their aperture is brown with a short siphon canal twisting to the left.

Ladder hornsnails *(Cerithidea scalariformis)* have regularly spaced ribs, light spiral bands, and a flared aperture lip.

Button snails *(Modulus modulus)* are buttonlike with a gray- or brown-streaked, ridge-sculptured body whorl and a low spire.

HABITAT: West Indian false ceriths are locally abundant in shallow lagoons with coral rubble. Ladder hornsnails prefer mangrove mudflats, and button snails like shallow seagrass.

DID YOU KNOW? West Indian false ceriths are a major food item for Caribbean flamingos. All three species feed on algae and detritus and deposit their eggs in gelatinous strings. The young hatch as free-swimming larvae, except for the button snail, which emerges as a miniature version of the adult.

Purple Sea Snails

RELATIVES: Purple sea snails (*Janthina* spp.) are in the family Janthinidae, distantly related to wentletraps.

IDENTIFYING FEATURES: These gastropods have violet, fragile shells. Live snails have a translucent, bubble-raft arcing from their aperture.

Common purple sea snails (*J. janthina*) have a low spire and D-shaped aperture. Their top whorls are pale and their base is violet.

Globe purple sea snails (*J. prolongata*) are all violet and have rounded whorls and a pointed spire.

HABITAT: Purple sea snails live adrift on the open ocean. Unbroken snails are found in freshly beached wrack.

DID YOU KNOW? Two other species are known from Florida beaches. Dwarf purple sea snails (*J. globosa*) have a deeply indented outer aperture, and pale purple sea snails (*J. pallida*) have large, round apertures. Purple sea snails sail along with, and prey upon, Portuguese man-o-war and by-the-wind sailors. When they are not attached to these floating hydrozoans, they construct a mucous-bubble raft for buoyancy. The snails' violet shell-tinting blends in with the color of deep ocean waters and presumably hides them from the birds and young sea turtles that eat them. Ancient Greeks used a violet fluid produced by *Janthina* snails as a dye for clothing.

Common purple sea snail, max 1.5 in (3.5 cm)

Common purple sea snail with bubble raft

Globe purple sea snail, max 3/4 in (20 mm)

Florida fighting conch, max 4 in (10 cm)

Hawk-wing conch, max 4 in (10 cm)

Juveniles: fighting conch (A), hawk-wing conch (B)

Conchs
(Florida Fighting and Hawk-wing)

Florida Fighting Conch   Hawk-Wing Conch

RELATIVES: These are true conchs in the family Strombidae.

IDENTIFYING FEATURES:

Florida fighting conchs *(Strombus alatus)* are thick-shelled with blunt-knobbed whorls. Colors vary from pale yellow to chestnut-brown with occasional light spots and zigzags. The body whorl has fine spiral cords (ridges).

Hawk-wing conchs *(Strombus rainus)* have coarse spiral cords on the body whorl and a rear projection to their widely flared aperture lip. The rough upper part of the "hawk wing" is mottled brown and white.

HABITAT: Florida fighting conchs live in sandy shallows, including the swash zone of low-energy beaches. Hawk-wing conchs prefer seagrass pastures.

DID YOU KNOW? Fighting conchs (pronounced "konks") get their name from occasional bouts between rival males. They are spry for snails and can quickly flip themselves and walk using their pointed operculum. Both species feed on algae and detritus. A similar southeast Florida and Caribbean species, the West Indian fighting conch *(S. pugilis),* has longer spines on the spire and is more orange. Fighting conchs are being farmed experimentally as an edible alternative to the rarer and slower-maturing queen conch.

Queen Conch

RELATIVES: These are true conchs in the family Strombidae.

IDENTIFYING FEATURES:

Queen conchs *(Strombus gigas)* are also known as pink conchs for their interior color, a hint of which can be seen on the exterior of fresh shells. Adults have a wide, thick, flaring aperture lip. Knobs on their whorl shoulders are especially pointed on the last three whorls. Juveniles have a more strongly pointed spire, a narrow, pointed base, and a sharp, unflared lip.

HABITAT: Queen conchs live in seagrass and coral rubble to moderate depths.

DID YOU KNOW? Florida's queen conchs have been nearly lost. Over-harvesting for meat and souvenirs has made this conch a rare beach find except for bleached old shells. Conch meat from the Bahamas continues to be sold as Keys cuisine, and Florida shell shops still stock Bahamian conch shells. Live queen conchs in Florida have been protected from harvest since 1985, but recovery has been limited by poor water quality surrounding the Keys. Adult conchs are active at night when they may make journeys of more than a hundred yards (about 100 m) before sunrise. Queen conchs reach adulthood in about 4 years. Those in deep water where harvest pressure is low can reach 26 years in age.

Queen conch, max 12 in (30 cm)

Juvenile queen conch (size 6 in, 15 cm)

Beach-worn adult

Atlantic slippersnail, max 2.5 in (6.5 cm)

Spotted slippersnail, max 1 in (2.5 cm)

Spiny slippersnail, max 1 in (2.5 cm)

Eastern white slippersnail, max 1 in (2.5 cm)

White hoofsnail, max 3/4 in (2 cm)

Slippersnails and Hoofsnail

White Hoofsnail

Slippersnails

RELATIVES: Hoofsnails (family Hipponicidae) are only distantly related to slippersnails (family Calyptraeidae).

IDENTIFYING FEATURES: Slippersnails *(Crepidula* spp.) are shoe-shaped, with a conspicuous ventral shelf.

Atlantic slippersnails *(C. fornicata)* have a coiled apex bent to one side, a smooth exterior, and a shelf with an indented edge.

Spotted slippersnails *(C. maculosa)* have a shelf with a straight edge angling away from the apex. Most spotted slippersnails have brown spots on white.

Spiny slippersnails *(C. aculeata)* differ in having roughened, sometimes spiny, radiating ridges.

Eastern white slippersnails *(C. atrasolea)* are white, thin, and flattened with a small pointy apex.

White hoofsnails *(Hipponix antiquatus)* are white, roughened, thick-shelled, and shaped like a floppy Santa hat.

HABITAT: Hoofsnails attach themselves to rocks in areas of moving water. Slippershells live in shallow waters on rocks and on other shells. White slippersnails prefer to be inside other shells.

DID YOU KNOW? Slippersnails begin life as males that grow into being female. Environmental conditions determine when they strategically switch sex.

Cowries and Trivias

Cowries and
Fourspot Trivia

Coffeebean Trivia

Atlantic deer cowrie, max 5 in (13 cm)

RELATIVES: Cowries (family Cypraeidae) are distantly related to trivias (family Triviidae).

IDENTIFYING FEATURES: Cowries have glossy, egg-shaped shells with a body-length, grinning aperture. Florida's trivias are cowrie-shaped with riblets wrapped between a back groove and the aperture.

Measled cowrie, max 4.5 in (11 cm)

Atlantic deer cowries *(Macrocypraea cervus)* are chocolate-brown with solid white spots or may be hazy brown with light bands.

Measled cowries *(Macrocypraea zebra)* are similar to deer cowries, but are more elongate (less domed) and have dark centers to their side spots.

Atlantic yellow cowrie, max 1.2 in (3 cm)

Atlantic yellow cowries *(Erosaria acicularis)* have a granular yellow pattern with marginal brown spots.

Coffeebean trivias *(Niveria pediculus)* are pale purple with 3 pairs of dark spots.

Fourspot trivias *(Niveria quadripunctata)* are pinkish-white with 2–4 dark spots straddling the back groove.

HABITAT: Cowries and trivias live on shallow reefs.

Coffeebean trivia, max 3/4 in (20 mm)

DID YOU KNOW? Trivias feed on tunicates and soft corals. Cowries feed on algae and colonial invertebrates. The Atlantic deer cowrie is the largest of the world's 190 cowrie species.

Fourspot trivia, max 3/8 in (10 mm)

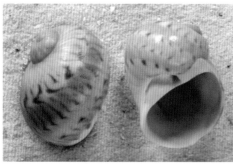

Colorful moonsnail, max 2 in (5 cm)

Milk moonsnail, max 1.5 in (4 cm)

White baby's ear, max 2 in (5 cm)

Maculated baby's ear, max 1.2 in (3 cm)

Moonsnails and Baby's Ears

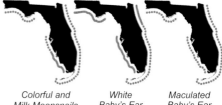

| Colorful and Milk Moonsnails | White Baby's Ear | Maculated Baby's Ear |

RELATIVES: Moonsnails and baby's ears share the family Naticidae with shark's eyes and naticas.

IDENTIFYING FEATURES: All have a large body whorl, gaping aperture, and low, smooth spire.

Colorful moonsnails *(Naticarius canrena)* have a deep umbilicus half-filled with a traguslike pad (callus). They are creamy white with brown zigzags that are faded in old beach shells.

Milk moonsnails *(Polinices lacteus)* have a deep umbilicus half-filled with callus. Shells are glossy white.

White baby's ears *(Sinum perspectivum)* are like a flattened moonsnail with an expansive aperture. The body whorl is sculptured with broad spiral grooves. Shells are dull white or stained.

Maculated baby's ears *(Sinum maculatum)* are like the white baby's ear but are smudged with brown and have a higher, slightly pointed spire.

HABITAT: Sandy shallows

DID YOU KNOW? Colorful moonsnails fade after being beached, but in life they have a lovely patterned shell and an enormous brown-streaked foot spreading ten times their shell size. Baby's ear snails have an equally big foot that cannot be withdrawn. These species prey on buried bivalves.

Shark's Eye

Shark's eye, max 3 in (7.5 cm)

RELATIVES: Shark's eyes (family Naticidae) are related to naticas, moon-snails, and baby's ears.

IDENTIFYING FEATURES:

Shark's eyes *(Neverita duplicata)* have a gaping aperture and a large body whorl that forms a smooth dome with their low spire. The umbilicus is nearly covered by a brown, traguslike pad (callus). Shells are brown-gray, blue-gray, or faded. Unfaded shells have a blue "eye" in the early whorls. Shark's eyes from the southern Gulf coast are browner with conelike spires and may be a distinct species.

HABITAT: Sandy shallows, including the swash zone

DID YOU KNOW? Shark's eyes plow through surf-zone sands in search of clams. Unlucky clams are enveloped by the snail's foot while an acidic secretion softens the clam shell and a tooth-studded tongue (radula) rasps a beveled hole. The hole allows a visit from a proboscis that injects digesting enzymes and later removes liquid clam. Shark's eyes breed in the surf zone by cementing their eggs with sand into a gelatinous sheet that cures into a rubbery **sand collar**, which is hydrodynamically engineered to remain upright on shifting surf sands. Collars disintegrate when eggs hatch, so whole collars found in the swash contain developing little snails.

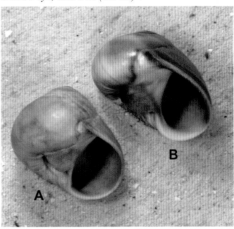

Southern Gulf coast (A), all other coasts (B)

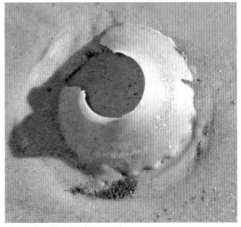

A sand collar in the swash zone

Scotch bonnet, max 4 in (10 cm)

Queen helmet, max 12 in (30 cm)

Reticulate cowrie-helmet, max 3 in (7.6 cm)

Scotch Bonnet and Helmet Shells

Scotch Bonnet   *Queen Helmet and Reticulated Cowrie-helmet*

RELATIVES: These gastropods are in the family Cassidae, distantly related to tun and fig shells.

IDENTIFYING FEATURES: All have a large body whorl with wide, toothy, grinning (or smirking) apertures.

Scotch bonnets *(Phalium granulatum)* are light shells with spiral grooves and a pointed spire. Colors range from white to cream with dark squares.

Queen (cameo) helmets *(Cassis madagascariensis)* are heavy shells with a low spire and a glossy, triangular aperture shield. Their whorl shoulders are studded with blunt knobs. Aperture teeth are light on chestnut. The remaining shield is light or salmon with no central dark blotch like the king helmet (*Cassis tuberosa,* Keys only).

Reticulate cowrie-helmets *(Cypraecassis testiculus)* are dense, egg-shaped shells with smooth spiral grooves and growth lines, and a rounded spire. They are chestnut to salmon with darker, blurry squares.

HABITAT: Scotch bonnets occur in sandy shallows. Queen helmets and cowrie-helmets live on rocky reefs.

DID YOU KNOW? These gastropods feed on sand dollars and sea urchins. Queen helmet populations are low and declining, perhaps due to trawling and habitat loss.

Tun Shells and Figsnail

Giant Tun Shell and Atlantic Figsnail

Atlantic Partridge Tun

RELATIVES: Tun shells (family Tonnidae) are distantly related to figsnails (family Ficadae).

IDENTIFYING FEATURES: All are fragile, spiral-ridged shells with a large body whorl and a low spire.

Giant tun shells *(Tonna galea)* are almost spherical in shape with a wide aperture, prominent spiral ridges, and a plain cream or brown color. Most beach finds are in pieces.

Atlantic partridge tuns *(Tonna maculosa)* are more elongate than the giant tun, with a blurry pattern of alternating, cream and brown rectangles.

Atlantic figsnails *(Ficus papyratia)* are delicately tapered at the front, have a low spire, and are sculptured with fine spiral ridges. Their colors range from cream to tan, sometimes with faint brown dots.

HABITAT: Giant tuns are most common offshore. Atlantic partridge tuns and figsnails live in sandy shallows.

DID YOU KNOW? Tun shells feed on other mollusks, sea cucumbers, and fishes by engulfing their prey within a large expandable proboscis. Figsnails feed on sea urchins, and in life their shells are covered by their large, soft mantle (the part of their body that produces the shell).

Giant tun shell, max 10 in (25 cm)

Atlantic partridge tun, max 5 in (13 cm)

Atlantic figsnail, max 5 in (13 cm)

67

Atlantic trumpet triton, max 12 in (30 cm)

Atlantic hairy triton, max 5 in (13 cm)

Giant hairy triton, max 3.5 in (9 cm)

Triton Shells

Atlantic Hairy and Trumpet Tritons

Giant Hairy Triton

RELATIVES: Tritons are in the family Ranellidae.

IDENTIFYING FEATURES:

Atlantic trumpet tritons *(Charonia variegata)* have a sharply spired, cone-shaped shell sculpted with wide spiral bands. The aperture has white teeth on chestnut-colored lips. Colors include rows of brown smears on a tan background.

Atlantic hairy tritons *(Cymatium aquatile)* have an elongate oval shell sculpted with spiral bands and strong axial ridges, 2/3 of a whorl apart, which represent former outer aperture lips. The current outer lip is also thick and bears paired whitish teeth. The inner lip has evenly spaced teeth.

Giant hairy tritons *(Cymatium parthenopeum)* have a thick, wavy outer lip.

HABITAT: Shallow to deep reefs.

DID YOU KNOW? Rome's Trevi fountain features the Greek mermangod Triton, blowing an Atlantic trumpet triton, which may have inspired the common name. Trumpet tritons feed on sea cucumbers and urchins. The "hairy" tritons are named for the coat of frilly periostracum that covers the living snail. Hairy tritons feed on bivalves.

Nutmeg and Cantharus Snails

RELATIVES: Nutmegs (family Cancellariidae) and cantharus snails (family Buccinidae) are distantly related to auger shells.

IDENTIFYING FEATURES:

Common nutmegs *(Cancellaria reticulata)* are egg-shaped shells with a cross-hatched texture and whorls indented at the sutures. The inner lip of the aperture has two white folds on the columella. Shell colors vary between tan with blurry brown streaks and cream white.

Tinted canthari *(Pollia tincta)* have a similar shape to nutmegs but without distinct whorl indentations. Their outer lip is toothed and the columella is glossy. Background shell color is cream or bluish gray. Most have streaks and smudges of brown.

Ribbed canthari *(Cantharus multangulus)*, also called false drills, have large ridges that are sharply angled at the whorl shoulders.

HABITAT: These snails live in sand, rubble, and seagrass to moderate depths.

DID YOU KNOW? Common nutmegs feed on soft-bodied animals buried in the sand. Canthari get their name from the cantharus, sacred cup of Bacchus, Roman god of wine. Cantharus snails prey on worms, barnacles, and other attached invertebrates.

Common nutmeg, max 1.7 in (4.5 cm)

Tinted cantharus, max 1.2 in (3 cm)

Ribbed cantharus, max 1.2 in (3 cm)

Common American auger, max 2.4 in (6 cm)

Shiny Atlantic auger, max 1.5 in (3.8 cm)

Sallé's auger, max 1.5 in (3.8 cm)

Sanibel turret, max 1 in (2.5 cm)

Augers

Common American
and Sallé's Augers

Shiny Atlantic
Auger

Sanibel
Turret Snail

RELATIVES: Augers (family Terebridae) are distantly related to turrets (family Turridae).

IDENTIFYING FEATURES: Augers are sharp glossy cones with smooth ribs and short, distinct siphon canals.

Common American augers *(Terebra dislocata)* are gray or orange-white with beaded spiral bands between whorls.

Shiny Atlantic augers *(Hastula hastata)* are shiny white with wide orange bands wrapping the bottoms of lower whorls. Their shape is more of a narrow bullet than a sharp cone.

Sallé's augers *(Hastula cinera)* are purple-gray with darker banded ribs below each whorl suture.

Sanibel turrets *(Zonulispira crocata)* have nine ribs crossed by dashlike cords.

HABITAT: Sandy shallows.

DID YOU KNOW? These augers feed on worms. Sallé's Auger is an active hunter. It has a long stride and quick pace, nearly one "footstep" per second, and lunges when it finds a worm above the sand. Like other augers, Sallé's subdues its prey with a stab from a venomous, radular tooth. Their summer mating swarms are in the style portrayed by Burt Lancaster and Deborah Kerr in *From Here to Eternity,* with embracing pairs rolling in the swash zone.

Mudsnails

Threeline and
Eastern Mudsnails | Bruised
Nassa Snail | White
Nassa Snail

Threeline mudsnail, max 7/8 in (22 mm)

RELATIVES: Mudsnails and nassas are in the family Nassariidae.

IDENTIFYING FEATURES: These are small oval snails with conical spires.

Threeline mudsnails *(Ilyanassa trivittata)* are yellowish-gray with shouldered (stepped) whorls and a basketlike texture.

Eastern mudsnails *(Ilyanassa obsoleta)* are solid brown with smooth, slanting, axial ribs. Their apex is typically worn.

Eastern mudsnail, max 1.2 in (3 cm)

Bruised nassas *(Nassarius vibex)* are light gray to dark with strong rounded axial ribs and a pointed spire. Their inner aperture lip is thickened by a wide glossy callus, which in darker shells bears a purple bruise.

White nassas *(Nassarius albus)* are white with brown on their distinct whorl shoulders.

HABITAT: Mudsnails live in muddy sand at the low-tide line. Bruised nassas are in shallow seagrass and white nassas live on sandy bottom to moderate depths.

Bruised nassa, max 3/4 in (20 mm)

DID YOU KNOW? Mudsnails and nassas eat algae, invertebrate eggs, carrion, and other easily outrun items. In Latin, *nassa* means wicker basket.

White nassa, max 1/2 in (13 mm)

Banded tulip, max 4 in (10 cm)

True tulip, max 5 in (13 cm)

Tulip snail egg capsules on a penshell

Tulip Snails

RELATIVES: Tulip snails (family Fasciolariidae) are related to spindle shells.

IDENTIFYING FEATURES: Tulip snails are pointed spindles with rounded curves and a stemlike siphon canal.

Banded tulips *(Fasciolaria lilium)* are cream to light gray with orange or gray splotches and distinctly fine spiral lines of reddish brown. Their whorls are smooth.

True tulips *(Fasciolaria tulipa)* are similar to banded tulips but have darker brown (or orange) splotches and interrupted, closer-set, spiral lines. Their whorls also differ in having fine ridges below each suture.

HABITAT: Banded and true tulips live on sand in water less than 100 ft (30 m).

DID YOU KNOW? True tulips prey on banded tulips, as well as on pear whelks and other mid-size gastropods. Tulip snails crawl into shallow waters during the winter to attach their clustered **egg capsules**, which look like tiny bouquets. The young, miniature tulip snails emerge from holes at the flat end of each frilly capsule. The capsules are formed of a tough, fingernail-like protein. If they rattle, the capsules are likely to contain tiny tulip shells. Several occupy each capsule.

Spindle Shells

Florida Horse Conch

Chestnut Latirus

RELATIVES: Spindle shells share the family Fasciolariidae with tulip snails.

IDENTIFYING FEATURES: Both of these snails are thick-shelled with knobbed whorls that form a pointed spire about half the total shell-length.

Florida horse conchs *(Triplofusus giganteus)* are unmistakably large as adults. They have a whitish spire and are often covered with brown, flaky periostracum. Beach-worn adult shells are white with a glossy tan interior. Living horse conchs have an orange-red body and a thick operculum (trap door).

Chestnut latiri *(Leucozonia nassa)* are dark golden-brown with lighter spiral cords beneath the knobs of its body whorl.

A **juvenile horse conch** resembles a **chestnut latirus** but is a lighter, more uniform, peach-gold, and has a much longer siphon canal.

HABITAT: Both live in waters as shallow as the low-tide line. Chestnut latiri prefer reefs. Horse conchs prefer sand.

DID YOU KNOW? As the largest snail in North America, horse conchs are able to prey on big gastropods like whelks. This impressive mollusk is Florida's state shell. Horse conch egg masses comprise dozens of flattened bugles clustered in a twisted clump. Chestnut latiri feed on barnacles and worms.

A horse conch's orange body and operculum (A)

Horse conch, max 19 in (48 cm), and egg masses

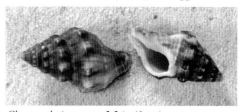
Chestnut latirus, max 2.2 in (6 cm)

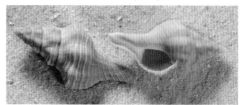
Juvenile horse conch

Knobbed whelk, max 9 in (23 cm), new and worn shells

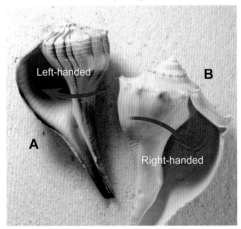

Lightning whelk (A), knobbed whelk (B)

Lightning whelk, max 16 in (40 cm), and egg masses

Whelks *(Knobbed and Lightning)*

Knobbed Whelk   Lightning Whelk

RELATIVES: These snails share the family Melongenidae with pear, channeled, and crown conch whelks.

IDENTIFYING FEATURES: Both species have large body whorls with distinct shoulders and a wide aperture tapering into their long siphon canal.

Knobbed whelks *(Busycon carica)* are light gray to gray-brown and have heavy shells with several triangular knobs on the shoulder of the body whorl. Beach-worn shells often remain intact although every edge is smoothed by surf-sanding.

Lighting whelks *(Busycon sinistrum)* are cream to gray with younger shells showing brown, lightning-bolt, axial streaks. They have a dozen or more petite knobs on their body whorl, which spirals to their left (their spire is rearward). Their left-handed aperture separates them from most other marine snails.

HABITAT: Both live in sandy shallows.

DID YOU KNOW? Knobbed whelks are common on beaches far from where they live. Worn shells from south Florida have probably tumbled south with the longshore current for well over 100 miles (160 km). Both whelks produce egg masses containing dozens of discs attached by a common string. The egg-discs strung together by lightning whelks have edge projections. Those from knobbed whelks are more angled.

Whelks
(Pear, Channeled, and Crown Conch)

Pear Whelk and
Crown Conch   Channeled Whelk

Pear whelk, max 5.5 in (14 cm)

RELATIVES: These snails share the family Melongenidae with other whelks.

IDENTIFYING FEATURES: All have a shouldered body whorl and a wide aperture tapering into their siphon canal.

Pear (fig) whelks *(Busycotypus spiratus)* are cream with brown, wavy, axial streaks. A channel along the suture disappears in earlier whorls.

Channeled whelks *(Busycotypus canaliculatus)* are gray to tan and have a deep channel along their body-whorl suture that goes well into their spire. Their angled whorl shoulders are edged by a lumpy spiral ridge.

Channeled whelk, max 7.5 in (19 cm)

Crown conchs *(Melongena corona)* have spiral bands of blue-gray or brown. Their shell is sculptured by axial ribs along the whorl shoulders that commonly project as hollow spikes, but may be only tiny nubs. Spiky shells also have points at their base. Juvenile crown conchs are least spiky.

HABITAT: Channeled whelks live on intertidal sands and nearby shallows. Pear whelks and crown conchs live on muddy sand in shallow, quiet bay waters.

DID YOU KNOW? These snails scavenge and are often captured in baited traps. Knobbed and channeled whelks are the local scungilli served in Italian restaurants.

Crown conch, max 5 in (13 cm)

75

Glossy dove snail, max 5/8 in (16 mm)

Common dove snail, max 7/8 in (22 mm)

Rusty dove snail, max 1/2 in (13 mm)

Greedy dove snail, max 3/4 in (20 mm)

Sparse dove snail, max 1/2 in (13 mm)

Dove Snails

| Glossy and Common Dove Snails | Rusty and Sparse Dove Snails | Greedy Dove Snail |

RELATIVES: Dove snails are in the family Columbellidae.

IDENTIFYING FEATURES: Dove snails have tubby shells the size of a pencil eraser with pointed spires, short siphon canals, and toothed aperture lips.

Glossy dove snails *(Nitidella nitida)*, are smooth and splotched with light on brown or brown on light.

Common (West Indian) dove snails *(Columbella mercatoria)* have a triangular body whorl wrapped in rounded spiral cords. Their cords are dashed with white and orange-brown.

Rusty dove snails *(Columbella rusticoides)* have rounded whorls and an outer aperture lip that is tinted and thickened in the center.

Greedy dove snails *(Costoanachis avara)* have 12 ribs on their body whorl highlighted by white splotches.

Sparse dove snails *(Costoanachis sparsa)* are orange and white and have 20 or more ribs with crossing cords.

HABITAT: Dove snails live in seagrass or rubble out to moderate depths.

DID YOU KNOW? Common and rusty dove snails graze on algae. Greedy and sparse dove snails are carnivores or scavengers. Dove snail eggs are laid within single capsules, and young emerge either swimming or crawling.

Murex Shells
(Giant Eastern, Apple, and Lace)

Giant Eastern Murex   Apple and
                            Lace Murices

RELATIVES: Murices share the family Muricidae with drills and rocksnails.

IDENTIFYING FEATURES: All have highly sculptured shells with round apertures and tubular siphon canals.

Giant eastern murices *(Murex fulvescens)* are turnip-shaped with a body whorl sculptured by about 8 axial ridges (varices), each bearing pronounced hollow spikes. Beached shells are white to gray and may have only worn knobs instead of spikes.

Apple murices *(Chicoreus pomum)* are cream with brown bands and have 3 lumpy varices per whorl. Their inner aperture lip has a thin, flared margin and a dark blotch opposite the siphon canal.

Lace murices *(Chicoreus dilectus)* are similar to apple murices but differ in having varices lined with hollow, scoop-shaped spines, and in having a simple, circular, unmarked aperture.

HABITAT: Giant eastern murices live on sand to about 325 ft (100 m). Lace murices live in shallow rubble. Apple murices inhabit intertidal sands.

DID YOU KNOW? These murices are predators of bivalves, which are devoured through holes rasped in their shells. Apple and giant eastern murices prefer oysters.

Giant eastern murex, max 7 in (18 cm)

Apple murex, max 4.5 in (12 cm)

Lace murex, max 3.2 in (8 cm)

77

Pitted murex, max 1 in (2.5 cm)

Pitted Murex and Drills
(Mauve-mouth, Sharp-ribbed, and Thick-lipped)

| Pitted Murex | Mauve-mouth and Sharp-ribbed Drills | Thick-lipped Drill |

RELATIVES: Murices and drills are in the murex family, Muricidae.

IDENTIFYING FEATURES: All have sculptured shells with pointed spires.

Pitted murices *(Favartia cellulosa)* are dull-white, have 5–7 lumpy varices per whorl, and have a narrow, upturned siphon canal.

Mauve-mouth drill, max 1.2 in (3 cm)

Mauve-mouth drills *(Calotrophon ostrearum)* are grayish-white with 7–10 axial ribs and two spiral cords on the lower half of each spire-whorl. The inside aperture is pinkish-purple.

Sharp-ribbed drills *(Eupleura sulcidentata)* are similar to thick-lipped drills but have smoother whorls and sharper lips.

Thick-lipped drills *(Eupleura caudata)* are pinkish with a long, thin siphon canal, an oval aperture, and a thick, toothed outer lip opposite an equally thick ridge (varix) on the body whorl.

Sharp-ribbed drill, max 7/8 in (22 mm)

HABITAT: Pitted murices and drills live near oyster beds in shallow bays.

DID YOU KNOW? Drills pierce oysters by secreting shell-softening acids and rasping with their toothy radula. The resulting hole is round and tapering to a small pinpoint, just wide enough for the drill to insert digestive enzymes and withdraw oyster soup.

Thick-lipped drill, max 1.5 in (4 cm)

Gulf Oyster Drill and Rocksnail

Gulf Oyster Drill and Florida Rocksnail

Gulf oyster drill, max 1 in (2.5 cm)

RELATIVES: Drills and rocksnails are in the murex family, Muricidae.

IDENTIFYING FEATURES:

Gulf oyster drills *(Urosalpinx perrugata)* are yellowish with 6–9 large, rounded, axial ribs around each whorl, crossed by numerous spiral cords.

Florida rocksnails *(Stramonita haemastoma)* have sculptured shells and wide apertures with a toothed outer lip. They are whitish to grayish and frequently show red-brown spots. Their shells are highly variable, but all have spiral cords and axial ridges that are most prominent at the shoulders, which may have knobs. Knob size ranges from none to large, aperture color ranges white to orange, and the outer lip interior may have tiny brown lines or fine white ribs. Some of these forms overlap in distribution and may represent as many as three species in Florida.

Florida rocksnail, max 3 in (8 cm)

HABITAT: Florida rocksnails and Gulf oyster drills live in rocky, intertidal areas and oyster bars. Rocksnails are common on jetties.

DID YOU KNOW? Rocksnails feed on bivalves, gastropods, and barnacles. Rocksnail eggs are contained in tan or purple-stained, vase-shaped capsules that are attached to rocks during communal gatherings of snails.

A living Florida rocksnail on a jetty boulder

79

Lettered olive, max 2.7 in (7 cm)

Lettered olives show color variation with wear

Variable dwarf olive, max 5/8 in (16 mm)

Olive Shells

RELATIVES: Olive shells are in the family Olividae, distantly related to vase, volute, marginella, and cone shells.

IDENTIFYING FEATURES: All have cylindrical, glossy shells with narrow, elongate apertures.

Lettered olives *(Oliva sayana)* have a thick shell with a small pointed spire about 1/9 total shell length. Unfaded shells are covered with overlapping, slightly blurry, brown zigzags that are darkest just below the suture and as part of two, broad, spiral bands. The similar netted olive, *Oliva reticularis* (southeast only), has no bands and a larger spire of about 1/7 total shell length.

Variable dwarf olives *(Olivella mutica)* are gray to brown, variably marked, and have a spire nearly half their shell length. Their aperture is triangular with an inner, ridged, parietal callus that extends beyond the aperture up to the next suture. Several other dwarf olive species occur in Florida.

HABITAT: Lettered and variable dwarf olives live within sand in waters as shallow as the low-tide mark.

DID YOU KNOW? An olive's glossy shell is covered in life by its body mantle and large foot. Their strong foot allows them to burrow easily through sand. Lettered olives prey on coquina clams in the surf zone, and both species scavenge when opportunities arise.

Junonia and Vase Shells

Junonia   Vase Shell

RELATIVES: Junonias are volutes, family Volutidae, and are only distantly related to vase shells, which are in the family Turbinellidae.

IDENTIFYING FEATURES:

Junonias *(Scaphella junonia)* have unmistakably flamboyant shells with squared, chestnut spots on a background of pinkish ivory. They have a wide aperture and rounded whorls that spin into a distinct spire with a rounded apex.

Caribbean vase shells *(Vasum muricatum)* have dense, cone-shaped shells with short, pointed spires, spiral cords, and numerous blunt knobs at the whorl shoulders. They are dull white with occasional purple tinges.

HABITAT: Junonias live on offshore reefs and Caribbean vases live on shallow reefs.

DID YOU KNOW? Junonia shells are a rare find but they inspire a common quest. Because Florida is the hotspot for this rare and spectacular shell, junonias receive much attention, especially from visitors to Sanibel where, island-wide, roughly one junonia per day is found. Like their shell, the soft parts of the living junonia are covered with spots. Junonias and vases are predators of bivalves.

Junonia, max 3.5 in (9 cm)

Beach-worn junonia shells

Caribbean vase shell, max 3 in (8 cm)

81

Florida cone, max 2 in (5 cm)

Jasper cone, max 1 in (2.5 cm)

Alphabet cone, max 3 in (7.5 cm)

Cone Shells

Florida and Alphabet Cones   *Jasper Cone*

RELATIVES: Cone shells are in the family Conidae, distantly related to volutes, olives, vases, and marginellas.

IDENTIFYING FEATURES: Cone shells are cone-shaped, with long, thin apertures.

Florida cones *(Conus anabathrum)* have a medium-high spire and a body whorl with orange or yellow streaks and splotches on a lighter background.

Jasper cones *(Conus jaspideus)* have a high spire and distinct spiral cords that bear dashes of white and orange or brown.

Alphabet cones *(Conus spurius atlanticus)* have a low, concave spire and spiral rows of orange dots, dashes, and checks.

HABITAT: These cones live in shallow to moderately deep sand and seagrass.

DID YOU KNOW? Cone shells have radular teeth that look and function like harpoons. They use this needle-like weapon to inject venom into the animals they eat, and into would-be attackers. Deadly neurotoxin venoms from fish-eating, Indo-pacific cones are used in medicine for treating stroke, heart disease, and chronic pain. Florida's tamer, worm-eating species have much milder venom. There are about 400 species of cone shells, 16 of which are found in Florida.

Melampus Snail and Marginellas

Coffee Malampus, White-spot,   Atlantic Marginella
and Orange Marginellas

Coffee melampus, max 3/4 in (19 mm)

RELATIVES: Melampus (family Marginellidae) and marginella shells (family Ellobiidae) are distantly related.

IDENTIFYING FEATURES:

Coffee melampi *(Melampus coffea)* have an egg-shaped shell with smooth, broadly conical spires. Their thin outer aperture lip has numerous fine ridges inside. Colors range from pale gray to brown with thin spiral bands.

Atlantic marginella, max 1/2 in (13 mm)

Atlantic marginellas *(Prunum apicinum)* have a glossy, egg-shaped shell with a low spire and a thick, smooth, outer aperture lip margin extending up past the preceding whorl. Colors range from gray to tan.

White-spot marginellas *(Prunum guttatum)* are pale to brown with numerous light spots.

Orange marginellas *(Prunum carneum)* are orange with a light mid-whorl band.

White-spot marginella, max 1 in (2.5 cm)

HABITAT: Coffee melampus snails live at the high tide line near mangroves. Marginellas live in shallow sand and seagrass areas.

DID YOU KNOW? Several other melampus and marginella species occur in Florida. Melampus snails have a lung instead of gills and spend most of their time out of water. Marginellas get their name from their wide margin (aperture lip). They feed as mostly as scavengers.

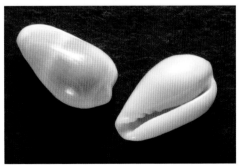

Orange marginella, max 3/4 in (2 cm)

83

Striate bubble shell, max 1 in (2.5 cm)

Bubble Shell and Sea Hare

Striate Bubble Shell   *Mottled Sea Hare*

RELATIVES: Bubble shells (family Bullidae) are related to headshield sea slugs. Sea hares (family Aplysiidae) are gastropods with internal shells.

IDENTIFYING FEATURES:

Striate bubbles *(Bulla striata)* have a fragile, smooth, mottled-brown, egg-shaped shell with a sunken apex and an aperture longer than the body whorl.

Mottled sea hares *(Aplysia brasiliana)* when beached look like a slippery, writhing, elongate blob with dark mottling background of green or brown. The blunt head has a rabbitlike face with a fleshy moustache (oral tentacles) and two beady eyes below two, soft, rabbit-ear horns (rhinophores). In water, they swim by undulating winglike parapodia that are dark and edged with light scallops. Sooty sea hares *(A. morio)* are dark purple and spotted sea hares *(A. dactylomela)* are yellow-green with dark rings.

Mottled sea hare, max 8 in (20 cm); arrow shows eye

HABITAT: Both striate bubbles and mottled sea hares live in shallow seagrass.

DID YOU KNOW? Sea hares beach after population booms and when rough seas sweep them from the shallows. They are among few animals that feed on toxic cynobacteria (blue-green algae). When stressed, seas hares release purple ink. Sea hares have both male and female working parts and perform as both in mating chains.

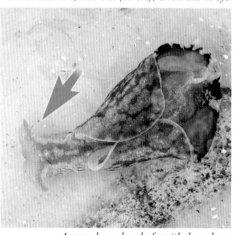

Arrow shows head of mottled sea hare

Glaucus, Pteropod, and Land Snail

Glaucus and Pteropod   *Gray Peanut Snail*

A beached blue glaucus, max 2 in (5 cm)

RELATIVES: Blue glaucus sea slugs (order Nudibranchia), pteropods (order Thecosomata), and land snails (order Stylommatophora) are distantly related gastropods.

IDENTIFYING FEATURES:

Blue glaucus sea slugs *(Glaucus atlanticus)* have tapered bodies and paired, handlike cerata. From above, they are deep blue on a silvery blue background. Below they are silver gray.

A beached blue glaucus placed in water

Straight-needle pteropods *(Creseis acicula)* have glassy, needle-shaped shells that occasionally beach in massive numbers. This tiny, shelled sea slug has paired winglike flaps for swimming.

Gray peanut snails *(Cerion incanum)* have a pale, lightweight, bullet-shaped shell with tight whorls and a rounded aperture bearing a thickened lip.

HABITAT: Pteropods and blue glaucus slugs inhabit the open ocean surface. Gray peanut snails live on terrestrial plants in salt-spray environments.

Straight-needle pteropod, max 3/8 in (1 cm)

DID YOU KNOW? The blue glaucus floats upside down (foot up) due to an air bubble in its stomach. Their cerata bear stinging cells taken in by feeding on Portuguese man-o-war. Pteropods feed by trapping plankton in a mucous web. Peanut snail shells reach the beach from land thanks to the travels of land hermit crabs (see page 128).

Gray peanut snail, max 1 in (2.5 cm)

Blood ark, max 3 in (7.5 cm)

Transverse ark, max 1.4 in (3.6 cm)

Ponderous ark, max 2.8 in (7 cm)

Arks
(Blood, Transverse, and Ponderous)

RELATIVES: Ark shells are allied within the family Arcidae.

IDENTIFYING FEATURES: All ark shells are thick to very thick with forward umbones and distinct ribs.

Blood arks *(Anadara ovalis)* have a very thick, oval shell with an arched hinge-line bearing about 7 teeth in front of the umbo and about 30 teeth behind. The most rearward hinge teeth are largest and angled backward.

Transverse arks *(Anadara transversa)* have an elongate oval shell with a relatively straight hinge-line bearing mostly vertical teeth below a thin ligament scar the length of the hinge.

Ponderous arks *(Noetia ponderosa)* have a very thick, triangular shell with flat, divided ribs and an arched hinge-line below a broad moustachelike, grooved, ligament area.

HABITAT: These arks live in nearshore sands as shallow as the low-tide line.

DID YOU KNOW? These ark shells are coated with a brown, fuzzy periostracum in life, worn white after beaching, or may be stained gray, rust, or black. Robust shells make blood and ponderous arks among the most common whole shells on high-energy beaches where waves pulverize most other mollusks. The blood ark gets its name from its uncommon, hemoglobin-red blood.

Arks *(Incongruous, Eared, Cut-ribbed, and White Miniature)*

Incongruous Ark

Eared, Cut-ribbed, and White Miniature Arks

Incongruous ark, max 3 in (7.5 cm)

IDENTIFYING FEATURES:

Incongruous arks *(Anadara brasiliana)* are thin-shelled for an ark. Their strong radial ribs have distinct dash-shaped beads.

Eared arks *(Anadara notabilis)* have shells with rounded ribs and a long, straight hinge-line that angles sharply with the front and rear edges. The upper rear of unworn shells has a flattened, pointed "ear."

Cut-ribbed arks *(Anadara floridana)* are similar to eared arks but have flattened ribs. Each of the forward ribs (toward umbo) has a deep central "cut."

White miniature arks *(Barbatia domingensis)* have rear-pointed shells with heavy growth lines that give it a scaly look.

HABITAT: Incongruous and eared arks live within shallow sandy bottom. Cut-ribbed arks live in offshore sands but are closer to shore in south Florida. White miniature arks grow under shallow-water rubble.

DID YOU KNOW? Young eared arks attach themselves to small bits of rubble using a threadlike byssus. As they grow they become unattached burrowers. White miniature arks remain attached for life.

Eared ark, max 3 in (7.5 cm)

Cut-ribbed ark, max 4.5 in (11.5 cm)

White miniature ark, max 7/8 in. (22 mm)

Mossy ark, max 2.5 in (6.3 cm)

Turkey wing, max 3.6 in (9 cm)

Red-brown ark, max 1.3 in (3.3 cm)

Arks *(Mossy, Turkey Wing, and Red-brown)*

Mossy and Turkey Wing Arks	*Red-brown Ark*

IDENTIFYING FEATURES: These arks have elongate, rectangular shells with long, straight, hinge-lines below a broad, triangular ligament area.

Mossy arks *(Arca imbricata)* have shells with beaded ribs and are mostly chestnut brown.

Turkey wings (zebra arks) *(Arca zebra)* have shells with rough ribs, but less beaded than in the mossy ark. Turkey wing shells are striped by nested, red-brown V's or W's at the umbo that turn into oblique lines or zig-zags rearward.

Red-brown arks *(Barbatia cancellaria)* are finely beaded and brown except for a light streak from the umbo down.

HABITAT: These arks live attached by byssal threads to shallow-water rubble.

DID YOU KNOW? The arched shell-gap opposite the umbo in these arks marks the opening where byssal threads anchor them to the bottom. In the Caribbean, thousands of tons of turkey wing arks are harvested each year to be canned and eaten. These filter-feeding bivalves are targets in one of the most important fisheries in Venezuela. Both mossy and turkey wing arks are ecologically important as plankton feeders, prey, and substrate for benthic animals.

Bittersweet Clams

RELATIVES: Bittersweets are in the family Glycymerididae, and may be distantly related to the arks.

IDENTIFYING FEATURES: Bittersweet clams have heavy, rounded shells with thick, arching hinge-lines bearing several prominent teeth on either side of the umbo.

Giant bittersweets (*Glycymeris americana*) have a nearly circular shell with a small, rounded umbo and roughly 50 flattened ribs. They are glossy cream with concentric, blurry necklaces of tan or rust.

Spectral bittersweets (*Glycymeris spectralis*) have a slightly triangular (or elliptical) shell with a large umbo and 30–40 smooth ribs. They range from white to brown and frequently show varied radiating, sunburst streaks of white on chestnut, or vice versa.

Comb bittersweets (*Glycymeris pectinata*) have a nearly circular shell with a small, relatively pointed umbo, and 20–30 raised ribs. They are slightly roughened by growth lines and are grayish-white with brownish spatters.

HABITAT: These bittersweet clams live in sand from shallow moderate depths.

DID YOU KNOW? Bittersweets are indeed named for their taste and are elements of recipes in many eastern Atlantic countries. They live unattached and have light-sensitive eyespots along their mantle.

Giant bittersweet clam, max 4 in (10 cm)

Spectral bittersweet clam, max 1.5 in (3.8 cm)

Comb bittersweet clam, max 1.2 in (3 cm)

Ribbed mussel, max 5 in (13 cm)

Scorched mussel, max 1.5 in (4 cm)

Southern (A) and American (B) horse mussels

Green mussel, max 3.5 in (9 cm)

Mussels

Ribbed Mussel *Scorched, Horse, and Green Mussels*

RELATIVES: Mussels (family Mytilidae) are distantly related to penshells.

IDENTIFYING FEATURES: Mussels have thin shells that fan out from their umbones and tend to retain their thin, shiny periostracum.

Ribbed mussels *(Geukensia demissa)* have shells with radiating ribs and no hinge teeth. Shells without the brown periostracum are yellowed gray with occasional purple tinges.

Scorched mussels *(Brachidontes exustus)* have shells with radiating ribs and 2 or 3 hinge teeth under the umbo.

Horse mussels *(Modiolus* spp.) have inflated shells and an umbo just shy of their upper end. Two similar species occur. **Southern horse mussels** *(M. squamosus)* reach 2.5 in (6.5 cm), have less-inflated umbones, and are whitish or purple after beach wear. **American horse mussels** *(M. americanus)* reach 4 in (10 cm), have bulbous umbones, and are bright red through their golden periostracum.

Green mussels *(Perna viridis)* have a smooth, green and brown exterior.

HABITAT: These mussels grow attached to rocks or pilings in estuarine waters as shallow at the intertidal zone.

DID YOU KNOW? Green mussels are alien invaders from Asia.

Penshells

Sawtooth Penshell   Half-naked   Stiff Penshell
Penshell

RELATIVES: Penshells (family Pinnidae) are distantly related to mussels.

IDENTIFYING FEATURES: Penshells have thin, amber-brown, fanlike valves.

Sawtooth penshells *(Atrina serrata)* have about 30 radiating ribs bearing hundreds of short, hollow prickles.

Half-naked penshells *(Atrina seminuda)* have about 15 radiating ribs bearing a few to dozens of long tubular spines. Their posterior (fan end) muscle scar is completely within their pearly (or cloudy) "nacreous" area. Amber penshells *(Pinna carnea,* southeast beaches only) have their hinge (dorsal) side much longer than the opposite open (ventral) side.

Stiff penshells *(Atrina rigida)* are darker and broader than half-naked penshells and have their posterior muscle scar outside the shiny nacre.

HABITAT: Penshells live in colonies with individuals buried in soft sediment out to 20 ft (6 m).

DID YOU KNOW? Pen shells anchor themselves with golden byssal threads, which lead from their pointed (front) end to a small bit of rubble beneath the sand. Like most bivalves, they are filter feeders. Many living penshells have pale, soft-bodied pen shrimp living within their mantle cavity.

Sawtooth penshell, max 9 in (23 cm)

Half-naked penshell, max 9 in (23 cm)

Stiff penshell, max 11 in (28 cm), arrow shows scar

Atlantic wing oyster, max 3.5 in (9 cm)

Atlantic pearl oyster, max 3.5 in (9 cm)

Flat tree-oyster, max 4 in (10 cm)

Oysters

Atlantic Wing and Atlantic Pearl Oysters   *Flat Tree-oyster*

RELATIVES: Wing and pearl oysters, family Pteriidae, are related to flat tree-oysters, family Isognomonidae.

IDENTIFYING FEATURES: These oysters have straight hinges and thin shells covered with scaly periostracum.

Atlantic wing oysters *(Pteria colymbus)* have valves with a triangular front wing near the umbo and a long rear wing extending past the rest of the shell.

Atlantic pearl oysters *(Pinctada imbricata)* have valves with short triangular front and rear wings and have a scaly, fringelike periostracum.

Flat tree-oysters *(Isognomon alatus)* have both valves equally flat and a straight hinge with 8–12 distinct grooves.

HABITAT: These free-swinging bivalves live attached by their byssal threads. Atlantic wing and Atlantic pearl oysters are attached mostly to offshore soft corals. Flat tree oysters attach to shallow-water rubble and mangrove prop roots.

DID YOU KNOW? These oysters are most commonly found after storms have washed in the soft corals, mangrove roots, and trap-float lines on which they grow. Southern Caribbean pearl oysters produce pearls and were harvested to depletion by the Spanish in the late 1500s.

Scallops *(Calico and Bay)*

Atlantic Calico Scallop   Bay Scallop

Atlantic calico scallop, max 2.7 in (7 cm)

RELATIVES: Scallops are allied within the family Pectinidae.

IDENTIFYING FEATURES: Scallops have round or oval shells with distinct ribs and winglike "ear" projections on either side of the umbo.

Atlantic calico scallops *(Argopecten gibbus)* have shells with 19–21 rounded ribs. Shell colors vary through white, yellow, orange, red, purple, and gray, generally with splotches of dark on light. Their ears are often worn.

Atlantic bay scallops *(Argopecten irradians)* have shells with 17–18 ribs that are squarish in comparison to calico scallops. Shell color may be white, gray-brown, or orange.

Atlantic bay scallop, max 4 in (10 cm)

HABITAT: Atlantic calico scallops live on sand bottom at depths to 1300 ft (400 m). Bay scallops live on muddy sands and seagrass in shallow waters.

DID YOU KNOW? The palest scallop shells are the right (lower) valves. Due to overharvest and habitat loss, once plentiful bay scallops are scarce in Florida except for the Big Bend region. A fishery for calico scallops off Cape Canaveral has taken as much as 40 million pounds (18 million kg) per year, but population busts bring about years when few are harvested. Scallops filter-feed on bits of organic stuff, and are eaten by gastropods, squid, octopi, sea stars, crabs, and people.

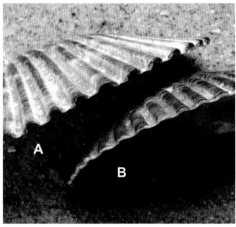

Bay scallop (A) and calico scallop (B)

Antillean scallop, max 2 in (5 cm)

A

Zigzag scallop, max 4 in (10 cm) lower valve (A)

Round-rib scallop, upper valve, max 2 in (5 cm)

Scallops
(Antillean, Zigzag, and Round-rib)

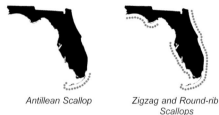

Antillean Scallop · Zigzag and Round-rib Scallops

IDENTIFYING FEATURES:

Antillean scallops *(Bractechlamys antillarum)* have shells colored yellow to peach with occasional purplish streaks. They have about 10 broad ribs separated by several fine lines.

Zigzag scallops *(Euvola ziczac)* have a domelike lower valve and an upper valve that looks as if it were melted flat. Their color pattern has distinct zigzags of purple on a background of cream, orange, or light purple.

Round-rib scallops *(Euvola raveneli)* are similar to zigzag scallops but have rounder, separated ribs on the flat, upper valve. The flat valve varies from light gray to purple with rayed streaks.

HABITAT: Antillean scallops live in shallow coraline sands. Round-rib and zigzag scallops live in waters as deep as 330 ft (100 m).

DID YOU KNOW? Round-rib and zigzag scallops lay with their flat upper valve flush with the sandy bottom. If disturbed by a potential predator, they launch from the bottom by clapping their valves to create jets of propulsion. Scallops are the swiftest of the bivalves. Most have numerous light-sensing eyes lining their mantle to detect predators and perhaps even steer their swimming.

Scallops *(Scaly and Rough)*

Scaly Scallop   Rough Scallop

IDENTIFYING FEATURES:

Scaly scallops *(Caribachlamys sentis)* have fan-shaped shells with numerous, finely beaded ribs and a front ear about 5 times longer than the rear one. They are most often a mottled orange-red but may also be pale, light orange, purple, or combinations of these colors.

Rough scallops *(Lindapecten muscosus)* have a rounder shape than scaly scallops, less lopsided ear lengths, and fewer (only about 19) ribs that are roughened by tiny spoon-shaped prickles. Beach-worn shells are less prickly. Most rough scallops are solid-colored lemon, peach, or tangerine, but some are mottled with plum.

HABITAT: Scaly scallops live attached beneath rubble in shallow to moderate depths. Rough scallops are free-living on offshore sand banks.

DID YOU KNOW? The eyes lining each mantle of the scaly scallop are as red as its shell. Scallops also have long tentacles for touch and taste that fringe their open shell. Both of these scallops are only moderately common but are conspicuous on the beach due to their sanguine colors.

Scaly scallop, max 1.6 in (4.1 cm)

Rough scallop, max 1.5 in (4 cm)

A rough scallop's rib prickles

95

Lion's-paw, max 6 in (15.2 cm)

Atlantic kittenpaw, max 1.2 in (3 cm)

Atlantic kittenpaw color and shape variation

Scallops *(Lion's-paw and Atlantic Kittenpaw)*

Lion's-paw Scallop

Atlantic Kittenpaw Scallop

IDENTIFYING FEATURES:

Lion's-paws *(Nodipecten nodosus)* have thick, flattened shells with 7–8 large, roughly ridged ribs bearing occasional hollow knuckles. Their outer shell color is commonly orange or brick red, but may range from pale to purple.

Atlantic kittenpaws *(Plicatula gibbosa)* have thick, tough, flattened shells with 6–10 curving, digitlike ribs. They are white to gray except for their tabby-orange ribs marked with numerous, thin, red-brown lines.

HABITAT: Lion's-paws live offshore in sandy rubble at depths up to 160 ft (50 m). Atlantic kittenpaws live attached to rocks in waters from intertidal depth to 300 ft (91 m).

DID YOU KNOW? Lion's-paws are impressive and rare enough to be a quest shell for many beachcombers. Although bits and pieces are moderately common on the Atlantic coast, whole shells are an unusual find. Kittenpaws are common on beaches in part due to their toughness. Left-valve kittenpaws are most common because the right valve often remains attached where the animal lived. The flat attachment site on the right valve retains an impression of the shell or rock on which it grew.

Atlantic Thorny Oyster, Common Jingle Shell, and Crested Oyster

Atlantic Thorny Oyster *Common Jingle Shell and Crested Oyster*

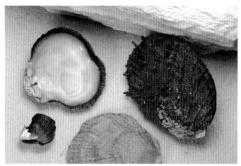

Atlantic thorny oyster, max 5.1 in (13 cm)

RELATIVES: Atlantic thorny oysters (family Spondylidae) are related to jingle shells (family Anomiidae) and crested oysters (family Ostreidae).

IDENTIFYING FEATURES:

Atlantic thorny oysters *(Spondylus* spp.) have thick, circular, lumpy valves with occasional thorns (long in unworn shells). The hinge on the cup-shaped lower valve has two large cardinal teeth separated by a split, and the upper valve hinge has two corresponding sockets. Colors are commonly orange and brick red.

Common jingle shell, max 2 in (5 cm)

Common jingle shells *(Anomia ephippium)* have round, translucent shells with no clear umbo or hinge. Their colors include silver-gray, white, yellow, and orange. Black shells have been stained by sulfurous sediments.

Crested oysters *(Ostreola equestris)* have oval, lumpy shells. Unworn shells have a rayed, flaky periostracum.

Crested oyster, max 2 in (5 cm)

HABITAT: Atlantic thorny oysters attach to rocky reefs and include two species: *S. ictericus* (shallow) and *S. americanus* (deep). Common jingle shells and crested oysters live attached in shallow marine waters to rocks, wood, and other shells.

DID YOU KNOW? Nearly all beached jingle shells are the unattached left valve.

Crested oysters attached to beached flotsam

97

Eastern oyster, max 6 in. (15 cm)

Frond oysters on sea whips, max 2.7 in (7 cm)

Frond oysters on a trap float

Antillean lima, max 1.1 in (2.8 cm)

Oysters and Antillean Lima

Eastern Oyster   Frond Oyster   Antillian Lima

RELATIVES: Oysters are in the family Ostreidae and limas are in the family Limidae.

IDENTIFYING FEATURES:

Eastern oysters *(Crassostrea virginica)* have lumpy shells that vary from oval to clown-shoe shapes. Their inner surface is smooth with a purple muscle scar.

Frond oysters *(Dendostrea frons)* have yellow- or purple-colored oval shells with strong radial ridges ending in interlocking scalloped margins. Those attached by fingerlike shell projections to the branches of soft corals have the most elongate shell shape.

Antillean limas *(Limaria pellucida)* have thin white shells with fine riblets.

HABITAT: These oysters live in shallow waters attached to rocks, debris, or other oysters. Eastern oysters prefer brackish waters. Frond oysters often grow on sea whips. Limas live in crevices.

DID YOU KNOW? Eastern oysters are common near inlets and in seafood raw bars. Frond oysters are beached with storm-tossed corals and trap parts. All are filter feeders and are preyed upon by a variety of animals. Northeast Florida barrier islands have 4000-year-old Timucuan middens piled 50 ft (15 m) high with eastern oyster shells.

Lucines *(Buttercup, Thick Buttercup, and Pennsylvania)*

Buttercup lucine, max 2.5 in (6.4 cm)

RELATIVES: Lucines are allied within the family Lucinidae.

IDENTIFYING FEATURES: Lucines have thick circular shells with forward-pointing umbones above a distinct, heart-shaped impression (the lunule) split by the valve opening.

Buttercup lucines *(Anodontia alba)* have a forward flare that forms a keel protruding more than the umbo. The outer shell is dull white with fine growth lines and the inner shell is butter yellow or cream.

Thick buttercup, max 2.7 in (6.7 cm)

Thick buttercup lucines *(Lucina pectinata)* are similar to buttercup lucines but are thicker shelled, more compressed, and have coarser growth lines. A furrow creases behind the umbo, which protrudes about as much as the keel in front of it. Colors are generally on the pale side of yellow or orange.

Pennsylvania lucines *(Lucina pensylvanica)* have very thick, off-white valves with a deep furrow either side of the umbo. Thin, scaly, growth lines are separated by smooth bands.

HABITAT: All live in sandy shallows. Buttercup lucines and Pennsylvania lucines can live as deep as 300 ft. (90 m).

DID YOU KNOW? Lucines are named for Lucina, an aspect of the Roman goddess Juno who represented light and childbirth.

Pennsylvania lucine, max 2 in (5 cm)

Tiger lucina, max 3.5 in (8.9 cm)

Cross-hatched lucine, max 1 in (2.5 cm)

Cross-hatched lucine detail

Lucines *(Tiger Lucina and Cross-hatched Lucine)*

Tiger Lucina   Cross-hatched Lucine

IDENTIFYING FEATURES:

Tiger lucinas *(Codakia orbicularis)* are compressed with thick, yellow-white valves sculptured with fine riblets and concentric growth ridges. Their lunule is a small deep pit beneath a pointed umbo. The insides of the youngest shells are yellow, rimmed with pink.

Cross-hatched lucines *(Divaricella quadrisulcata)* are moderately inflated with relatively thin valves sculptured by numerous, parallel lines that make the shell appear covered with fingerprints. Beached shells are glossy white, chalky, or ivory.

HABITAT: Both of these lucines live in muddy sand in shallow waters. Cross-hatched lucines occur the deepest to about 300 ft (90 m).

DID YOU KNOW? Tiger lucinas are most common on beaches with coraline sands. Lucines filter plankton and detritus from water drawn into a mucus-lined tube that is maintained by their long foot.

Jewelboxes and Cardita

Florida Spiny Jewelbox and Broad-ribbed Cardita

Leafy and Corrugate Jewelboxes

Florida spiny jewelbox, max 2.5 in (6.3 cm)

RELATIVES: Jewelboxes (family Chamidae) and carditas (family Carditidae) are allied with clamlike bivalves.

IDENTIFYING FEATURES:

Florida spiny jewelboxes *(Arcinella cornuta)* are shaped like tubby commas bearing about 8 radiating ridges with hollow spines (or knobs, if beach-worn). They are white with a pinkish interior.

Leafy jewelboxes *(Chama macerophylla)* have thick, oval shells covered in numerous scaly ridges. Beach-worn shells are lumpy, but new shells may have long, hollow scales. They are generally yellow or chalky, but are often orange or lavender.

Leafy jewelbox, max 3.1 in (8 cm)

Corrugate jewelboxes *(Chama congregata)* have a corrugated exterior, fine ridges within the inner valve margins, and are reddish outside, purplish inside.

Broad-ribbed carditas *(Carditamera floridana)* have very thick valves with about 15 strong, beaded ribs. They are most often white with bands of chestnut.

HABITAT: Jewelboxes live cemented to reefs and debris to moderate depths. Florida spiny jewelboxes detach when young to grow free within sandy rubble. Carditas live in shallow sands.

Corrugate jewelbox, max 1 in (2.5 cm)

DID YOU KNOW? Spines and scales help bivalves avoid being drilled by gastropod predators.

Broad-ribbed cardita, max 2.5 in (6.3 cm)

101

Atlantic strawberry-cockle, max 2 in (5.1 cm)

Atlantic giant cockle, max 5.2 in (13.2 cm)

Spiny papercockle, max 1.8 in (4.5 cm)

Cockles

Atlantic Strawberry-cockle and Spiny Papercockle *Atlantic Giant Cockle*

RELATIVES: Cockles are allied within the family Cardiidae.

IDENTIFYING FEATURES: Cockle shells are oval, inflated, and have a large umbo with one central tooth and socket.

Atlantic strawberry-cockles *(Americardia media)* are cream with red-brown specks and have numerous flattened ribs that feel like sandpaper. An angled ridge runs from the umbo across the longest part of the shell.

Atlantic giant cockles *(Dinocardium robustum)* are cream with brown or tan in segments along their shell ribs, which are rounded and bumpy on one side (the front) flattened and smooth on the other (the rear).

Spiny papercockles *(Papyridea soleniformis)* are compressed for a cockle with rear ribs ending in protruding spines. They are mottled with pale pink, purple, orange, or red-brown.

HABITAT: These cockles live in sandy shallows off beaches. Atlantic giant cockles may occur as deep as 100 ft (30 m).

DID YOU KNOW? Giant cockles are also called heart cockles. Shells of this species found on Gulf beaches have more pronounced color patterns than Atlantic shells and are often separated as a subspecies called Van Hyning's cockle *(Dinocardium robustum vanhyningi)*.

Pricklycockles

Florida and Yellow Pricklycockles   Even Pricklycockle

RELATIVES: Pricklycockles are allied with other cockles in the family Cardiidae.

IDENTIFYING FEATURES: Pricklycockles have inflated valves with a large umbo and a lone tooth and socket. Their ribs bear sharp, cuplike scales, which are reduced to bumps when beach-worn.

Florida pricklycockles *(Trachycardium egmontianum)* have about 30 pronounced ribs covered by strong scales (in unworn shells) and ending in a hind margin that is deeply serrated. Their external color is cream with tan or purple-brown splotches. Their valves inside are salmon and/or purple.

Even pricklycockles *(T. isocardia)* are similar to Florida pricklycockles but are heavier, more elongate, and have more ribs (about 35).

Yellow pricklycockles *(T. muricatum)* have about 35 ribs with small scales. They have tinges of yellow inside and out and may tend toward peach with occasional red-brown streaks.

HABITAT: These pricklycockles live in sandy shallows near beaches and out to about 100 ft (30 m).

DID YOU KNOW? Cockles live just beneath the sand surface and are often washed ashore after storms. Their prickles may help anchor them in place, or they may deter gastropod predators, or both.

Florida pricklycockle, max 2.7 in (6.9 cm)

Even pricklycockle, max 3 in (7.5 cm)

Yellow pricklycockle, max 2.5 in (6.4 cm)

103

Common egg cockle, max 3 in (7.6 cm)

Painted egg cockle, max 1 in (2.5 cm)

Morton's egg cockle, max 1 in (2.5 cm)

Egg Cockles

Common Egg Cockle   Painted and Morton's
                            Egg Cockles

RELATIVES: Egg cockles are allied with other cockles in the family Cardiidae.

IDENTIFYING FEATURES: Egg cockles are smooth with only faint riblets.

Common egg cockles *(Laevicardium laevigatum)* have valves with an oblique oval shape and ridges along the inner margin. They are glossy white or yellow with occasional rosy tinges. Older beached shells are white and less glossy.

Painted egg cockles *(Laevicardium pictum)* are compressed for a cockle and have a triangular-like shape. They are cream with blurry zigzags and spatters of brown or yellow-orange.

Morton's egg cockles *(Laevicardium mortoni)* are almost evenly rounded with a central umbo and are colored by relatively distinct rows of brown, purple, or orange zigzags.

HABITAT: Common and painted egg cockles occur in sandy areas out to moderate depths. Morton's egg cockles prefer shallow inlet areas and lagoons.

DID YOU KNOW? These cockles can literally leap about using their muscular foot. The response does not always allow Morton's egg cockle to escape ducks, who have this bivalve on their favorite-foods list.

Atlantic Mactra Clam, Southern Surfclam, and Dwarf Surfclam

Fragile Atlantic mactra clam, max 4 in (10.2 cm)

RELATIVES: Mactra and surfclams are allied within the family Mactridae.

IDENTIFYING FEATURES: These clams have a spoon-shaped pit behind the central hinge teeth.

Fragile Atlantic mactras *(Mactra fragilis)* are relatively thin-shelled with a forward umbo. Beached shells are cream with some remaining periostracum behind a ridgeline on the hind end.

Southern surfclams *(Spisula raveneli)* have strong shells with a central umbo and fine growth lines. They range from white to dirty cream with rusty tones.

Dwarf surfclams *(Mulinia lateralis)* have an umbo forward of center and a tapered hind end. Colors may be white, cream, gray, or purple-gray, with highlighted growth bands.

HABITAT: All live in sand from just off the beach out to moderate depths (165 ft or 50 m). Dwarf surfclams are also common in shallow lagoons.

DID YOU KNOW? Some surfclam species are commercially harvested for food in the southeast US. The abundant dwarf surfclam feeds a host of estuarine animals including ducks, and a hefty shell-crunching fish called the black drum *(Pogonias cromis)*.

Southern surfclam, max 5.1 in (13 cm)

Dwarf surfclam, max 3/4 in (20 mm)

Channeled duckclam, max 3.2 in (8.1 cm)

Smooth duckclam, max 3 in (7.6 cm)

Atlantic rangia clam, max 2.7 in (7 cm)

Duckclams and Atlantic Rangia

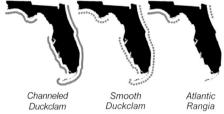

| Channeled Duckclam | Smooth Duckclam | Atlantic Rangia |

RELATIVES: These clams are allied with surfclams in the family Mactridae.

IDENTIFYING FEATURES: These clams all have a distinct spoon-shaped pit behind the central hinge teeth.

Channeled duckclams *(Raeta plicatella)* have white, thin, ear-shaped shells with strong concentric growth ridges.

Smooth duckclams *(Anatina anatina)* have thin, off-white, ear-shaped shells with relatively smooth growth lines. Their highly flared hind end has a distinct ridge leading from the umbo.

Atlantic rangia clams *(Rangia cuneata)* have thick shells with inflated, forward-pointing umbones. Their front hinge tooth is large and rectangular and their rear tooth is a long, flat ridge. Beach shells are white, yellow, variously stained, and generally worn.

HABITAT: Channeled duck clams live in sand just outside the surf zone. Smooth duck clams live offshore to depths of about 250 ft (75 m). Atlantic rangia live in the muddy sands of brackish bays.

DID YOU KNOW? Duckclams gape open at their flared hind end from which their siphons protrude. Atlantic rangia are abundant as fossils and in Indian middens, and are a base material for many Gulf coast roadbeds.

Tellins *(Alternate, Rose Petal, Sunrise, and Candystick)*

Alternate Tellin   Rose Petal and   Sunrise Tellin
                    Candystick Tellins

Alternate tellin, max 2.7 in (6.9 cm)

RELATIVES: Tellins are allied with macomas in the family Tellinidae.

IDENTIFYING FEATURES: Valves in each of these species have a rounded front end and a tapered rear that has a recognizable rightward bend at the rear (outward in the right valve).

Alternate tellins *(Tellina alternata)* are a pearly yellow-white with numerous concentric grooves between flattened concentric ridges. They may have yellow or pink radiating from the umbo.

Rose petal tellin, max 1.3 in (3.3 cm)

Rose petal tellins *(Tellina lineata)* are rosy white to deep pink.

Sunrise tellins *(Tellina radiata)* are elongate with glossy, ivory shells that may be rayed with yellow and/or pink, emanating from a pink-tipped umbo.

Candystick tellins *(Tellina similis)* have thin, pearly shells with pink rays.

HABITAT: Each of these tellins lives in sand off beaches out to moderate depths.

Sunrise tellin, max 4.5 in (11.4 cm)

DID YOU KNOW? Tellins lie beneath the sand on their left valve so that their posterior curves upward. This accommodates their long intake siphon, which draws in surface morsels. Their blade-like form and strong foot allow rapid burrowing should a predator approach. Like the arks, tellin bodies are red from the oxygen binding pigment, hemoglobin.

Candystick tellin, max 1 in (2.5 cm)

Speckled tellin, max 2.3 in (6 cm)

Favored tellin, max 4 in (10 cm)

Tampa tellin, max 1 in (2.5 cm)

Tellins *(Speckled, Favored, and Tampa)*

Speckled Tellin   Favored Tellin   Tampa Tellin

IDENTIFYING FEATURES: Like other tellins, each of these shells is less rounded in the rear where they bend right (outward in the right valve).

Speckled tellins *(Tellina listeri)* have strong concentric growth lines and two ridges at their posterior (pointed) end where they bend sharply right. Inside they are yellow and outside they are cream with blurry brown zigzags.

Favored tellins *(Tellina fausta)* have large, thick shells with crowded growth lines that are coarse near the outer margin. They are white with an occasional hint of yellow inside and at the umbo.

Tampa tellins *(Tellina tampaensis)* have thin, strong, cream-colored shells that are smooth except for outer growth lines.

HABITAT: Speckled and favored tellins live in sand or seagrass out to moderate depths (100 ft, 30 m). Tampa tellins prefer shallow bays and lagoons.

DID YOU KNOW? The speckled tellin is also known as Lister's tellin for Martin Lister, a British medical doctor who in 1685 published the first detailed book on shells. Favored tellins are favored by octopi, who find them delicious. Tampa tellins are often the dominant mollusk in enclosed hypersaline lagoons. They are one of many shells that only occasionally make it to the beach even though they are highly abundant where they live.

Coquina Clams and Minor Jackknife Clam

Variable Coquina and
Minor Jackknife Clams

Giant
Coquina Clam

Living variable coquina clams, max 1 in (2.5 cm)

RELATIVES: Coquina clams (family Donacidae) are related to tellins. Minor jackknife clams (family Cultellidae) are related to razor clams.

IDENTIFYING FEATURES:

Variable coquina clams *(Donax variabilis)* have glossy, wedge-shaped shells with faint riblets and groove-teeth lining their inner margins. Patterns vary between solids, radial rays, and concentric bands, and may include any color.

Giant coquina clams *(Iphigenia brasiliana)* have smooth, thick shells with an umbo just rear of center. Worn shells are cream with hints of purple inside.

Minor jackknife clams *(Ensis minor)* have fragile shells with a curved straight-razor shape, purplish inside and whitish outside. The similar green jackknife *(Solen viridis,* family Solenidae, north Florida) has a straight upper shell edge.

Giant coquina clam, max 2.6 in (6.6 cm)

HABITAT: Variable coquinas live in the swash zone. Giant coquinas live in deeper water out to about 13 ft (4 m).

DID YOU KNOW? Variable coquinas are one of the most abundant and ecologically important mollusks on Florida beaches. Specialized for life in wave-washed sand, they filter-feed on algae and bacteria swept to shore. They are a critical food for shore birds and surf fishes.

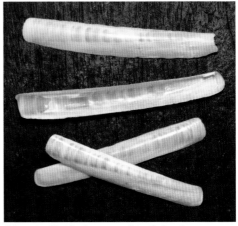

Minor jackknife clam, max 3 in (7.6 cm)

Purplish semele, max 1.5 in (3.8 cm)

Cancellate semele, max 3/4 in (1.9 cm)

White Atlantic semele, max 1.5 in (3.8 cm)

Tellin semele, max 1 in (2.5 cm)

Semeles

Purplish and White Atlantic Semeles	*Cancellate Semele*	*Tellin Semele*

RELATIVES: Semeles (family Semelidae) are related to tellins and coquinas.

IDENTIFYING FEATURES: Like tellins, a semele's hind end bends right. Their hinges have a diagonal depression angling back from the umbo.

Purplish semeles *(Semele purpurascens)* have smooth oval shells with an umbo toward the rear. They have smudge-streaks of blurry purple, brown, or orange.

Cancellate semeles *(Semele bellastriata)* are cream or gray with concentric ridges and radial riblets front and rear.

White Atlantic semeles *(Semele proficua)* have a central umbo and are cream with occasional nervous purple lines.

Tellin semeles *(Cumingia tellinoides)* are dirty white and have a distinct point at the rear shell. At their hinge, a spoon-like depression beneath the umbo protrudes into the inner shell.

HABITAT: Purplish and cancellate semeles live in sand banks off beaches out to moderate depths. Tellin and white Atlantic semeles prefer inlet areas and shallow bays open to the sea.

DID YOU KNOW? A semele's slash- or spoonlike hinge depression (chondrophore) bears a cushiony pad that springs the valves open when the animal's adductor muscles relax.

Tagelus (Short Razor) Clams, and Gray Pygmy-venus Clam

RELATIVES: Tagelus clams (family Solecurtidae) are related to semeles and tellins and are distant kin to pygmy-venus clams (family Veneridae).

IDENTIFYING FEATURES: These clams have central umbones and elongate shells that gape at each end.

Stout tagelus clams *(Tagelus plebeius)* have thick, lumpy shells with smooth growth lines. They are white, ivory, or light gray with a greenish periostracum on margins of freshly beached shells.

Purplish tagelus clams *(Tagelus divisus)* have smooth, thin shells that are tinted purple inside and out. A darker purple ray from the umbo marks a slightly raised internal rib. Small shells may have a covering of brown periostracum.

Gray pygmy-venus clams *(Timoclea grus)* have ribs crossed by growth lines and are cream or gray, often with a purple-brown streak covering the hind end.

HABITAT: These clams live in the sand or mud of shallow embayments. Stout tagelus clams prefer closed lagoons and purplish tagelus clams prefer bays open to the sea.

DID YOU KNOW? Tagelus clams live with only their siphons exposed and feed on suspended particles. Pygmy venus clams leave only their dark hind end exposed.

Stout tagelus, max 3.9 in (10 cm)

Purplish tagelus, max 1.6 in (4.0 cm)

Gray pygmy-venus clam, max 3/8 in (10 mm)

111

Calico clam, max 3.5 in (8.9 cm)

Sunray venus clam, max 6 in (15.2 cm)

Imperial venus clam, max 1.4 in (3.6 cm)

Venus Clams *(Calico, Sunray, and Imperial)*

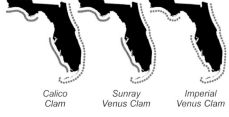

| Calico Clam | Sunray Venus Clam | Imperial Venus Clam |

RELATIVES: Venus clams are allied within the family Veneridae.

IDENTIFYING FEATURES: These venus clams have sturdy shells with forward-pointing umbones behind a conspicuous lunule (a rounded patch divided by the hinge line).

Calico clams *(Macrocallista maculata)* have smooth, creamy shells with blurry brown rectangles and smudges.

Sunray venus clams *(Macrocallista nimbosa)* have smooth, elongate shells that are purplish-brown with darker, narrow rays streaking from the umbo. Beach-worn shells may be bone white.

Imperial venus clams *(Chione latilirata)* have their shells thickened by 5–9 concentric, chunky rolls. They are whitish, light gray, or mottled tan with a few blurry rays.

HABITAT: Calico clams and imperial venus clams live in sand off beaches out to moderate depths. Sunray venus clams live in the muddy sands of shallow bays.

DID YOU KNOW? The sunray venus is abundant in the Panhandle where it is popular with hungry gulls and other local chowder fans. The thick shell rolls of the imperial venus may help this shallow burrowing clam avoid predation by drilling gastropods.

Venus Clams *(Lady-in-waiting, Cross-barred, Pointed, and Princess)*

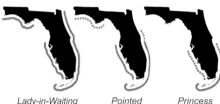

Lady-in-Waiting
and Cross-barred
Venus Clams

Pointed
Venus Clam

Princess
Venus Clam

Lady-in-waiting venus clam, max 1.6 in (4.1 cm)

IDENTIFYING FEATURES:

Lady-in-waiting venus clams (*Chione intapurpurea*) have strong concentric ridges that are serrated beneath on the hind end. Colors are cream, tan, or gray, often with brownish streaks.

Cross-barred venus clams (*Chione elevata*) have sharp, concentric ridges that cross radial riblets. Even beach-worn shells show a distinct cross-hatched look. Most are gray-white with a white or purple interior. South Florida shells have the most purple and may have colorful rays.

Cross-barred venus clam, max 1.3 in (3.3 cm)

Pointed venus clams (*Anomalocardia auberiana*) are rounded in front and tapered behind. They have strong concentric ridges and teeth at the inner margins. Colors are cream, tan, or gray with a white, brown, or purple interior. Some have faint blue-gray lines outside.

Princess venus clams (*Periglypta listeri*) have radial ribs and sharp ridges that form blades on the hind end.

HABITAT: These clams live in shallow waters. Cross-barred and pointed venus clams are common in coastal lagoons.

Pointed venus clam, max 3/4 in (20 mm)

DID YOU KNOW? Given the abundance of cross-barred venus shells, both fossil and recent, this species has been the most abundant clam in many Florida lagoons for about two million years.

Princess venus clam, max 3 in (7.5 cm)

Lightning venus clam, max 2 in (5.1 cm)

Disc dosinia, max 3 in (7.6 cm)

Elegant dosinia, max 3 in (7.6 cm)

Thin cyclinella, max 1 in (2.5 cm)

Venus Clams *(Lightning, Disc Dosinia, Elegant Dosinia, and Thin Cyclinella)*

Lightning
Venus Clam

Disc and Elegant Dosinias
and Thin Cyclinella

IDENTIFYING FEATURES:

Lightning venus clams *(Pitar fulminatus)* have smooth concentric growth ridges and are thin-shelled for a venus. They are typically whitish with brown rays or dripping zigzags.

Disc dosinias *(Dosinia discus)* have ivory, circular shells with sharp forward-pointing umbones. They have fine concentric ridges too narrow for most folks to count without a hand lens.

Elegant dosinias *(Dosinia elegans)* are similar to disc dosinias, but their flattened concentric ridges are broad, easily seen, and readily felt.

Thin cyclinellas *(Cyclinella tenuis)* are flat white with fine but irregular growth lines. They are smaller and have thinner shells than the dosinias.

HABITAT: Each of these clams lives in sand or muddy sand from outside the surf zone out to moderate depths.

DID YOU KNOW? Dosinias have a hinge ligament strong enough to keep their valves attached long after their demise, surf tumble, and beaching. These events commonly follow encounters with predatory gastropods like moon snails. Many dosinia shells show the telltale holes from these meetings.

Quahogs *(Hard Clams)*

RELATIVES: Quahogs and other venus clams are in the family Veneridae.

IDENTIFYING FEATURES: Quahogs have thick shells with forward umbones, numerous concentric growth lines, and a heart-shaped lunule.

Southern quahogs *(Mercenaria campechiensis)* have their mid-shell growth lines clearly visible, the largest of which are as wide as a pencil lead. They are gray outside with occasional purple zigzags and broad rays. Inside they are mostly white but may have hints of purple.

Northern quahogs *(Mercenaria mercenaria)* are similar to their southern cousins, but they differ in having finer growth lines that are smooth in the center of larger clams. Their inner margin tends to be deep purple.

HABITAT: These clams live in the muddy sands of shallow bays and lagoons.

Southern quahog, max 5.9 in (15 cm)

Northern quahog, max 4.2 in (10.7 cm)

DID YOU KNOW? The southern quahog is our native Florida hard clam. Yankee quahogs are used by surf fishers for bait, which is why their broken bits are common on Florida beaches. Northern clams also have been commercially "seeded" in Florida lagoons, resulting in northern-southern hybrids. The genus *Mercenaria* translates to "payment," a reference to the wampum (wampumpeg, Algonquin for valuable string of beads) made from the quahog's purple parts.

Northern quahog "bait clam" remnants

Angelwing, max 6.7 in (17 cm)

Campeche angelwing, max 5 in (12.7 cm)

Fallen-angelwing, max 2.8 in (7.1 cm)

False angelwing, max 2 in (5 cm)

Angelwings and False Angelwing

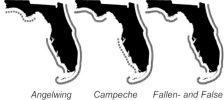

| Angelwing | Campeche Angelwing | Fallen- and False Angelwings |

RELATIVES: False angelwings (family Petricolidae) are closer kin to venus clams than to angelwings (Pholadidae), which are allied with shipworms.

IDENTIFYING FEATURES: All have fragile, whitish, winglike shells with radial ribs.

Angelwings *(Cyrtopleura costata)* have a flared shell margin near the hinge that curves out at the umbo.

Campeche angelwings *(Pholas campechiensis)* have a flared margin in front of the hinge that curves out to cover the umbo. This membranous shell over the umbo is divided into several delicate compartments.

Fallen-angelwings (Atlantic mud-piddocks) *(Barnea truncata)* are stubby, with pronounced shell gapes both front and rear.

False angelwings *(Petricolaria pholadiformis)* have a simple hinge margin with 3 (left valve) or 2 (right valve) cardinal teeth.

HABITAT: All bore into muddy clay, peat, or rotten wood on the bottoms of open bays. Campeche angelwings also occur in shallow offshore clays.

DID YOU KNOW? True angelwings live with much of their soft parts outside their shells. The siphons of the fallen-angelwing extend 12 times its shell length.

Geoduck and Shipworm

Atlantic Geoduck   Shipworm

RELATIVES: Geoducks (family Hiatel-lidae) and shipworms (family Tere-dinidae) are bivalves related to angel-wings and piddocks.

IDENTIFYING FEATURES:

Atlantic geoducks *(Panopea bitruncata)* are beached as large, off-white, lumpy, oblong shells that clearly did not close without large gapes at either end.

Shipworms *(Bankia* spp. or *Teredo* spp.) are evident as snaking tunnels through beached driftwood. The tunnels of these bivalves are lined with white, fragile, shell material. These mollusks are worm-shaped, having small, wing-like, shell valves (generally deep in wood and not easily seen) in front and paddle-like "pallets" in the rear. *Teredo* has its pallets hollowed like a vase and *Bankia* has pallets composed of about 16 stacked funnels.

HABITAT: Geoducks live in burrows 4 ft (1.2 m) deep in muddy sand off beaches out to moderate depths. Shipworms live in submerged or drifting wood.

DID YOU KNOW? Geoducks are sel-dom beached until severe storms erode them from their deep burrows. Ship-worms tunnel for protection and feed by filtering outside water taken in by siphon tubes. Their shell valves close like jaws to grind wood and their rear pallets plug their tunnel to prevent dehydration.

Atlantic geoduck, max 9 in (23 cm)

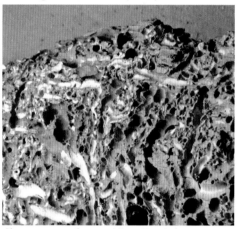

Shipworm tunnels, max 3/8 in (1 cm) diameter

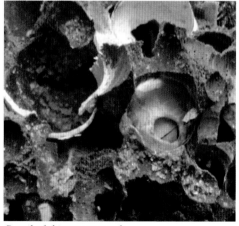

Detail of shipworm tunnels

117

Circular Chinese-hat

Dwarf olive

Spotted pheasant

Snubnose corbula

Lunate crassinella

Atlantic nutclam

Atlantic abra

White strigilla

Miniature lucine

Many-line lucine

Itty-Bitty Shells

RELATIVES: Gastropods and bivalves

IDENTIFYING FEATURES: These shells are too small to be seen by folks on a casual stroll and are all less than about 1/4 inch (8 mm) as adults. The path into the amazing world of itty-bitty shells is traveled by those on their hands and knees. Peering into drift piles at the recent strand line will reveal many of this page's petite species in addition to miniature versions of the larger species shown on previous pages.

Dinky gastropods:

Circular Chinese-hat *(Calyptraea centralis),* all Florida beaches, family Calyptraeidae

Dwarf olive *(Olivella lactea),* all Florida beaches, family Olividae

Spotted pheasant *(Eulithidium affine),* SE Florida and Keys, family Trochidae

Wee bivalves:

Snubnose corbula *(Corbula caribaea),* all Florida beaches, family Corbulidae

Lunate crassinella *(Crassinella lunulata),* all Florida beaches, family Crassatellidae

Atlantic nutclam *(Nucula proxima),* all Florida beaches, family Nuculidae

Atlantic abra *(Abra aequalis),* all Florida beaches, family Semelidae

White strigilla *(Strigilla mirabilis),* all Florida beaches, family Tellinidae

Miniature lucine *(Lucina amianta),* all Florida beaches, family Lucinidae

Many-line lucine *(Parvilucina multi-lineata),* all Florida beaches, family Lucinidae

Shell Wars (Shell Bioerosion)

Beached mollusk shells often bear clues to how they met their demise and who made use of them after their death. This evidence includes boreholes, perforations, and grooves.

Shells with single, circular **boreholes** were likely eaten by a predatory gastropod. Oyster drills *(Urosalpinx* spp.) leave a straight hole, whereas thick-lipped drills *(Eupleura caudata)* leave a slightly beveled hole. Shark's eye snails *(Neverita duplicata)* leave a countersunk, circular borehole that has an outer diameter about twice the inner diameter. Two tactics for hole-boring gastropods include edge drilling and umbo drilling. Drilling at the valve edge is fastest (because the shell is thinner) but is risky because closing valves could pinch the snail's proboscis. Umbo drilling is safer, but in the time it takes to bore through the thick umbo, a snail may have its prey stolen by a larger gastropod or become a meal itself (note the bored shark's eye in the top image).

Scattered **perforations** in a shell were likely made by boring sponges *(Cliona* spp.). These sponges partially acid-digest living and dead shells and invade them as living space.

Other animals that use shells as living space include polychaete worms like polydorids, which leave snaking **groove** marks. The router-tool indentations are made as the worm rasps with its bristled body aided by acids it secretes. Bivalve shells may also be penetrated by other bivalves like *Gastrochaena,* which leave oblong boreholes **(A)** in either shell or rock. This bean-shaped clam lives out its life within the pit it forms.

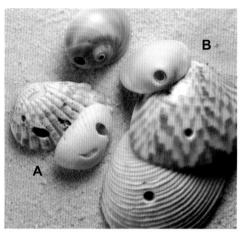

Boreholes from bivalves (A) and gastropods (B)

Boring sponge perforations in a quahog

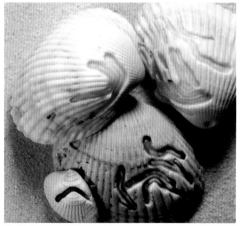

Polychaete worm grooves

Colorful incongruous arks from the same beach

Shell Color Variation and Mollusk Bits and Pieces

Although some shells are most colorful in life, other shells turn a variety of colors after they die. These colors depend on the shell's afterlife experiences. Black shells were likely darkened by iron sulfide after burial in sulfurous muck. A beach speckled with numerous black shells indicates that the surf zone was once the lagoon behind the barrier island. Pink, rust, or brown are the colors most shells turn after decades of exposure to air. Although glossy white shells are probably recent, bone-white shells may be fossils. After millennia under ground and water, shells are slowly converted to the most stable form of calcium carbonate, calcite, the lime in limestone.

For every whole shell found on a beach there are thousands of bits and pieces. Some surf-worn shards have the clear distinguishing features of the original shell. Do you recognize these?

Some readily recognizable shell fragments

A. **Operculum** (trapdoor) from a horse conch *(Triplofusus giganteus)*

B. **Giant tun shell** *(Tonna galea)*

C. **Queen helmet** *(Cassis madagascariensis)*

D. **Hawk-wing conch** *(Strombus rainus)*

E. **Lettered olive** *(Oliva sayana)*

F. **Shark's eye** *(Neverita duplicata)*

G. **Angelwing** *(Cyrtopleura costata)*

H. **Junonia** *(Scaphella junonia)*

I. **Nacre from a penshell** *(Atrina spp.)*

J. **Atlantic giant cockle** *(Dinocardium robustum)*

K. **Crown conch** *(Melongena corona)*

Tuskshells and Ram's Horn Squid

RELATIVES: Tuskshells are scaphopods (a separate class from the gastropods and bivalves) in the family Dentaliidae. The ram's horn squid is in a fourth class, the cephalopods (cuttlefishes, octopods, nautili), family Spirulidae.

IDENTIFYING FEATURES:

Tuskshell, max 1.4 in (3.5 cm)

Tuskshells (most commonly *Dentalium* spp.) are white, delicate, curved and tapered tubes open at each end. The foot and mouth of the living tuskshell were formerly located at the wide end.

Ram's horn squid *(Spirula spirula)* are beached as white, chambered coils. The coil lies within the posterior end of the squid opposite its two large eyes and ten tentacles. The coil takes up almost half the squid, minus outstretched tentacles.

HABITAT: Some tuskshell species live in shallow bay sediments and others live in deep offshore seabottom. Ram's horn squid live in the deep open ocean.

Ram's horn squid shell, max 1 in (2.5 cm)

DID YOU KNOW? Tuskshells live with their wide (anterior) end in the seabottom where they use their oral tentacles to feed on forams (protozoa). Ram's horn squid use their buoyant, chambered coil to suspend themselves head-down in the water column. For protection, the squid can pucker up by withdrawing its head and tentacles into its body. They range worldwide.

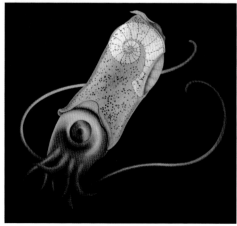

A living ram's horn squid

Sargassum sea mat on sargassum algae

Gulf staghorn bryozoan

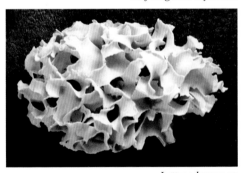

Lettuce bryozoan

Common bugula

Moss Animals (Bryozoans)

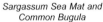

Sargassum Sea Mat and Common Bugula	Gulf Staghorn and Lettuce Bryozoans

RELATIVES: Moss animals are in the phylum Bryozoa and are most closely related to annelid worms and mollusks.

IDENTIFYING FEATURES: All are colonies of individual animals (zooids).

Sargassum sea mat *(Membranipora tuberculata)* is a lacy crust covering sargassum algae and other drifters. Colonies may span 1 in (2.5 cm) and are composed of tiny rectangular compartments.

Gulf staghorn bryozoan *(Schizoporella pungens)* colonies grow in cylindrical form attached to sea whips, but also stand free as 6-in (15-cm) branched tubes. They are brownish-white when beached. The zooids live in compartments surrounding the tubes.

Lettuce bryozoan *(Thalamoporella gothica)* colonies form sand-colored, potato-sized bunches of brittle, crinkled, leaves.

Common bugula *(Bugula neritina)* are palm-sized and brownish with tough branches. The zooids live in alternating positions on dual rows. Other *Bugula* species are white.

HABITAT: Most bryozoans live attached to substrates in shallow waters. Sargassum sea mat lives at the ocean surface.

DID YOU KNOW? Florida has about 300 species of marine bryozoans. Zooids filter-feed using a semicircle of mouth tentacles.

Polychaete Tube Worms

Parchment, Calcareous, and Spiral Tube Worms

RELATIVES: Tube worms are in the phylum Annelida, class Polychaeta, which includes segmented worms with bristles (setae).

IDENTIFYING FEATURES: Casual beachcombers can expect to identify these worms by the tubes they make.

Parchment tube worms *(Chaetopterus variopedatus,* family Chaetopteridae) leave whitish, curved, limp, paperlike tubes up to 12 in (30 cm) long. Each tube was formerly U-shaped beneath the sand and was home to a worm with specialized segments employing paddle-like flaps, lobes, and cups. Storms erode the sands where these worms live and can fill the beach with their parchment tubes.

Calcareous tube worms (family Serpulidae) secrete an inch-long (2.5 cm) whitish, calcareous, tube adhering to shells, rocks, or debris. Some of these worms form dense masses of parallel and intertwined tubes.

Spiral tube worms (family Spirorbidae) live within tiny, pinhead-sized, shelly coils that are stuck to rocks, shells, seagrass, or sargassum algae. They are very common in the wrack line. A handful of sargassum weed may have hundreds of worm coils (mostly *Spirorbis corrugatus)*, covering every surface in tiny white dots.

Parchment tube worm tube

Calcareous tube worms encrusting a cockle shell

Spiral tube worms on seagrass

123

Honeycomb tubeworm reef

Honeycomb Tubeworms   *Plumed Worms*

Honeycomb tubeworms *(Phragmatopoma caudata,* family Sabellariidae) create rocklike mounds with a honeycomb texture that are occasionally exposed in the surf zone at low tide. The "rocks" are masses of tubes made of cemented sand and shell bits.

Plumed worms (family Onuphidae) live within soda-straw-sized tubes that project from the sand near the low-tide line. Layers of glued shell bits and other debris thicken the end of each tube.

HABITAT: Parchment tube worms live near the surf zone. Calcareous and spiral tube worms encrust a variety of objects out to moderate depths and attach to floating objects adrift on the open ocean. Honeycomb tubeworms build reefs in the surf zone and slightly deeper. Plumed worms live below the low tide line on beaches with mild surf.

DID YOU KNOW? Although blind, parchment tube worms glow in the dark, emitting a luminous blue cloud of mucous when disturbed. Honeycomb tubeworms create reef habitat that is critical for many species of animals including mollusks, reef fish, sport fish, and sea turtles. The swimming larvae of these worms are chemically attracted to their own kind and prefer to settle within an already bustling worm colony.

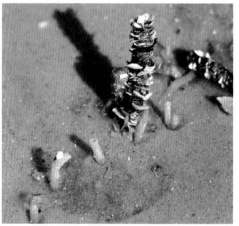

Plumed worm tubes

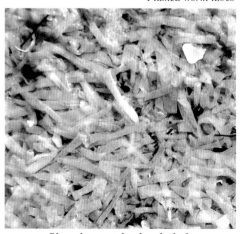

Plumed worm tubes beached after a storm

Barnacles *(Without Stalks)*

Skeletons of half-buried ivory acorn barnacles

RELATIVES: Barnacles (subclass Cirripedia) are crustaceans related to crabs, shrimp, and beachhoppers.

IDENTIFYING FEATURES:

Ivory acorn barnacles *(Balanus eburneus)*, 1.2 in (3 cm), are white and steep-sided with distinct plates.

Rock acorn barnacles *(Megabalanus coccopoma)*, 2 in (5 cm), are large dome-like, and purplish, with distinct plates.

Striped acorn barnacles *(B. amphitrite)*, 0.4 in (10 mm), are conical with purple stripes on their distinct plates.

Ribbed barnacles *(Tetraclita stalactifera,* family Tetraclitidae), 1.6 in (4 cm), have fused plates that form a rough-ribbed volcano with a small opening.

Star barnacles *(Chthamalus stellatus,* family Chthamalidae), 0.4 in (10 mm), are flattened cones with six ribbed plates.

Rock (rear) and striped (front) acorn barnacles

HABITAT: Striped and ivory acorn barnacles reach beaches by being attached to driftwood or flotsam like lobster traps. Other species live on intertidal rocks like those forming groynes and jetties.

DID YOU KNOW? Barnacles live attached for life, head down within their shells. They feed by gathering plankton with their feathery legs, which also act as their gills. At low tide their shells close to conserve water until the sea returns.

Ribbed (large) and star (small) barnacles

125

Freshly beached Lepas hilli *goose barnacle*

L. anserifera *showing feathery legs (cirri)*

Living duck barnacles on floating pumice

Barnacles *(With Stalks)*

| L. anserifera Goose Barnacle | L. hilli *Goose Barnacle* and Duck Barnacle |

RELATIVES: Stalked barnacles are in the family Lepadidae, related to the other barnacles (subclass Cirripedia).

IDENTIFYING FEATURES: All have leaflike shells on fleshy stalks.

Goose barnacles *(Lepas hilli)*, 1.5 in (3.8 cm), have a dark stalk and bluish-gray shell plates with growth lines.

Goose barnacles *(Lepas anserifera)*, 1.5 in (3.8 cm), have white shells with radial grooves, and an orange stalk.

Duck barnacles *(Lepas pectinata)*, 1 in (2.5 cm), have scaly, dark ridges and a spiny edge to their opening.

HABITAT: These barnacles never live on the seabottom. Their habitat consists of wood, seabeans, and other flotsam adrift on the open ocean. They reach the beach when their ride does. For some reason, the duck barnacle is the most common species growing on the floating spiral of the ram's horn squid.

DID YOU KNOW? These stalked barnacles feed on plankton and other tiny drifting food bits. They grow from swimming larva to adult size in a matter of weeks. Loggerhead sea turtles eat goose barnacles, and also provide a home for them on their carapace. Some little loggerheads adrift in the open Atlantic are known to host masses of barnacles heavier then themselves.

Beachhoppers, Dock Roaches, and **Ghost Shrimp**

Beachhoppers and
Dock Roaches

Ghost Shrimp

Beachhoppers uncovered

RELATIVES: Beachhoppers are amphipods, dock roaches are isopods, and ghost shrimp are decapods related to mole and hermit crabs. All are crustaceans.

IDENTIFYING FEATURES:

Beachhoppers *(Talorchestia* spp.), 0.8 in (2 cm), are the sand-colored, humpbacked critters that bounce by the dozens as moist wrack is disturbed.

Dock roaches *(Ligia exotica),* 1.5 in (3.8 cm), are charcoal-colored, swift-running, insectlike isopods.

Ghost shrimp *(Callianassa* spp.), 3.2 in (8 cm), are best identified by their pencil-sized burrow openings, which are surrounded by regurgitated pellets easily confused with chocolate ice-cream sprinkles. The animal itself is elongate, pale, and soft-bodied.

Dock roach

HABITAT: Beachhoppers live under seaweed piles. Dock roaches scurry about on jetties and beach wrack. Ghost shrimp burrow in fine, intertidal sands.

DID YOU KNOW? Beachhoppers eat seaweed remnants, and although they look like fleas, they don't bite. Dock roaches live in the shadows by day and feed at night. Ghost shrimp burrow as deep as six feet (1.8 m). Their pellets feed hermit crabs and their burrows house commensal crabs and copepods.

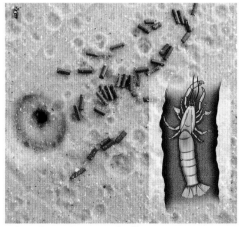

Ghost shrimp burrow and pellets, cross-section (inset)

127

Land hermit crab in a juvenile crown conch

Striped hermit at home in a crown conch shell

Giant red hermit housed in a lightning whelk shell

Long-wristed hermit crab in an oyster drill

Hermit Crabs

Land Hermit Crab   Striped, Giant Red, and
Long-wristed Hermit Crabs

RELATIVES: Hermit crabs are crustaceans in the infraorder Anomura, shared with mole crabs.

IDENTIFYING FEATURES:

Land hermit crabs *(Coenobita clypeatus),* 1.5 in (3.5 cm), have orange-tipped walking legs. The left claw is largest and is purple with orange tips.

Striped hermit crabs *(Clibanarius vittatus),* 1.2 in (3 cm), have brown-green legs with light stripes. Their claws are about equal in size.

Giant red hermit crabs *(Petrochirus diogenes),* 7 in (18 cm), are red with heavy, knobby, unequal claws.

Long-wristed hermit crabs *(Pagurus longicarpus),* 1 in (2.5 cm), have tan legs and an elongate right claw.

HABITAT: Land hermits stroll the beach and dune, and striped hermits stay seaward of high tide. Both are out at low tide when scuffles fueled by shell envy break out. Long-wristed hermits stay in tidepools. Giant red hermits live on reefs and are beached after storms.

DID YOU KNOW? Adult land hermits do not need seawater. Striped hermits walk about on the low-tide flat but require seawater replenishment to breathe. Hermit crabs eat detritus and carrion. Long-wristed hermits are known to harvest the fats and protein in sea foam.

Mole Crabs

Common Mole Crab

Slender-eyed Mole Crab

RELATIVES: Mole crabs are crustaceans related to ghost shrimp and hermit crabs.

IDENTIFYING FEATURES:

Common mole crabs *(Emerita talpoida),* 1.5 in (3 cm), also known as sand fleas, are teardrop-shaped little digging machines with short, fuzzy antennae. They are mottled green-gray on tan above, and white below.

Slender-eyed mole crabs *(Albunea paretii),* 1 in (2.5 cm), have long antennae, slender eyestalks, and spiny projections across the carapace behind their head. They are an iridescent, pinkish-gray.

HABITAT: Common mole crabs are locally abundant in the swash zone, even on beaches with big surf. Slender-eyed mole crabs burrow in fine sands at inlet areas and low-energy beaches.

DID YOU KNOW? Both species feed on plankton and detritus driven into the surf. Common mole crabs swim-dig backwards through flooded sands but are helpless if placed above the receding swash. They position themselves tail down and head seaward so their net-like antennae can inflate with the backwash from each spent wave. The crabs move with wave crashes so that they follow the tide up and down the beach. Surf fishers scoop mole crabs as preferred bait for whiting and pompano (see page 147).

Common mole crabs

As the wave recedes / the mole crab digs / Head

Common mole crab swim-digging

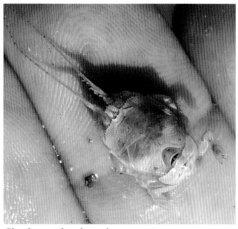
Slender-eyed mole crab

129

Calico box crab, 3 in (7.5 cm) carapace width

Mottled purse crab, 2.5 in (6 cm) carapace width

Spider crab, 4 in (10 cm) carapace width

Box, Purse, and Spider Crabs

Calico and Purse Crabs　　　*Spider Crab*

RELATIVES: These short-tailed crabs are allied within the infraorder Brachyura.

IDENTIFYING FEATURES:

Calico box crabs *(Hepatus epheliticus)* have stout, smooth, variably speckled bodies, short legs, and wide claws that partially hide their faces.

Mottled purse crabs *(Persephona mediterranea)* have clean, bumpy, rounded bodies, long legs, and narrow claws.

Spider crabs *(Libinia* spp.) look like their name and are covered with seabottom growth. Longnose spider crabs *(L. dubia)* have six bumps on the carapace midline, whereas portly spider crabs *(L. emarginata)* have nine.

HABITAT: Calico box crabs and mottled purse crabs bury themselves in surf-zone sands on relatively calm beaches. Spider crabs are common in shallow waters and are swept onto beaches after rough weather.

DID YOU KNOW? Box crabs hide their faces to keep sand out of their gill chambers. Purse crabs may get their name from Persephone (winter-bringing Greek goddess) or their egg-protecting, purse-like, under-curled abdomen. Small juvenile spider crabs ride and feed on cannonball jellies. Larger juveniles move sluggishly on the bottom and decorate themselves with sponges and algae.

Blue Crab, Speckled Crab, and Stone Crab

Blue and Speckled Crabs   Stone Crab

RELATIVES: Blue and speckled crabs are swimming crabs in the family Portunidae. Stone crabs are in the family of mud crabs, Xanthidae.

IDENTIFYING FEATURES:

Blue crabs *(Callinectes sapidus)* have pointed projections on the sides of their carapace and swimming paddles on their hind legs. They are greenish and blue. Females have orange highlights and clawtips, and are more commonly beached than males.

Speckled crabs *(Arenaeus cribrarius)* are shaped like blue crabs but are grayish-tan with white spots.

Stone crabs *(Menippe mercenaria)* are stout-bodied crabs with claws seemingly enhanced by steroids and Popeye's spinach. Juveniles are deep purple and adults become olive with black spots. Like most xanthid crabs, stone crabs have black claw-tips.

HABITAT: Female blue crabs are occasionally beached after migrating from estuaries to spawn at sea. Speckled crabs bury themselves in swash-zone sands. Stone crabs live amongst rubble and frequent nearshore reefs and jetties.

DID YOU KNOW? Blue and speckled crabs are swift predators that eat mollusks, fishes, and other crabs. Stone crabs crush and eat barnacles and clams.

Blue crab, 8 in (20 cm) carapace width

Speckled crab, 5.5 in (14 cm) carapace width

Stone crab, 5 in (13 cm) carapace width

131

Blue land crab, 4.5 in (11 cm) carapace width

Adult ghost crab, 2 in (5 cm) carapace width

A cryptic, juvenile ghost crab

Blue Land Crab and Ghost Crab

Blue Land Crab	Ghost Crab

RELATIVES: Land crabs (family Gecarcinidae) are distantly related to ghost crabs (family Ocypodidae).

IDENTIFYING FEATURES: These crabs move about on land and have one claw (left or right) larger than the other.

Blue land crabs *(Cardisoma guanhumi)* found near beaches are migrating adults, which are blue-gray, blue and white, or violet with orange highlights beneath.

Ghost crabs *(Ocypode quadrata)* are lightweight, swift-footed crabs with pale, square bodies and yellowish legs. Juveniles are mottled.

HABITAT: Blue land crabs live in burrows near coastal lagoons and migrate to beaches to breed. Ghost crabs use the entire beach and dune. Young ghost crabs prefer the lower beach.

DID YOU KNOW? Land crab migrations occur during rainy periods, several days before full or new moons, June–December. The events include mating, and the release of larvae into the ocean by females. Formerly spectacular mass migrations in Florida have diminished, and land crabs are missing from many coastal locations. Blue land crabs eat shoots, berries, and mangrove leaves. Ghost crabs eat coquina clams, mole crabs, and wrackline treats. Both crabs must keep their gills moist to breathe.

Ghost Crab Signs

Ghost crab tracks

IDENTIFYING FEATURES: Ghost crab tracks appear as six rows of widely spaced commas. Tracks wider than hand-width may be from blue land crabs (if in south Florida). **Burrows** from juvenile ghost crabs are finger-sized, and the largest adult burrows might accommodate a tennis ball. Upper beach burrows have spoil-mound aprons, often with radiating tracks from the rolling of excavated sand balls. Tides that have washed over lower beach burrows leave only a hole.

A burrow under construction

HABITAT: Favorite burrowing locations include moist sand (close but not too close to the swash zone); next to driftwood, dead fish, and other groceries; and sand tilled by nesting sea turtles. Over-wintering crabs may have burrows well behind the dune. Burrows from males are closer to the swash zone. This puts them on the route that potential mates take as they re-moisten their gills.

Males burrow into low, wet sand

DID YOU KNOW? Ghost crab burrows are up to 4 ft (1.2 m) deep and may be nearly straight down or U-shaped. A male entering another male's burrow often leads to ritualized combat. A female entering a male's burrow often leads to crab love. At mid-day and over the winter, crabs retire in their burrows behind a plug of sand. Ghost crabs leave their burrows to feed before dusk and are active through dawn. Because of their close ties to the dune, beach, and surf, and because of their predatory dependence on swash-zone filter-feeders, ghost crabs are important indicators of beach health. Numerous burrows are signs of a healthy, lively beach.

A well-planned burrow ensures several herring meals

133

A female horseshoe crab

A mating pair with the smaller male behind

Molts are perfect replicas of the growing animal

Horseshoe Crab

RELATIVES: These arthropods are not crustaceans, but are chelicerates (class Merostomata), more closely related to spiders than to crabs. Horseshoe crabs are likely the closest living relatives to the ancient trilobites.

IDENTIFYING FEATURES:

Horseshoe crabs *(Limulus polyphemus),* 24 in (61 cm), have an unmistakable domed, U-shaped head (cephalothorax), a spine-edged abdomen, and a stiff, pointed, tail spine (telson). Live animals are chestnut brown or olive. Molted exoskeletons are lightweight, tan, complete versions of the animal that shed them.

HABITAT: Horseshoe crabs live in Florida's coastal lagoons, bays, and waters of the Big Bend region. Their habitats vary between sand, mud, rubble, and seagrass. Adults mate and nestle eggs into the upper swash zone of low-energy beaches. In winter, horseshoe crabs move into deeper waters.

DID YOU KNOW? Horseshoe crabs nearly identical to those seen today preceded the dinosaurs by millions of years. Although they look a little creepy, horseshoe crabs are gentle and safe to handle. Females take a decade or more to mature and live 20–40 years. The species is valuable in both pharmaceutical and biomedical research. Intense harvest for eel and whelk bait has caused severe population declines.

Biting Flies

Salt-marsh Mosquito and   Stable Fly
Biting Midge

RELATIVES: These insects are flies in the order Diptera. Insects are arthropods like crustaceans and horseshoe crabs.

IDENTIFYING FEATURES: Flies have one pair of wings. These particular flies have a taste for blood and are willing to hurt you to get it.

Salt-marsh mosquitoes *(Ochlerotatus* spp.), 1/4 in (7 mm), have long, striped legs and are either golden-brown *(O. sollicitans)* or black *(O. taeniorhynchus)*.

Biting midges *(Culicoides* spp.), 1/8 in (3 mm), also known as sandflies or noseeums, are tiny and gray with black eyes.

Stable flies *(Stomoxys calcitrans)*, 1/4 in (7 mm), also called dog flies, look like a housefly with slightly lighter coloration (they are in the same family, Muscidae).

HABITAT: Coastal. Salt marsh mosquitoes lay eggs in wet soil and eggs hatch with rising water. Biting midges prefer to lay eggs in mud. Stable flies lay eggs in rotting grasses or livestock manure.

DID YOU KNOW? Bad news—salt marsh mosquitoes actually prefer people to other mammals and birds. Good news—folks bitten about a zillion times gain resistance to the injected saliva that causes itching. Stable flies bite only in daylight, biting midges prefer dawn and dusk, and saltmarsh mosquitoes take the night shift, as well as dawn and dusk.

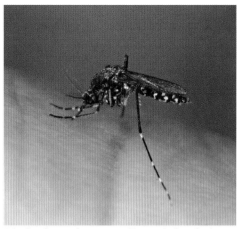

Black salt-marsh mosquito (O. taeniorhynchus)

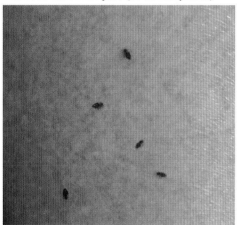

Biting midge or no-seeum

Stable fly (dog fly)

135

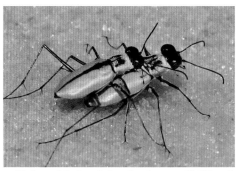

Mating white beach tiger beetles on a Gulf beach

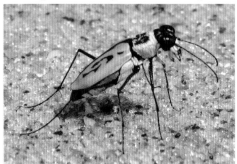

White beach tiger beetle on an Atlantic beach

Salt-marsh tiger beetle, Keys

Darkling beetles

Beetles

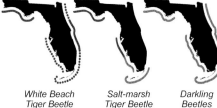

White Beach   Salt-marsh   Darkling
Tiger Beetle   Tiger Beetle   Beetles

RELATIVES: Beetles are insects in the order Coleoptera.

IDENTIFYING FEATURES: When not flying, beetles have their flight wings hidden by hard wing-covers called elytra.

White beach tiger beetles *(Cicindela dorsalis)* are pearly colored and **salt-marsh tiger beetles** *(C. marginata)* are dark. Each is 1/2 in (13 mm) with long legs and large eyes. They make short, awkward flights and are among few beach insects active in daylight.

Darkling beetles (family Tenebrionidae), 1/4 in (7 mm), are sluggish, brown or black beetles with glossy, grooved wing-covers and tapered hind ends.

HABITAT: Adult tiger beetles hunt between the swash zone and dune. Their larvae ambush prey from tiny burrows between the wrack and the dune. Darkling beetles live under moist wrack.

DID YOU KNOW? Florida has two subspecies of white beach tiger beetles: Gulf and Atlantic. Glaring lights (which attract and kill adults) and foot/vehicle traffic (which destroys larval burrows) have eliminated tiger beetles from many beaches. Adults eat beachhoppers, flies, and wrack treats (carrion). Darkling beetles feed on fungi and carrion beneath moist seaweed and burrow into the sand as conditions become dry.

Drowned Insects

IDENTIFYING FEATURES: Occasionally, lots of dead insects wash in with the tide. These **mass-drowning** events commonly involve **fire ants** *(Solenopsis invicta,* which have wings during reproductive flights), honeybees *(Apis mellifera),* and love bugs *(Plecia nearctica,* flies in the family Bibionidae). Some individual insects found include waterbeetles (Dytiscidae), and butterflies, especially the monarch *(Danaus plexippus),* and **Gulf fritillary** *(Agraulis vanillae).*

Drowned insects are found after strong winds have blown offshore. Fire ants are found when these winds follow summer rains that prompt winged sexuals (alates) to fly.

HABITAT: Nearly all these insects live in terrestrial or freshwater habitats. They reach the sea as lost members of the aerial plankton.

DID YOU KNOW? Insects were the first animals to take flight and are still the only invertebrates to truly fly. It may not be coincidence that the insects most involved in mass drownings are not native to Florida (fire ants, honeybees, and lovebugs). Insects familiar with the local neighborhood are believed to hug the coast rather than disperse seaward when offshore winds blow. This coast-hugging explains the clustering of migrating insects along beaches, including the unpleasant massing of biting stable flies occasionally seen at Panhandle beaches.

Strong offshore winds account for mass drownings

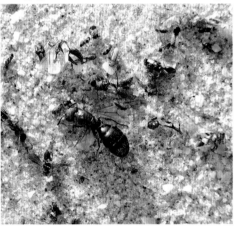

A winged fire ant among other drowned insects

Gulf fritillary butterflies

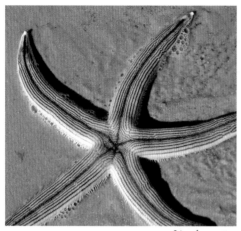

Lined sea star

Nine-armed sea star

Thorny starfish

Sea Stars

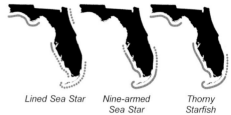

| Lined Sea Star | Nine-armed Sea Star | Thorny Starfish |

RELATIVES: Sea stars are echinoderms, related to sea cucumbers and sea urchins.

IDENTIFYING FEATURES:

Lined sea stars *(Luidia clathrata),* 6 in (15 cm), are grayish, brownish, or salmon with a dark stripe down each of their five arms.

Nine-armed sea stars *(Luidia senegalensis),* 12 in (30 cm), are tan with gray lines radiating into nine, pointed arms, each with a spiny fringe.

Thorny starfish *(Echinaster spinulosus),* 6 in (15 cm), are red to purple with stubby arms and widely spaced spines.

HABITAT: All live in sandy shallows or seagrass but are common near the swash zone after storms and at low tide.

DID YOU KNOW? Like all echinoderms, sea stars have an internal skeleton of calcium carbonate. Their movement is aided by a water-vascular system that provides hydraulic pressure for their many tube feet. These hydraulic tube feet can pull on the closed valves of a clam without fatigue, outlast the clam's closing (adductor) muscles, and allow the sea star to poke its stomach into the open shell. Lined and nine-armed sea stars differ from this "arm-wrestling" feeding pattern and often swallow their prey whole.

Brittle Stars and Sea Cucumbers

Smooth Brittle Star *Brown and Green Sea Cucumbers*

RELATIVES: Brittle stars are echinoderms that share the class Stelleroidea with sea stars, although they are only distantly related. Sea cucumbers are in the echinoderm class Holothuroidea.

IDENTIFYING FEATURES:

Smooth brittle stars *(Ophioderma* spp.), 4 in (10 cm), have five serpentine arms attached to a central pentagon-shaped disk. They are green or gray with darker highlights including arm bands.

Brown (hairy) sea cucumbers *(Sclerodactyla briareus),* 4 in (10 cm), are soft, gray-brown lumps. The surf rubs away the tube feet that cover them in life.

Green (striped) sea cucumbers *(Thyonella gemmata),* 10 in (25 cm), are elongate, gray or green lumps with their tube feet in five relatively organized rows (stripes). They often retain the boomerang shape they had while in their burrows.

HABITAT: Smooth brittle stars live in seagrass beds. The sea cucumbers here live within burrows in shallow sandy areas. All are swept onto beaches following rough weather.

DID YOU KNOW? Brittle stars can regenerate an entire animal from just an arm and part of their central disk. Some divide this way on their own to reproduce. Sea cucumbers gather plankton with their tentacles.

Smooth brittle star

Brown sea cucumber

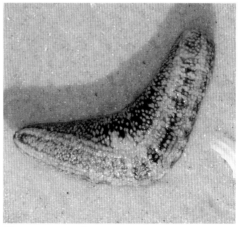

Green sea cucumber

Notched sand dollar with Aristotle's lantern pieces

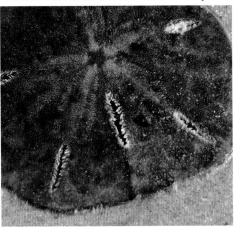

Living five-holed keyhole urchin

Five-holed keyhole urchin test

Sand Dollars

Notched Sand Dollar

Five-holed Keyhole Urchin

RELATIVES: These echinoderms are related to sea urchins, class Echinoidea.

IDENTIFYING FEATURES: All have flat, round, bone-white tests (skeletons).

Notched (arrowhead) sand dollars *(Encope michelini),* 5.5 in (14 cm), have four marginal notches and one hole.

Five-holed keyhole urchins *(Mellita quinquiesperforata),* 4 in (10 cm), have five slot-like holes.

HABITAT: Sand dollars and keyhole urchins live in sandy shallows and sea-grass. Many live just off the beach.

DID YOU KNOW? In life, these animals have a feltlike coating of fine, brown, moveable spines. Tiny tube feet gather their planktonic food and carry it below to their mouth. The gathered bits are crunched by a chewing apparatus made of five bird-shaped elements, collectively known as Aristotle's lantern. Their notches and holes provide a short-cut for food bits traveling from their topside to their mouth. The holes also allow these disc-shaped animals to sink into the sand. The conspicuous petals on the upper surface of a sand dollar are traced by dual lines of pores for tube feet which the animal uses only for breathing.

Sea Urchins

Short-spined and Purple Urchins   *Inflated Sea Biscuit*

A short-spined urchin adorned with shell bits

RELATIVES: Sea urchins share the class Echinoidea with sand dollars.

IDENTIFYING FEATURES:

Short-spined (variegated) urchins *(Lytechinus variegatus)*, 4 in (10 cm), are whitish, greenish, brownish, or mauve, with tubular spines that are lighter at their base and relatively blunt.

Purple sea urchins *(Arbacia punctulata)*, 4 in (10 cm), have longer spines and smaller tests than the short-spined urchin. Their purplish spines are sharp cones above and flattened paddles underneath.

Inflated sea biscuits *(Clypeaster rosaceus)*, 6 in (15 cm), are an elongate biscuit shape with five radiating petals.

HABITAT: Purple sea urchins live among rocks near turbulent water and are common on nearshore reefs and jetties. Short-spined urchins and sea biscuits prefer seagrass beds.

DID YOU KNOW? None of these urchins is dangerous to humans. Both short-spined urchins and sea biscuits often hold shells and other debris over themselves using their suckered tube feet. They are important grazers on seagrasses. Purple sea urchins graze on sponges and algae using their strong beaklike teeth. This urchin senses light and will point its spines toward a looming shadow.

Purple sea urchin

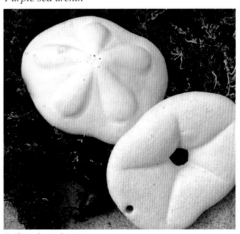

Inflated sea biscuit tests

Short-spined urchin tests and spines

Purple sea urchin tests and spines

Rock-boring urchin tests

Heart urchin tests

Sea Urchin Tests

Rock-boring
Urchin Test

Mud Urchin Test

IDENTIFYING FEATURES:

Short-spined urchin tests *(Lytechinus variegatus),* 3 in (7.5 cm), are greenish when fresh and bone-white when sun-bleached.

Purple sea urchin tests *(Arbacia punctulata),* 1.5 in (3.8 cm), are whitish with purple highlights.

Rock-boring urchin tests *(Echinometra lucunter),* 2.5 in (6.3 cm), are oval and white. Fresh tests may have brownish highlights. Their thick, purple-brown spines are about an inch (2.5 cm) long.

Heart (mud) urchin tests *(Moira atropos),* 2.5 in (6 cm), are egg-shaped with five radiating petal grooves. Most beached tests are bone white. In life, mud urchins are covered with short, delicate, tan spines.

HABITAT: Rock-boring urchins use their teeth to bore into shallow reefs. Heart urchins live in offshore muddy sediment. Both are most common on beaches only as their skeletal tests.

DID YOU KNOW? It seems an immutable law that urchin tests can survive the pounding surf but are crushed into dust in a beachcomber's pocket. The tests are made of 10 fused plates scattered with tiny holes for the urchin's tube feet. Each bump (tubercle) on the test is a former spine-attachment point.

142

Acorn Worms and Tunicates

Acorn Worms,
Leathery Sea Squirt, and
Sandy-skinned Tunicate

Sea Pork

Acorn worm poop

RELATIVES: Acorn worms (not really worms) are in the phylum Hemichordata, linked to both echinoderms and tunicates. Tunicates share the phylum Chordata with fishes, birds, and us.

IDENTIFYING FEATURES:

Acorn worms (commonly *Balanoglossus aurantiacus)* are evident from their finger-width, sandy poops (fecal casts) that lie in coiled piles. The burrowing animals are wormlike with an acorn-shaped proboscis and reach 40 in (1 m) in length. The area surrounding an acorn worm burrow smells like medicinal iodine.

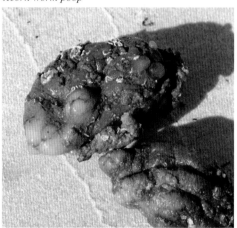

Leathery sea squirt

Leathery (rough, pleated) sea squirts *(Styela plicata),* 4 in (10 cm), look like wrinkled potatoes. They have a basal (formerly attached) end opposite a puckered end with 4 lobes around a siphon, which squirts when squeezed. They wash ashore in singles and in attached groups.

Sandy-skinned tunicates *(Molgula occidentalis),* 2 in (5 cm), look like soft potatoes rolled in the sand. Their thin test is imbedded with mud, sand, and shell bits and they are often still attached to shells and rocks.

Sea pork *(Aplidium stellatum),* 10 in (25 cm), is a colony of tiny tunicate animals individually known as zooids. The

Sea squirts squirt when squeezed

143

Sandy-skinned tunicates

Sandy-skinned tunicates en masse

Sea pork

colonies arrive at the beach as white, pink, yellow, green, red, or purple, rubbery lumps. They generally have a flattened side and may have several lobes. The zooids are imbedded within the collectively shared rubbery tunic.

HABITAT: Acorn worms live in U-shaped burrows in the inter-tidal zone of low-energy beaches. Leathery sea squirts and sandy-skinned tunicates live in shallow waters attached to rocks, docks, shells, and debris. Sea pork is common on rocks and jetties.

DID YOU KNOW? Acorn worms swallow sand just below the surface creating a depression that accumulates bits of organic stuff coming in with the tide. The animal takes in this food along with a lot of sand. Their odor of iodine comes from a bromine compound that may be an antibiotic protecting the animal's soft, naked body from infections.

Although sea squirts may be barely recognizable as a living animal, they have a lot in common with humans, including gill slits, a rigid notochord, and a hollow nerve cord (traits we each have during early development). Larval tunicates swim like tadpoles before settling into an attached existence. As adults, they are wrapped in tunics made of tough, fibrous cellulose.

All tunicates make a living by filtering particles from seawater. Even a plum-sized sea squirt can filter bathtubs of water each day, removing (and eating) about 95% of the suspended bacteria.

Sea pork resembles salt pork in appearance, but not in flavor. Tunicates are an acquired taste appreciated by tulip snails, stingrays, and sea turtles.

Sharks and Skates

Sharks

Skate Egg Cases

Sharks enter the surf to feed on schooling fish.

RELATIVES: These fishes are in the class Chondrichthys and are related to others with skeletons of cartilage.

IDENTIFYING FEATURES:

Sharks in the surf zone include: Bonnethead sharks *(Sphyrna tiburo)*, 3.2 ft (1 m), with a shovel-shaped head; Atlantic sharpnose sharks *(Rhizoprionodon terraenovae)*, 3.5 ft (1.1 m), with a relatively long snout; lemon sharks *(Negaprion brevirostris)*, 9 ft (2.7 m), with similar dorsal-fin sizes; and blacktip sharks *(Carcharhinus limbatus)*, 8 ft (2.4 m), with black fin-tips.

Skate egg cases (mermaids purses), 3.5 in (9 cm), are commonly from the clearnose skate *(Raja eglanteria)*, which breeds December–May. The plasticlike egg cases are black with four tendrils. Fresh ones without exit-slits may have a spherical yolk or wiggling embryo.

Mermaid's purse bundle, clearnose skate (inset)

HABITAT: Sharks are most common in deeper waters but will enter the surf when small fish are plentiful. Skates attach their egg cases, sometimes in clusters, to soft corals and other anchored objects.

DID YOU KNOW? Seashells lacerate more beach-goers than sharks do, and falling coconuts kill more people. But just the same, exit the water when small fish abound. A skate embryo pumps water through its egg case by beating its tail down one of the hollow tendrils.

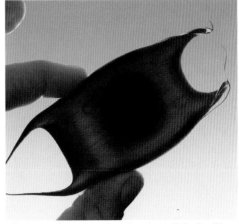

Skate egg showing yolk and embryo (left of yolk)

145

Waves of mullet in the surf

A tarpon slashes through desperate mullet

Pelicans and gannets feast on fingerlings

The Fall Mullet Run

RELATIVES: Mullets (family Mugilidae) are related to other bony fishes.

IDENTIFYING FEATURES: Mullet taking part in fall migrations off beaches are predominantly **striped (black) mullet** *(Mugil cephalus)*. The migration draws other fishes and diving birds into a grand biological phenomenon. Shadowy schools each may contain thousands of hand-sized mullet that periodically burst into the air like exploding fireworks. Mullet aerials commonly precede the rushes and boils of predatory fishes like jack crevalle or tarpon.

HABITAT: Mullet live most of the year in coastal lagoons, marshes, and fresh-water streams. The surf serves as a migration corridor for fingerling mullet seeking deeper waters to overwinter and for adult mullet (16 in, 41 cm) moving offshore to spawn.

DID YOU KNOW? Fingerling mullet are nearing their first year. A big mullet run follows high success from the previous spawn. Mullet are catadromous, living in fresh or brackish water and migrating to the sea to breed. Mullet jump even when they are not leaping for their lives. Because they jump more in waters with little dissolved oxygen, it is thought that frolicking mullet are launching, burping, and gulping as a way to get oxygen from the air. Then again, maybe they jump just to feel wind blowing through their scales.

Surf Catches

Hardhead Catfish, Whiting,
Pompano, and Jack Crevalle   Bluefish

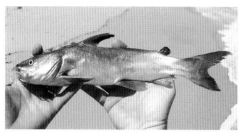

Hardhead catfish

RELATIVES: These surf catches are related to other bony fishes in the class Osteichthys.

IDENTIFYING FEATURES:

Hardhead (sea) catfish *(Arius felis),* 24 in (61 cm), have harpoonlike dorsal and pectoral spines, and relatively short whiskers (barbels). The related gafftop-sail catfish *(Bagre marinus)* has long barbels and extended rays from its forward fins.

Bluefish

Bluefish *(Pomatomus saltatrix),* 18 in (46 cm) near shore, are blue-green above and light below with a large toothy mouth.

Whiting (Gulf kingfish) *(Menticirrhus littoralis),* 12 in (30 cm), are silvery above and white below with a single chin barbel.

Whiting

Pompano *(Trachinotus carolinus),* 17 in (43 cm), have a low-slung jaw and are silvery with a yellowish anal fin and tail.

Jack Crevalle *(Caranx hippos),* 18 in (46 cm) near shore, are similar to pompano (same family) but have a larger eye and mouth.

HABITAT: These are generally coastal fishes. Whiting live almost exclusively in the surf zone.

Pompano

DID YOU KNOW? Catfish spines can cause pain. Polite fishermen toss them back into the surf to reduce foot pokes.

Jack Crevalle

Atlantic midshipman

Anchovy

A discarded bonnethead shark

Fish out of Water

Atlantic Midshipman   Anchovy and
                                  Bonnethead Shark

RELATIVES: Many fish species are found stranded on beaches.

IDENTIFYING FEATURES:

Atlantic midshipman *(Porichthys plectrodon),* 8 in (20 cm), have a large head and a limp body lined with pearly dots (photophores). The related toadfish *(Opsanus* spp.) is darker with no dots.

Striped anchovies *(Anchoa hepsetus),* 5 in (13 cm), have a silvery body stripe and an enormous mouth for their size.

Bonnethead Sharks *(Sphyrna tiburo),* 4 ft (1.2 m), have shovel-shaped heads.

HABITAT: Atlantic midshipman strand on the beach after their fall spawn in nearshore waters. Anchovies and other fishes migrating in the surf are chased onto the beach by predators. Surf-zone sharks caught by vengeful fishermen have their last gasp on the upper beach.

DID YOU KNOW? Male Atlantic midshipman sing (using air-bladder contractions) and flash (using their luminescent photophores) to court potential mates. Females become spent following egg-laying and males exhaust themselves guarding eggs and fry. Both sexes have poisonous cheek spines; live fish should be handled carefully. Anchovies are frail fish that die in great numbers if schools are swept onto the beach. Their large mouths are used to filter plankton from the water.

American Crocodile and Gopher Tortoise

American Crocodile

Gopher Tortoise

RELATIVES: Crocodiles and alligators (order Crocodilia), and turtles and tortoises (order Chelonia), are reptiles.

IDENTIFYING FEATURES:

American crocodiles *(Crocodylus acutus)*, 16 ft (5 m), have a tapered snout and clearly exposed teeth. American alligators *(Alligator mississippiensis)* have a rounded snout and their teeth are less evident.

Gopher tortoises *(Gopherus polyphemus)*, 14 in (36 cm) shell-length, are dark brown or grayish with shovel-like forelimbs and elephantine hind limbs.

HABITAT: American crocodiles live in warm brackish waters near mangroves and nest on sandy banks and beaches with low wave-energy. Gopher tortoises dig burrows in sandy scrub habitat including coastal dunes.

DID YOU KNOW? Florida's crocodiles are federally listed as Endangered, and gopher tortoises are considered Threatened. Crocodiles are shy around humans and eat mostly fish. Cape Sable is the only remaining open beach where crocodiles regularly nest and bask. Nesting occurs March–May. Females return to nests to free their hatchlings and carry them to the water. Gopher tortoises from the dune wander onto beaches but rarely feed there.

American crocodile

Gopher tortoise

Tracks from a gopher tortoise

149

A female loggerhead scatters sand over her nest

A typical loggerhead nest the morning after

A late-emerging hatchling scurries to the surf

Loggerhead Sea Turtle

RELATIVES: Sea turtles are reptiles in the order Chelonia and share the family Cheloniidae with green turtles.

IDENTIFYING FEATURES:

Loggerhead sea turtles *(Caretta caretta)* as adults (37 in, 95 cm, shell length) are orange-brown with a large head and a stout, tapered shell, which typically has scattered barnacles. Nests are circular or slightly elongate mounds with adjacent shallow pits. The hatchling's lumpy, walnut-sized shell is gray, tan, or charcoal above.

HABITAT: Most loggerheads nests are between the wrack line and the dune toe. Loggerheads nesting on Florida beaches have migrated from southernmost Florida, the Bahamas, throughout the Gulf of Mexico, or the Greater Antilles.

DID YOU KNOW? Loggerheads are Threatened, and are Florida's most common nesting sea turtle. Nests have 70–150 ping-pong-ball-sized eggs buried about 18 in (46 cm) beneath the sand. Each female loggerhead makes an average of four nests separated by two-week intervals during the May–August nesting season. Migrating hundreds of miles and laying hundreds of eggs is strenuous, which is why loggerheads typically take off 1–3 years between nesting trips. Hatchlings emerge from nests July–October, 45–60 days after eggs are laid. Both nesting and hatchling emergence occurs mostly at night.

Green Turtle

RELATIVES: Green turtles share the family Cheloniidae with loggerheads and other "hard-shelled" sea turtles.

IDENTIFYING FEATURES:

Green turtles *(Chelonia mydas)* as adults (39 in, 100 cm, shell length) are olive or brownish with a smallish head and a smooth, oval, domelike shell, which may have scattered dark spots. Nests are large, elongate mounds with adjacent deep pits. The 3-inch (7.6-cm) long hatchlings have a smooth, dark shell, outlined in white, as are the flippers.

HABITAT: Most green turtle nests are near the toe of the dune or higher. Green turtles nesting in Florida come from foraging areas in southernmost Florida and the Bahamas.

DID YOU KNOW? Florida's green turtles are federally listed as Endangered, and are our second most common nesting sea turtle. Nests have 100–180 eggs buried about 21 in (53 cm) beneath the sand. The females make an average of four nests separated by two-week intervals during the June–September nesting season. Our green turtles take a year off between nesting migrations. Hatchlings emerge from nests late July through November, 50–65 days after eggs are laid. Nesting is nocturnal, but the two-hour process occasionally leaves females on the beach past dawn. Adult green turtles eat seagrasses and algae.

Sunrise catches a late nester covering her eggs

An exhausted female returns to the surf after nesting

A drop in temperature cues hatchlings to emerge

151

Leatherbacks average about 750 lbs (340 kg)

A female turns a circle over her nest

Leatherback hatchlings crawl with a butterfly stroke

Leatherback Turtle

RELATIVES: Leatherbacks are in the family Dermochelyidae, separate from the other sea turtles.

IDENTIFYING FEATURES:

Leatherback turtles *(Dermochelys coriacea)* as adults (5.5 ft, 1.7 m, shell length) are black with blurry white spots and have a tapered, skin-covered shell bearing seven ridges. Nests are broad, lumpy areas of cast sand and tracks. The hand-sized hatchlings are covered with dark, beadlike scales and have oversized front flippers with white trailing edges.

HABITAT: Most leatherback nests are between the wrack line and the dune toe. Leatherbacks complete their nesting on Florida beaches and leave to forage on jellyfish in the cold waters between New England and Newfoundland. They are likely to wander thousands of miles and even circle the Atlantic before returning to nest again.

DID YOU KNOW? Leatherbacks are Endangered. Their nests have 65–85 billiard-ball-sized eggs about 2.5 ft (75 cm) beneath the sand. Each female makes 4–9 nests separated by 9- or 10-day intervals during the nesting season, which lasts March–July. Leatherbacks take off 1–2 years between nesting trips. Hatchlings emerge from their nests May–September, 55–70 days after eggs are laid. About 5% of Florida leatherbacks nest in daylight.

Sea Turtle Tracks

IDENTIFYING FEATURES:

Loggerhead tracks (39 in, 100 cm, wide) have a smooth, wavy center straddled by alternating commalike swooshes from the turtle's rear flippers. The rear flippers erase most of the front-flipper marks at the track's margins as the turtle crawls forward.

Green turtle tracks (47 in, 120 cm, wide) have a relatively straight set of central ridges (either low or pronounced) that straddle a thin, straight, tail-drag line, which is punctuated by regularly spaced tip-pokes. Both the rear flipper prints (either side of the center ridges) and front flipper slashes (at the margins) are in parallel sets. Front-flipper slash marks are conspicuous all along the track edges.

A loggerhead track to the sea

Leatherback tracks (6.5 ft, 2 m, wide) look like green turtle tracks but are much wider. The slashlike front-flipper marks make up almost half of the track width.

TURTLES AND THEIR TRACKS:

Loggerheads crawl baby-style, leave alternating flippersteps, and have relatively short front flippers and tails. Green turtles and leatherbacks crawl with a butterfly stroke, leave parallel flipper marks, and have longer front flippers and tails. Leatherbacks are enormous and have very long front flippers. If undisturbed, loggerheads and green turtles will nest during about half of their beach visits. When leatherbacks haul out, they make a nest about 80% of the time. Turtles leave the deepest tracks in the softest sands. Take care not to disturb sea turtle tracks and nests; they are counted by biologists each morning.

A green turtle track up the beach

Leatherback tracks often weave down the beach

153

A raccoon-depredated loggerhead nest

A nest eroded by a severe storm

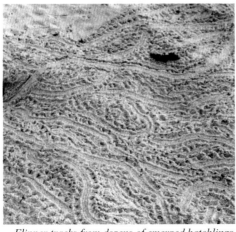

Flipper tracks from dozens of emerged hatchlings

Other Signs of Sea Turtles

IDENTIFYING FEATURES:

Depredated nests are a hole in the beach with numerous scattered eggshells and animal footprints. Raccoons dig into nests from many angles and scatter eggs in all directions. Foxes and dogs dig from one side only. Ghost crabs leave a burrow with only a few eggshells near the entrance. Fish crows commonly feast on nests opened by other predators.

Washed-out eggs are white, pinkish, yellowish, or grayish spheres, or are gray-yellow and deflated (and stinky). Although some white eggs may be viable, many are not due to jostling and exposure.

Hatchling emergence sign is typically a bowl-like depression with hatchling tracks fanning out seaward. Hatchlings leave their eggshells buried during a 1–5 day escape from the nest. The tracks of loggerhead hatchlings are 2–3 fingers wide and like miniature versions of the adult tracks. Unfortunately, it is common for hatchling tracks to circle, meander, and spread out toward the dune when artificial lighting is visible from the beach at night.

DID YOU KNOW? In Florida, raccoons eat more sea turtle eggs than any other predator. Ghost crabs are a distant second. Storm erosion washes out many eggs, but because nests are spread out spring through fall, Panhandle to Georgia, fewer than a third of Florida's eggs are destroyed by the surf even in the stormiest years. Hatchlings emerge at night and orient toward the brightest horizon. Beachfront lights lure hatchlings landward and kill tens of thousands each year in Florida.

Stranded Sea Turtles

Washbacks   Strandings

IDENTIFYING FEATURES:

Washbacks are weeks-old, hand-sized sea turtles that wash onto beaches during late hurricane-season storms, August through November. They are slightly bigger than hatchlings right out of the nest and often have sea stuff, like hydroids and bryozoans, growing on them.

A washback loggerhead following a hurricane

Sea turtle strandings also occur when larger sea turtles become trapped, entangled, diseased, struck by boats, hooked by fishing gear, or drowned in trawl nets.

DID YOU KNOW? Approximately 85% of little loggerheads washed in during storms have ingested bits of plastic from disintegrated marine litter. Like manatees, sea turtles are struck and killed by boat propellers, which provide the most common recognizable cause of death. Nesting sea turtles also get into trouble when they encounter groynes, revetments, and other rocks. The loggerhead in the middle photo became entrapped while returning from her nest, but was rescued and released into the surf. Stranded sea turtles of all kinds should be reported to Florida FWC by calling 1-888-404-FWCC (3922). Conservation workers who have recorded data from a sea turtle carcass may mark it with bright-colored spray paint.

A loggerhead female, stranded in rocks, was rescued

A painted carcass means biologists have recorded it

A male green anole

A male brown anole displaying his dewlap

Six-lined racerunner

Lizards

Green Anole and Racerunner

Brown Anole

RELATIVES: Lizards are reptiles that share the order Squamata with snakes.

IDENTIFYING FEATURES:

Green anoles *(Anolis carolinensis),* 7 in (18 cm), are flat brown or spring-leaf green with a long tapered head. Males have a pink throat fan (dewlap).

Brown anoles *(Anolis sagrei),* 6 in (15 cm), are gray to dark brown with a wedge-shaped head. Females often have a rusty head and contrasting markings down their back. Males have an orange-red dewlap with a yellow border.

Six-lined racerunners *(Cnemidophorus sexlineatus),* 9 in (23 cm), are brownish-gray whiptail lizards with six light lines down their back. They are fidgety and occasionally sprint at blazing speeds.

HABITAT: All are most common on the dune. Green anoles are slinky climbers and prefer leafy canopies. Brown anoles are leaping runners that prefer lower levels. Racerunners are found on the ground in open dune areas.

DID YOU KNOW? Green anoles are Florida natives and have been pushed out of many areas by the brown anole, an alien from Cuba and the Bahamas. This invader is now the most common lizard seen on beaches, as well as just about everywhere else in Florida. All of these lizards feed on small insects.

Snakes

Black Racer   Other Snakes

RELATIVES: Snakes are reptiles that share the order Squamata with lizards.

IDENTIFYING FEATURES:

Black racers *(Coluber constrictor),* 5 ft (1.5 m), are indeed black and racy. They are nervous, sleek-bodied snakes with shiny scales and a white chin and belly. Juveniles (to 12 in, 30 cm) are tan with gray-brown blotches.

Two similar snakes occur more rarely on beaches. **Eastern indigo snakes** *(Drymarchon corais),* 6 ft (1.8 m) are heavy bodied and reddish around the face and throat. Eastern coachwhips *(Masticophis flagellum),* 6 ft (1.8 m), have a black front half and tan rear half.

Snake tracks are either sinusoidal, wavy slithers, or relatively straight caterpillar crawls. Snakes make caterpillar crawls as they compress their body in waves like an accordion, using belly scales for traction.

HABITAT: These snakes live in the dune and only occasionally hunt on the beach.

DID YOU KNOW? Each of these snakes is harmless. The venomous eastern diamondback rattlesnake is a rare beach visitor. Do not approach a snake that rattles. Black racers are the best-known snake to Floridians because they are diurnal and get along well in folks' backyards. Racers on the beach are likely hunting brown anoles.

Black racer

Eastern indigo snake

Snake tracks

Adult common loon, winter

Common loon during its first winter

Red-breasted merganser

Common Loon and Red-breasted Merganser

Common Loon

Red-breasted Merganzer

RELATIVES: Loons (Gaviiformes) belong to a different order of birds from mergansers (Anseriformes), which are related to ducks and other waterfowl.

IDENTIFYING FEATURES:

Common loons *(Gavia immer),* 24 in (61 cm), are diving birds the size of a large duck and have a straight, pointed bill. Their winter plumage is a drab charcoal pattern with a whitish throat and breast. Loons sit low in the water.

Red-breasted mergansers *(Mergus serrator),* 16 in (41 cm), are diving ducks with a thin reddish bill and shaggy head-crest. All but breeding males have a cinnamon head and gray back. Common mergansers *(M. merganser)* are not common in saltwater and have lighter bodies with a white chin.

HABITAT: Loons and mergansers are occasionally found diving for fish in the surf but are more common in lagoons.

DID YOU KNOW? Loons from the northeastern US and Canada winter in Florida. They are often stressed by the long migration and end up stranding on our beaches. On land, even healthy loons can't walk. Their feet are behind them, like an outboard motor, and can only make swimming movements. Mergansers work in groups to herd fish and often paddle with their heads under water.

Northern Gannet

RELATIVES: Gannets and boobies (family Sulidae) are in the order Pelecaniformes, which includes pelicans, cormorants, and frigatebirds.

IDENTIFYING FEATURES:

Northern gannets *(Morus bassanus),* 31 in (79 cm), are big, sleek seabirds with thick bills. Their tapered wings span six feet (1.8 m). Adults are white with black wingtips and have a wash of pastel yellow covering the head. Juveniles are brown with white flecks.

Juvenile in flight

HABITAT: Gannets are oceanic birds that are sighted off beaches when the fishing is good. They are recognizable at a distance due to their steep, forceful, folded-wing dives into offshore waters. Sick and injured gannets often strand on the beach during the winter. Summer breeding for northern gannets occurs on steep cliffs and rocky islands around Newfoundland. The birds nest in dense colonies and reuse their nest-site annually until it becomes piled high with feathers and fish remains.

A juvenile's flecks expand into solid, adult white

DID YOU KNOW? Gannets are supreme divers: their eyes aim forward for binocular fish-spotting, they have no nostril holes, and bills that are watertight upon impact. Their smack into the water is cushioned by a system of air cells beneath their skin. Dives begin as high as 100 ft (30 m) above and end as deep as 50 ft (15 m) below the water's surface.

Adult

159

Juvenile in flight

Juvenile diving

Adults in breeding plumage (L), non-breeding, (R)

Brown Pelican

RELATIVES: Pelicans share the order Pelecaniformes with gannets, cormorants, and frigatebirds.

IDENTIFYING FEATURES:

Brown Pelicans *(Pelecanus occidentalis),* 41 in (104 cm), are bulky birds with a long, pouched bill and stubby legs. They are one of Florida's largest birds and have a wingspan to 7 ft (2.1 m). Winter adults have grayish bodies, a white neck, and a pale yellow cap. During summer breeding, the back of the bird's long neck turns chestnut brown in both sexes. Juveniles are brown above and light below. Pelicans fly with their head resting back on their shoulders. White pelicans *(Pelecanus erythrorhynchos)* are rare at the beach and are mostly white with yellow bills.

HABITAT: Brown pelicans dive for fish off the beach, float just outside the surf, and use the beach for resting. They are equally common in coastal lagoons. Their colonial nesting sites are mostly in mangroves on small coastal islands.

DID YOU KNOW? Yes, their bill can hold more than their belly can: about three gallons of fish and water, twice the capacity of their stomach. Before a pelican swallows its catch it drains its bill from the corners of its mouth. Fish are carried in its gullet, never in its bill pouch.

Double-crested Cormorant and Magnificent Frigatebird

Double-crested Cormorant   Magnifcent Frigatebird

RELATIVES: Cormorants (family Phalacrocoracidae) and frigatebirds (family Fregatidae) are distantly related to pelicans and gannets.

IDENTIFYING FEATURES:

Double-crested cormorants *(Phalacrocorax auritus),* 27 in (69 cm), are snake-necked waterbirds with a hooked bill. They fly with rapid wingbeats. Adults are blackish. Juveniles are lighter, especially on the throat and breast.

Magnificent frigatebirds *(Fregata magnificens),* 35 in (89 cm), are dark seabirds with a hooked bill and thin, tapered wings spanning up to 8 ft (2.5 m). Their long forked tail is typically folded to a point. Males have an inflatable red throat sac and females have a white patch across the breast. Juveniles have a white head and breast.

HABITAT: Cormorants surface-dive for fish outside the surf but are most common in lagoons. They nest in trees on coastal islands. Frigatebirds soar offshore and rarely fly near the mainland, although they are common in the Keys. They nest in summer within mangroves of the Marquesas and Dry Tortugas.

DID YOU KNOW? With poor oil glands, cormorants must hang their wings out to dry before flying. Frigatebirds can remain aloft for hours without a wingbeat.

Double-crested cormorant in flight

Double-crested cormorant drying its wings

Juvenile frigatebird (L), adult male (R)

Black vulture soaring

Turkey vulture soaring

Adult black vulture

Adult turkey vulture

Vultures

Black Vulture

Turkey Vulture

RELATIVES: Our vultures (family Cathartidae) are newly thought to be more closely related to storks and other waders (order Ciconiiformes) than to the vultures of Asia and Africa.

IDENTIFYING FEATURES: Vultures are dark, broad-winged, soaring birds.

Black vultures *(Coragyps atratus),* 22 in (56 cm), are black with whitish wingtips and a stubby, squared tail. Adults have a gray, wrinkled face, and juvenile faces have a less-wrinkled, youthful look. Black vultures soar with straight wings and give quick flaps between glides.

Turkey vultures *(Cathartes aura),* 25 in (64 cm), are blackish-brown with pale flight feathers and have a long, rounded tail. They have a bare head (red in adults, dark in juveniles) with large nostrils. These vultures soar with wings held in a V, rocking erratically as if trying to maintain a drunken balance.

HABITAT: Both vultures catch dune updrafts and use the beach as a travel corridor. Vultures on the beach are there because of dead fish and other stranded delicacies. Eggs are laid on the ground in spring, often in thick palmettos.

DID YOU KNOW? Turkey vultures find carrion by smell and are often first to arrive. Black vultures find carrion by sight and in groups they are tougher competitors at a carcass.

Great Egret

RELATIVES: Egrets share the family Ardeidae with other herons and are distantly related to storks and new world vultures (together with egrets in the order Ciconiiformes).

IDENTIFYING FEATURES:

Great egrets *(Ardea alba),* 32 in (81 cm), are tall, white wading birds with a long slender neck, yellow, spearlike bill, and long, dark legs. In breeding adults, the bill is more orange, the skin in front of the eyes (the lores) is lime green, and long, wispy plumes extend from the back beyond the tail (both sexes). Great egrets fly with their neck folded into an S shape.

HABITAT: Great egrets stalk the surf and other coastal waters for fish but are more common inland. They nest in trees May–August and share island colonies with other herons and ibises.

DID YOU KNOW? Egrets specialize in skewering fish with their sharp-pointed bill. At the turn of the twentieth century plume hunters killed 95% of Florida's egrets. The newly formed National Audubon Society began a mission to protect these birds from hunting, which has resulted in the recovery of great egrets and in the selection of this bird as the symbol of the Society. Florida's population of great egrets increases slightly in winter due to an influx of migrants from the north.

In flight, an egret's neck is held in a crook

Great egret with mullet

Breeding plumage shows long plumes past the tail

163

Adult

Juvenile showing yellow leg-stripes

Adult with a surf-caught, Atlantic thread herring

Snowy Egret

RELATIVES: Egrets share the family Ardeidae with herons.

IDENTIFYING FEATURES:

Snowy egrets *(Egretta thula),* 20 in (51 cm), are delicate, medium-sized wading birds with a shaggy head and all-white plumage. They have a thin neck and a black bill with yellow skin in front of their eyes. Their legs are black with yellow toes. Adults in breeding plumage have especially long, lacy plumes, and the skin on their face develops a tinge of red or orange. Juveniles look similar to adults except for a paler bill and a yellow stripe up the back of each leg.

HABITAT: Snowy egrets stalk calm shallows in the swash zone, runnels, and near inlets. They also occur in freshwater systems. Their nests are made January through August in trees, often hanging over water.

DID YOU KNOW? Snowy egrets were decimated by plume hunters during the late 1800s but recovered dramatically following a ban on plume hunting. In the last couple of decades, snowy egrets have resumed their decline, losing almost three-fourths of their numbers due to loss of coastal wetlands. These egrets use a foot-stirring method to rake up small fish and shrimp from the bottom in shallow waters. Their golden toes may help achieve success by either spooking or luring their potential prey.

Reddish Egret and Yellow-crowned Night-heron

Reddish Egret　　*Yellow-crowned Night-heron*

RELATIVES: Egrets and herons are in the family Ardeidae.

IDENTIFYING FEATURES:

Reddish egrets *(Egretta rufescens),* 25 in (64 cm), are mid-sized wading birds with dark legs and a long neck. Their two color forms, dark and white, are not related to age. Dark-form adults are gray with a rusty head and neck, and dark juveniles are pale gray. White-form birds (least common) are all white with a pinkish, dark-tipped bill. Breeding adults get shaggy neck plumes.

Yellow-crowned night-herons *(Nyctanassa violacea),* 21 in (53 cm), are small, short-necked wading birds with stout black bills. Adults have a black head with a yellowish crown and a white streak below a blazing red eye. Their body plumage is blue-gray. Juveniles are gray-brown with streaks of white and have amber eyes.

HABITAT: Reddish egrets chase fish in the swash zone. Yellow-crowned night-herons lurk on the upper beach between dusk and dawn. Both birds are more common in mangrove habitats.

DID YOU KNOW? Reddish egrets run in circles and flail their wings to herd fish. As their name suggests, night-herons prefer hunting in the dark.

Adult reddish egret, dark phase

Juvenile reddish egret, dark phase

Yellow-crowned night-heron with ghost crab

165

A great blue heron, just taking flight

Adult great blue heron

Great white heron

Great Blue Heron and Great White Heron

Great Blue Heron   Great White Heron

RELATIVES: Herons are allied with egrets and bitterns in the family Ardeidae.

IDENTIFYING FEATURES:

Great blue herons *(Ardea herodias)*, 38 in (97 cm), are tall, grayish wading birds with a long neck, and a thick, pointed bill. Adults have a shaggy foreneck, rusty nape, and a white face. Breeding adults have stylish black streaks that trail thin, ponytail plumes. Bands of three colors at the shoulders and down the legs share the pattern of Neapolitan ice cream. Juveniles have a subdued cast to the adult colors. **Great white herons** occur in the Keys and have all-white plumage. Genetics suggests these great-blue and great-white forms may be distinct species, which would make an uncommon intermediate form, Würdemann's heron, a hybrid.

HABITAT: These herons stalk the swash zone, giving an intent sideways scan to each spent wave. Although great blue herons are common in freshwater, great white herons are almost exclusively marine. Most nesting is in trees, but nests in the Keys may be only a pile of sticks on the ground.

DID YOU KNOW? These are America's largest herons. They specialize in fish but also eat snakes and rodents. Those claiming surf fishermen as territory will give intimidating displays to interlopers.

White Ibis

RELATIVES: Ibises are distantly related to herons, storks, and vultures, and they share the family Threskiornithidae with Florida's roseate spoonbill.

IDENTIFYING FEATURES:

White ibises *(Eudocimus albus),* 22 in (56 cm), are medium-sized wading birds with a long neck and long, down-curved bill. Adults are white with black wingtips. In breeding, their pinkish legs and faces turn scarlet, and their normally pink bill becomes black toward the tip. Juveniles are brown with a white belly and have a dusky orange bill and grayish legs. As juveniles mature, white patches grow to replace their brown plumage.

HABITAT: White ibis groups stroll along the swash zone using their bills to probe the wet sand. Their long legs and bills allow them to capture buried mole crabs as waves surge around them. They also feed in marshes, swamps, mud flats, mangroves, and occasionally, on lawns and golf courses. They make their nests in trees, generally near water, during spring and summer.

DID YOU KNOW? These are social birds. Feeding flocks may contain dozens, separate flying V-formations may comprise hundreds, and Everglades nesting colonies may include thousands of pairs. This bird, once highly abundant, has suffered 90% declines since the 1940s.

A group of adults probing for mole crabs

Juvenile

Adults have red faces and blue eyes

Adult showing contrasting wing pattern

Adult

Adult showing scaly, featherless head

Wood Stork

RELATIVES: Wood storks are in the family Ciconiidae.

IDENTIFYING FEATURES:

Wood storks *(Mycteria americana),* 35 in (89 cm), are large wading birds with a dark, bald head and a thick, down-curved bill. Adults have a naked, wrinkled neck, and white body plumage with black feathers bordering the trailing edges of their wings. The sexes look alike, although males are slightly larger. Juveniles have a grayish, feathered neck. Flying wood storks extend their necks and trail their long legs.

HABITAT: Coastal wood storks are most common near inlets. Nesting occurs in late winter and early spring (the dry season) throughout the peninsula excluding the Keys. Nesting in the Panhandle is rare.

DID YOU KNOW? Wood storks hunt in shallow waters using a method called "grope feeding" to catch fish and other small animals. Aquatic critters touching a stork's submerged, open bill get snapped up in one of the fastest reflex moves known for any vertebrate. Unfortunately, many wood storks occupy beaches because they are fed fish carcasses, which are not good for them (see page 195). These birds have declined in number by about 75% in the last several decades and are federally listed as Endangered.

Osprey (fish hawk)

RELATIVES: Ospreys are allied with hawks, eagles, and kites within the family Accipitridae.

IDENTIFYING FEATURES:

Ospreys *(Pandion haliaetus),* 22 in (56 cm), are large raptors with long, narrow wings. Their upperparts are dark brown, and their breast, belly, and leg feathers are mostly white. Ospreys have a white head and a dark stripe behind each eye. In flight, an osprey holds its wings with a characteristic crook at the wrist (the bending point in the wing). Females are slightly larger than males and have a more streaked breast. Juveniles look similar to adults but have streaked breasts and lighter backs.

HABITAT: Ospreys live and breed near open water. They are most likely to nest in dead trees, normally the tallest in the area. But where tall trees have been removed, ospreys nest atop towers, electrical poles, and channel markers. Some ospreys in the Keys nest on the ground.

DID YOU KNOW? Ospreys hover over water to target fish, then plunge feet-first to grab their prey. In addition to oversized, curved talons, an osprey's feet have spiked pads for gripping slippery fish. In flight, fish are held aerodynamically head-forward, as if they were a bomb ready to be dropped. This fore-and-aft grip is possible due to the osprey's reversible outer toes.

A feet-first catch

Fish are carried as aerodynamic cargo

An adult showing its fish-gripping talons

169

Nonbreeding plumage showing white rump

Adult with post-migration breeding plumage

Nonbreeding plumage

Black-bellied Plover

RELATIVES: Plovers are in the family Charadriidae and are allied within the order Charadriiformes, which includes other shorebirds, gulls, and terns.

IDENTIFYING FEATURES: Plovers of all stripes have a habit of running in straight lines and stopping abruptly in a still, head-up posture.

Black-bellied plovers *(Pluvialis squatarola),* 9.5 in (24 cm) tail to bill tip, are medium-sized, stocky shorebirds that have gray legs and a dark, thick bill. Most beach birds have a pale, mottled back and breast with white underparts and a white rump. In spring and late summer, many show either the beginnings or vestiges of breeding plumage, which is black from face to belly, with a thick white border around the face and throat. Sexes appear similar although the female breeding plumage is less vibrant than the male. Juveniles look similar to nonbreeding adults but have more contrast to their upperparts.

HABITAT: These plovers breed in Arctic tundra. Florida beaches are one of many wintering locations. They feed on worms and mole crabs in the swash zone.

DID YOU KNOW? Black-bellied plovers are sensitive to disturbance and end up being sentinels for other shorebird species. They are the only American plover to have a hind toe (albeit tiny) on its foot.

Snowy Plover and Piping Plover

Snowy Plover   Piping Plover

Adult male snowy plover in breeding plumage

RELATIVES: These plovers share the family Charadriidae with other plovers.

IDENTIFYING FEATURES:

Snowy plovers *(Charadrius alexandrinus),* 5.25 in (13 cm) tail to bill tip, are dainty shorebirds the color of pale sand. They have white underparts, a black bill, and gray legs. In breeding, males have a black patch behind each eye.

Piping plovers *(Charadrius melodus),* 5.5 in (14 cm) tail to bill tip, are similar to snowy plovers but have a white collar and orange legs. During summer breeding (outside Florida) the piping plover sports a black bar across the forehead, a dark breastband, and a dark orange bill with a black tip. Juveniles look like non-breeding adults.

A female snowy plover on her sand-colored eggs

HABITAT: These plovers are found in coastal areas and require barren dry sand near dunes for their nesting. They rest on the upper beach and forage for small invertebrates in the wrack, swash zone, beach lagoons, and nearby mudflats. Snowy plovers breed in Florida March–September. Piping plovers nest April–August from North Carolina to Canada.

DID YOU KNOW? These plovers are state listed as Threatened and the piping plover has a federal Threatened designation. Both species have lost undisturbed areas for breeding, feeding, and resting.

Adult piping plover in nonbreeding plumage

171

Winter nonbreeding plumage

Female on eggs within a "scrape" nest

Precocious days-old chicks stay close to parents

Wilson's Plover

RELATIVES: Other plovers, family Charadriidae.

IDENTIFYING FEATURES:

Wilson's plovers *(Charadrius wilsonia),* 6.25 in (16 cm) tail to bill tip, are small shorebirds with grayish-brown upperparts and white underparts. They have a white collar, and a white patch between their eyes. The stout black bill and tan legs of Wilson's plover distinguishes it from other small plovers. In breeding, the male has a black chest band; the female's band is brown. Juveniles look like nonbreeding adults but with scaly-patterned upperparts.

HABITAT: Wilson's plovers nest mid-March through June near the dune on sandy beaches. They feed on fiddler crabs and other invertebrates on beaches and tidal mudflats.

DID YOU KNOW? Wilson's plover chicks are precocial, fleeing the nest almost immediately after hatching, and flying at about 21 days of age. Like other beach-nesting birds in Florida, Wilson's plover has lost undisturbed areas for breeding, feeding, and resting. There is concern that this species is threatened, although it has yet to be federally listed. The bird's name memorializes Alexander Wilson, Father of American Ornithology, who in 1813 collected a specimen and died shortly afterward at Cape May, New Jersey.

Semipalmated Plover

Semipalmated plover showing wingstripes

RELATIVES: Other plovers, family Charadriidae.

IDENTIFYING FEATURES:

Semipalmated plovers *(Charadrius semipalmatus),* 6 in (15 cm) from tail to bill tip, are small shorebirds commonly seen on many beaches. They have brown upperparts with a white collar and white underparts. Their bill is short and thin and their legs are yellow-orange. In flight, white stripes are visible on the wings and the dark tail has a fringe of white. In breeding plumage, semipalmated plovers have a thick, black, breast band and an orange base to their bill. The sexes look similar although the female is larger and duller in color. Juveniles resemble adults but have yellower legs and scaly plumage on the upperparts.

Breeding plumage before spring migration

HABITAT: These active little plovers breed during summer in open areas near the lakes of Alaska through northern Canada. They forage on small invertebrates found in the wrack and swash zone of varied beaches. They are also common in salt marshes, lakeshores, and on tidal mudflats.

DID YOU KNOW? In their northern breeding areas, semipalmated plover parents swim with their chicks across water channels to forage on islands and land spits. They are aided by a partial webbing between their toes, which is how the semipalmated plover got its name.

Winter nonbreeding plumage

Juvenile

Adult

Adults have a bright orange ring around the eye

American Oystercatcher

RELATIVES: Oystercatchers are alone in the family Haematopodidae and are distantly related to plovers, sandpipers, gulls, and terns.

IDENTIFYING FEATURES:

American oystercatchers *(Haematopus palliatus)*, 16 in (41 cm), are large, boldly colored, long-billed shorebirds. Their back is a deep brown, their neck and head are black, and their belly is stark white. They have an unmistakable red-orange bill, orange rings encircling their yellow eyes, and robust, pinkish legs. Breeding and nonbreeding plumage are almost identical and the sexes look similar. In comparison to adults, juveniles have a darker end to their bill, a darker eye with a less conspicuous eye ring, and lighter upperparts. American oystercatchers are usually seen on beaches in pairs or in small groups.

HABITAT: These skittish shorebirds forage for oysters, clams, crabs, sea urchins, marine worms, and mole crabs along estuarine shores and beaches. They nest on undisturbed beaches and exposed shell/sand bars between March and July.

DID YOU KNOW? Oystercatchers nest in Florida, but many leave in summer to nest in coastal South Carolina. As their name suggests, oystercatchers use their chisel-like bill to open oysters and other bivalves.

Willet

RELATIVES: Willets are allied with other sandpipers in the family Scolopacidae and are distantly related to plovers, gulls, and terns.

IDENTIFYING FEATURES:

Willets *(Tringa semipalmata),* 14 in (35 cm), are long-legged, long-billed, somewhat drab-looking shorebirds. Most birds are gray-brown above and white below with a gray chest. Their long, straight bill is dark and their legs are bluish-gray. In flight willets show a striking wing pattern with a deeply contrasting white band. In breeding plumage, willets are mottled on the upperwings, back, neck and head. The sexes look alike with the female being slightly larger. Juveniles resemble adults but are browner with scaled, white edges on their back.

HABITAT: Most Florida willets breed along our coast April through mid-June. Some willets seen in winter are from a western race that breeds on the prairies of the northern US and southern Canada. Florida willets nest in grassy dunes and saltmarsh. They forage in coastal waters and are common on beaches in the swash zone, where they probe for coquina clams and mole crabs.

DID YOU KNOW? The willet gets its name from the alarming and repetitious *pill-will-willet* call it produces while aggressively defending its nesting area.

Adult in winter

Juvenile

Adult in summer breeding plumage

175

Ruddy turnstones reveal bold patterns in flight

Winter nonbreeding plumage

Post-migration breeding plumage

Ruddy Turnstone

RELATIVES: Ruddy turnstones are sandpipers in the family Scolopacidae.

IDENTIFYING FEATURES:

Ruddy turnstones *(Arenaria interpres),* 7 in (18 cm) tail to bill tip, are stocky shorebirds with orange legs and a dark, wedge-shaped bill. In flight they show a bold set of white wing stripes and a white rump. Juveniles and winter adults are white below with a brownish head, bib, and back. Breeding turnstones before and after their spring migration have a black and white head, white belly, black bib, and a rusty red back and wings. The sexes look similar and juveniles resemble nonbreeding adults.

HABITAT: Turnstones forage on both the lower and upper beach but favor the wrack line. They are also common near other coastal waters. These birds migrate to nest on islands in the Canadian Arctic and return to winter on Florida beaches.

DID YOU KNOW? Ruddy turnstones earn their name by flicking aside beach wrack that may hide amphipods and other tasty invertebrates. These birds often allow close observations by cautious beachcombers and are a joy to watch. On their Arctic breeding grounds, male turnstones make nestlike scrapes in the ground as part of their courtship ritual, but the female constructs the actual nest.

Red Knot

RELATIVES: Red knots are sandpipers in the family Scolopacidae.

IDENTIFYING FEATURES:

Red knots *(Calidris canutus),* 10 in (25 cm) tail to bill tip, are stout, robin-sized sandpipers with greenish legs and a straight black bill. Red knots in flight show a pale, mottled-gray rump as their key identifier. Birds in Florida are generally pale gray above and light below. Some Florida red knots may show hints of breeding plumage during the spring and late summer: a brick-red head, neck, and breast, and a gray back with rusty spots.

Red knots have mottled rumps

HABITAT: Red knots prefer the lower beach for foraging and roost on upper beaches that are broad, flat, and undisturbed. They migrate to nest in the high, open tundra of the central Canadian Arctic.

Winter adult

DID YOU KNOW? Red knots wintering in southern South America fly over 20,000 miles (32,000 km) on each circuit. Keep this in mind when you see a flock on the upper beach being "lazy." Chances are, the birds are taking some critical downtime between connecting flights. Many red knots on Florida beaches during spring and fall are just passing through. Some of their most important staging areas for spring migration lie north in Delaware Bay where formerly massive flocks fed on eggs from spawning horseshoe crabs.

Most Florida red knots are just passing through

177

Spring adult gaining breeding plumage

Post-migration breeding plumage

Winter nonbreeding plumage

Sanderling

RELATIVES: Sanderlings are sand-pipers in the family Scolopacidae.

IDENTIFYING FEATURES:

Sanderlings *(Calidris alba),* 7 in (18 cm) tail to bill tip, are frantic, wave-chasing little sandpipers with black legs and a straight, black bill. In winter, adult plumage is pale gray above and white below. Juveniles are dark gray above and white below. In summer, adults are rusty on the back, head and breast. Juveniles in summer have black centers to their back feathers.

HABITAT: Sanderlings probe for mole crabs like tiny sewing machines in the wet sand briefly exposed between swash and backwash. They migrate in spring to nest on the Arctic tundra.

DID YOU KNOW? Female sanderlings feeling sufficiently plump will lay eggs in nests of multiple males, although most birds are monogamous. At the opposite extreme, some birds not ready to nest will remain in winter foraging areas while most other birds migrate. Sanderlings dodge waves to catch mole crabs and other small invertebrates that burrow within swash-zone sands. They may either swash-run in groups, or go it alone. Lone birds may be defending a patch of beach with lots of mole crabs. These territorial birds can be seen chasing others around in a hunched-over run.

Semipalmated Sandpiper and Western Sandpiper

Semipalmated sandpiper, fall

RELATIVES: These sandpipers are in the family Scolopacidae.

IDENTIFYING FEATURES: Both birds are small, rust-mottled to grayish-brown shorebirds with a black bill and dark legs. They are "peeps"—diminutive sandpipers that are tough to tell apart.

Semipalmated sandpipers *(Calidris pusilla),* 6 in (14 cm), have a bill that is short, stout, and straight. Like the western sandpiper, adults in winter are gray-brown above and in late summer are rufous above with dark mottling and a streaked breast. Semipalmated sandpipers taking flight give out a *cherk* call.

Western Sandpipers *(Calidris mauri),* 6 in (14 cm), have a bill that is moderately long with a slight droop. Otherwise, they look similar to semipalmated sandpipers and are most reliably distinguished by their flight call, which is a high-pitched *cheep*.

Semipalmated sandpiper, spring

HABITAT: Both of these peeps breed in Arctic tundra. Semipalms fly to central Canada and westerns travel to western Alaska. The birds seen on Florida beaches in spring and fall are probably passing through on flights to South America.

DID YOU KNOW? Semipalmated sandpipers get their name from the webs between their toes. Although this trait is rare, western sandpipers have it too.

Western sandpiper, spring

179

Dunlins in flight, winter

Winter nonbreeding plumage

Post-migration breeding plumage

Dunlin

RELATIVES: Dunlins are sandpipers in the family Scolopacidae.

IDENTIFYING FEATURES:

Dunlins *(Calidris alpina),* 7.5 in (19 cm) tail to bill tip, are medium-sized sandpipers with dark legs and a slightly droopy, long, black bill. Flying dunlins show their white rump with a dark central line. Adults with rusty-red backs and black belly patches are seen in Florida before and after their summer breeding migrations. The sexes look similar, although the female is slightly larger.

HABITAT: Dunlins prefer to probe for invertebrates on low-wave-energy tidal flats and are uncommon on steep, coarse-grained beaches. These birds migrate to nest in the Arctic tundra, May through July.

DID YOU KNOW? Although they are occasionally found with sanderlings, dunlins are much slower and more methodical in their feeding. In the late fall and winter, beach flocks of dunlins may number in the thousands. Bill length in this bird can differ between individuals 30% or more, which may reflect connections between the world's dunlin populations. Some American dunlins overlap their breeding areas with birds that winter in Asia.

Least Sandpiper and Short-billed Dowitcher

Least Sandpiper

Short-billed Dowitcher

Least sandpiper

RELATIVES: These birds are sandpipers in the family Scolopacidae.

IDENTIFYING FEATURES:

Least sandpipers *(Calidris minutilla),* 5 in (13 cm), are the smallest of Florida's sandpipers and are similar in appearance to other "peeps." Least sandpipers differ in having yellow-green legs. The other peeps have longer bills and dark legs.

Short-billed dowitchers *(Limnodromus griseus),* 10 in (25 cm), are medium-sized shorebirds with a plump body, greenish-yellow legs, and a long, straight, dark bill. Winter birds are grayish and birds ready to breed become flecked with cinnamon and black. Adult sexes look similar.

Short-billed dowitcher in nonbreeding plumage

HABITAT: As the tiniest peep on the beach, least sandpipers rarely enter the wave wash. Both birds prefer probing for invertebrates in runnels and on tidal flats and are uncommon on steep, coarse-grained beaches. Short-billed dowitchers nest near water in central Canada. Least sandpipers breed across subarctic North America.

DID YOU KNOW? More so than other sandpipers, dowitchers have a flexible, sensitive tip to their upper bill that allows them to grasp deeply buried prey (and do the Elvis lip-curl).

Short-billed dowitcher in post-migration plumage

181

Adult winter plumage

Adult in breeding plumage

Juvenile before its first winter

Laughing Gull

RELATIVES: Gulls are allied with terns and skimmers in the family Laridae and are distantly related to plovers and sandpipers.

IDENTIFYING FEATURES:

Laughing gulls *(Larus atricilla),* 16 in (40 cm), are slender, long-winged gulls. Adults have a smooth gray back and dark legs. Juveniles are brownish with a scaly back. Like most gulls, their bill tip droops. In breeding plumage, laughing gulls have a black head and a deep red bill and legs.

HABITAT: These gulls are common on beaches and throughout other coastal areas. They nest in May and June on partially bare islands within bays and lagoons.

DID YOU KNOW? Laughing gulls are the beach bird most likely to steal food from your hand, and their call will make you think that they've thoroughly enjoyed the prank: *ha-ha-ha-hah-haah-haah.* Their forward nature is promoted by beachgoers who keep these birds addicted to high-test junkfood. Their natural forage is opportunity seafood, including relatively fresh wrack-line treats (sea carrion). The largest nesting colonies for laughing gulls are in Tampa Bay, where some islands host over 50,000 pairs.

Ring-billed Gull

Adult in spring

RELATIVES: These gulls share the family Laridae with terns and skimmers.

IDENTIFYING FEATURES:

Ring-billed gulls *(Larus delawarensis),* 18 in (45 cm) are medium-sized, large-headed gulls with pale gray backs. Their light bill has a distinct black ring at its tip. Juveniles have brownish scalloping above, a black band on their grayish tail, pink legs, and a wide ring at the end of their pinkish bill. Adults are lighter, have a yellow bill with a narrow band, and sport yellowish legs. Sexes look alike, although the male is slightly larger.

HABITAT: Ring-billed gulls loaf and search for food at beaches, bays, lagoons, lakes, and urban areas. They migrate to breed in southeastern Canada and nearby US border states.

First winter plumage

DID YOU KNOW? This gull is a resourceful scavenger with the reputation of being the "fast food gull." This comes from their habit of hanging out at beach-side burger joints where they will gladly ensure that dropped french fries don't go to waste. The healthier part of their diet comes from fish dipped on-the-fly from surface waters and from treats gleaned from wracklines and mudflats. These birds show orientation to the Earth's magnetic field as youngsters, and adults return to nest sites within a few paces of the previous year's location.

Adult winter plumage

Nonbreeding adult

First-year plumage

Bonaparte's gulls often paddle along the surf

Bonaparte's Gull

RELATIVES: These gulls share the family Laridae with terns and skimmers.

IDENTIFYING FEATURES:

Bonaparte's gulls *(Larus philadelphia),* 11 in (28 cm), are dainty, ternlike gulls with a gray back and wings, pinkish-orange legs, and a thin, black bill. Their head is white with a distinct dark spot behind the eye. Juveniles are brown above with dark markings on the head and paler legs. First-year birds look similar to juveniles but have gray, dark-patterned upperparts. Adults in breeding plumage (not generally seen in Florida) have a jet-black head with white crescents above and below the eyes. Their sexes appear similar.

HABITAT: Bonaparte's gulls are winter visitors to Florida beaches, where they loaf near quiet tidepools or pluck small fish from the water, either on-the-fly or while paddling the surf. They breed during summer in middle Canada where they nest in fir and spruce trees.

DID YOU KNOW? This gull is named for Charles Lucien Bonaparte (a nephew of Napoleon), who made important contributions to ornithology in America. Bonaparte's is the only gull that commonly nests in trees. During the summer breeding season, most of their diet consists of insects.

Black-backed Gulls

Greater
Black-backed Gull

Lesser
Black-backed Gull

RELATIVES: These gulls share the family Laridae with terns and skimmers.

IDENTIFYING FEATURES:

Great black-backed gulls *(Larus marinus)*, 28 in (71 cm), are extra-large gulls with a thick bill and pink legs. Juvenile birds have brownish plumage with a checkerboard back and a dark bill. Over three winters, maturing gulls gradually assume adult plumage: white underparts and a sooty black back. Breeding adults have a yellow bill with a red spot on the lower tip.

Lesser black-backed gulls *(Larus fuscus)*, 20 in (52 cm) are similar in appearance to great black-backed gulls but are much smaller. Other differences are that adult lesser black-backed gulls have a dark gray (not black) back, more head-streaking in winter, and yellow legs.

HABITAT: Both gulls are seen loafing on beaches either alone or in small groups. Lesser black-backs nest on the Icelandic tundra. Great black backs breed on small islands and beaches of the northeastern US and eastern Canada, and in winter may feed far out to sea.

DID YOU KNOW? The great black-backed gull is the largest gull species and was hit hard by the feather trade prior to the 1900s. Lesser black backs are much more common in Europe.

Greater black-backed gull 2nd winter, left, adult right

Lesser black-backed gull, winter adult

Lesser black-backed gull, juvenile

185

Nonbreeding adult in winter

Adult winter nonbreeding plumage

Juvenile first-year plumage

Herring Gull

RELATIVES: These gulls share the family Laridae with terns and skimmers.

IDENTIFYING FEATURES:

Herring gulls *(Larus argentatus),* 23 in (59 cm), are our most commonly seen large gull. Juveniles and first-year birds are brownish and have a dark bill with a pale base. Second-year birds become paler with a hint of gray and have a pinkish, black-tipped bill. Adults have a light gray back, pink legs, and a yellow bill with a red spot on the lower tip. Although the adult's head is streaked in winter, breeding birds have a head that is an immaculate white. The sexes look alike with the male being slightly larger.

HABITAT: Our herring gulls breed in summer on islands across the northern US and Canada. They feed most commonly near water but also frequent garbage dumps. They loaf on open beaches as well as beach-side parking lots.

DID YOU KNOW? Herring gulls are moving south. Some of their northern-most breeding areas have been taken by great black-backed gulls and their southern shift has displaced some laughing gulls. Most herring gulls seen on Florida beaches are immatures and non-breeders. Breeding birds often stay near nesting areas. These birds inspired Richard Bach's novel *Jonathan Livingston Seagull* (despite the title there are no "seagulls," only gulls).

Caspian Tern

Adult in winter

RELATIVES: Terns share the family Laridae with gulls and skimmers, and are distantly related to plovers, oyster-catchers, and sandpipers.

IDENTIFYING FEATURES:

Caspian terns *(Hydroprogne caspia),* 20 in (49 cm), have black legs, a black cap, and a thick, pointed, reddish bill with a dark tip. They are our largest terns. Juveniles have black edging to their back feathers but adults are silvery gray and white. In winter, their cap fades into speckles, beginning on their forehead. The sexes look alike.

Adult in spring

HABITAT: These terns loaf on beaches and sandbars as singles or in small groups where they are often outnumbered by royal terns. They feed on fish by plunge-diving into coastal waters. Caspian terns nest in summer near water around the Great Lakes, in eastern Newfoundland, and on artificial islands in Tampa Bay (several other Florida colonies have been lost).

DID YOU KNOW? The Caspian tern is a Species of Special Concern in Florida. Their nesting here most commonly takes place within laughing gull colonies with other terns and skimmers occasionally included. They can live a long life. One wild Caspian tern was resighted over a 26-year period.

Caspian terns are larger than royal terns

Winter adult

A juvenile (right) begs a parent for food

Royal terns shun "the comb-over"

Royal Tern

RELATIVES: Terns share the family Laridae with gulls and skimmers.

IDENTIFYING FEATURES:

Royal Terns *(Thalasseus maximus)*, 18 in (45 cm), are large terns with a dark cap and a relatively slender orange bill. They are similar to Caspian terns but differ in that royal terns are smaller with a lighter bill. In winter, the royal tern's cap trails shaggy feathers in the style of wind-blown male-pattern baldness. Juveniles look similar to nonbreeding adults, and the sexes look alike.

HABITAT: Royal terns feed on fish from coastal waters. A few breeding colonies occur in Florida on both Gulf- and Atlantic-coast islands. Most nesting is April–July. Many of our wintering birds migrate to breed on the coastal islands of Virginia and North Carolina. Royal terns make a scrape-nest on sandy or shelly islands. The mated pair surrounds their egg (often only one) with a circular nest rim that is cemented with their own guano.

DID YOU KNOW? After hatching, young royal terns from many nests hang out together in a group known as a crèche, which may eventually accept every chick in the colony. Parents find their own chick among hundreds by recognizing its call. Juveniles are fed by parents for months, even after migrating away from the breeding colony.

Sandwich Tern

Winter adult

RELATIVES: Terns share the family Laridae with gulls and skimmers.

IDENTIFYING FEATURES:

Sandwich Terns *(Thalasseus sandvicensis),* 16 in (40 cm), are medium-sized terns with a black cap, black legs, and a long, thin, black bill. Adults have a pale yellow tip to their bill. Their black cap is complete during summer breeding and shows a male-pattern baldness style during winter. Juveniles look like nonbreeding adults, and the sexes look alike.

HABITAT: These terns plunge-dive for fish in the surf and other shallow coastal waters. They nest May–July on coastal islands from Virginia to Florida. Most Florida nesting occurs with royal terns on a few islands in Tampa Bay. Young sandwich terns group in crèches with royal terns.

Juvenile (L), adult (R)

DID YOU KNOW? You can remember this bird by its mustard-tipped bill, as in sandwich mustard. The tern is named for the Sandwich Islands (as Captain James Cook named them), now known as the Hawaiian Islands. Both the islands and the sandwich were named for the Earl of Sandwich (one of Cook's financial backers and a fan of meals between bread slices). Ponder that full circle as you eat your picnic lunch and watch the terns dive for theirs. Sandwich terns are rare enough to be a Species of Special Concern in Florida.

Adult with mustard-colored bill tip

Adult in breeding plumage

An early-winter adult

In late winter, heads darken from masks to caps

Forster's Tern

RELATIVES: Terns share the family Laridae with gulls and skimmers.

IDENTIFYING FEATURES:

Forster's Terns *(Sterna forsteri)*, 13 in (33 cm), are medium-small terns with a long forked tail and orange legs. Winter birds have a black eye mask, which turns into a cap by the spring breeding season. The bill is dark with an orange base. Immatures resemble winter adults, and the sexes look alike.

HABITAT: These terns feed on small fish in shallow coastal waters and commonly loaf on Florida beaches in winter. Forster's terns nest on floating mats of grass in marshes scattered from the western Gulf to the Great Lakes and New York State. They nest singly or in loose colonies and feed on insects while at inland breeding sites.

DID YOU KNOW? Although the range of a Forster's tern can span the US from north to south, this bird has one of the smallest ranges of our tern species. They breed in the same areas as black terns *(Chlidonias niger)* where cross-species feeding of chicks has been reported. Their nests are often atop old muskrat dens or abandoned waterbird nests. Johann Reinhold Forster was a pastor and naturalist who made many ornithological discoveries with Captain Cook on his world voyage in 1772.

Least Tern

RELATIVES: Terns share the family Laridae with gulls and skimmers.

IDENTIFYING FEATURES:

Adult hovering above the surf before a plunge

Least terns *(Sternula antillarum),* 9 in (23 cm), are tiny terns with short yellow legs and a yellow bill with a black tip. During spring and summer breeding, adults have a black cap with a white forehead. Nonbreeding adults have a black eyestripe, a white cap, and a dark bill. Immature birds resemble winter adults, and the sexes look alike.

A male courts a female with a gift anchovy

HABITAT: These terns feed on small fish in coastal waters. Florida's least terns winter in South America from Venezuela to Brazil. Their nesting here once occurred mostly on beaches, but due to human disturbance most nesting now takes place on the gravel rooftops of large buildings built near water. Breeding takes place from late April to early August.

A female succumbs to her fisherman's charm

DID YOU KNOW? Breeding least terns are sensitive to disturbance and will dive-bomb nest-colony intruders. With undisturbed beaches rare, and with gravel rooftops being replaced with more modern roofing, the future of Florida's littlest tern is uncertain. They are considered a Threatened Species. A few beaches remain where signs and string protect tern colonies from human visitors who are able to enjoy the bird's aerial feats and family life from a distance.

A least tern chick tries to look like the beach

191

A bridled tern searches a sargassum line out at sea

Adult bridled tern on flotsam

Breeding roseate terns on a Keys spoil island

Bridled Tern and Roseate Tern

Bridled Tern   Roseate Tern

RELATIVES: Terns share the family Laridae with gulls and skimmers.

IDENTIFYING FEATURES:

Bridled terns *(Onychoprion anaethetus),* 15 in (38 cm), are medium-sized terns with dark upperparts, a deeply forked tail, black legs, a black bill, and a bridle-like cap. Immature birds have a white head streaked with black. The sexes look alike.

Roseate terns *(Sterna dougallii),* 16 in (41 cm), are medium-sized terns with pale gray upperparts and a long, deeply forked tail. Breeding adults have a dark bill with an orange base, a black cap, and red legs. Immature birds have scaly-looking backs and a partial cap. The sexes appear similar.

HABITAT: Bridled terns feed by surface-dipping within lines of floating *Sargassum* long before it washes onto the beach. Florida's bridled terns nest on isolated rock-islands in the West Indies. They are generally seen near beaches only after severe storms. Roseate terns feed in coastal waters and breed on sandy, shelly spits throughout the Caribbean. Their breeding in Florida is limited to the Keys.

DID YOU KNOW? Roseate terns are named for their rose-flushed breast plumage. They are a Threatened species in Florida because of their small population and limited range.

Black Skimmer

RELATIVES: Skimmers are in the family Laridae with gulls and terns.

IDENTIFYING FEATURES:

Black skimmers *(Rynchops niger),* 16 in (41 cm), are medium-sized, short-legged sea birds decked out in Halloween colors. They have a long, unmistakable, scissorlike bill with a red-orange base and dark tip. Their lower bill is knife-thin and much longer than the upper bill. Adults have a black cap and upperparts, and immatures are darkly mottled above. Sexes look alike, although males are slightly larger and have a longer bill.

HABITAT: Skimmers feed by gracefully skimming their lower bill through surface waters where small fish are caught unaware. They are year-round Florida residents that nest May through August on beaches, exposed sand bars and gravel rooftops, often with least terns. In the fall and winter, Florida's skimmer population increases with migrants from Georgia and the Carolinas.

DID YOU KNOW? Skimmers are able to fish by feel during dawn, dusk, and at night. Birds resting during the day have probably returned from a very early morning of fishing. They appreciate each other's company, and if disturbed will yip like a pack of excited chihuahuas. The black skimmer is a Species of Special Concern in Florida due to disappearing nesting habitat.

Skimmers take their breakfast on the fly

Skimmers are gregarious birds

Skimmers have a unique style

193

A fish crow in flight

In sun, a crow's black plumage appears iridescent

Fish crows are social birds with strong family ties

Fish Crow

RELATIVES: Crows are in the order Passeriformes with the many other perching birds, and share the family Corvidae with jays.

IDENTIFYING FEATURES:

Fish Crows *(Corvus ossifragus),* 16 in (41 cm), are robust, dark, broad-winged perching birds. They are similar to the inland American crow *(C. brachyrhynchos)* but are slightly smaller and have a different call. Fish crows express a two-toned, nasal-sounding *UH-uh,* a bit like the negative indication children give when they don't want to do something. They commonly stroll and hop about on beaches, dig with their bill, and hold treats under their feet to peck them into bite-sized bits.

HABITAT: Fish crows haunt a wide variety of coastal habitats, and on beaches they frequent the wrackline. They make their nests high in trees, usually near water, during April and May. In winter, Florida receives flocks of fish crows from up north that add to our year-round residents.

DID YOU KNOW? Crows seem clever because they *are* clever, with smarts to rival chimpanzees. These birds use imagination and forecasting of future events to solve problems. They are known to use stick tools and have been observed to carefully drop nuts ahead of auto traffic in order to crack the shells.

For the Birds

Birds are beautiful but vulnerable. As much as we appreciate them, they are among the first elements lost from a living beach. Keeping birds part of the beach experience requires accommodating some of their needs and offering occasional assistance.

LEAVE SOME SPACE: In part, birds hang out on beaches to relax (sound familiar?). Birds that seem to be "loafing" are probably desperate to get a little rest after an exhausting flight, swim, or run. Give resting birds a wide berth, enjoy them from a distance (get close with binoculars), and never allow dogs or children to scatter a flock. Breeding birds (May–August) need extra room. When intruders approach, agitated tern parents take flight and plovers feign wing injury to distract predatory attention. These are clues that you are too close. Their nests are mere scrapes, eggs are cryptically beach-colored, and chicks resemble fluffy, sand-colored cotton swabs that virtually disappear when still. Both eggs and chicks are easily stepped-on or run-over, and continual harassment forces parents to leave their young to die.

LEND A HAND: Don't feed bony fish carcasses to begging birds (exposed spines can pierce their insides), don't fish where birds will go after your bait, and never miss the opportunity to pick up discarded fishing line. If you hook a bird, never just cut the line. Reel the bird in and toss a shirt or towel over it (to calm the bird and control its bill). To complete the rescue of hooked, entangled, or otherwise troubled birds, phone 411 and ask for your local wildlife hospital.

A stranded gannet

A cryptic but vulnerable snowy plover chick

A laughing gull entangled by fishing line

Armadillos are armored mammals

Armadillos leave tracks with a tail-drag mark

An eastern spotted skunk in the dune

Armadillo and Spotted Skunk

Armadillo   Spotted Skunk

RELATIVES: Armadillos (family Dasypodidae) are distantly related to anteaters. Skunks share the family Mustelidae with otters and weasels.

IDENTIFYING FEATURES:

Nine-banded armadillos *(Dasypus novemcinctus),* 28 in (71 cm), are hump-backed, armor-plated, troll-like critters with stubby legs, a long, tapered tail, and cup-shaped ears. This squinty-eyed Mister Magoo of the animal world is likely to be found with its sensitive nose (and most of its head) probing the ground in a seemingly oblivious search for small subsurface animals and eggs.

Eastern spotted skunks *(Spilogale putorius),* 20 in (51 cm), are shy, bushy-tailed, nocturnal animals with broken white stripes marking their black bodies. They have a bold white spot on their forehead and in front of each ear.

HABITAT: Armadillos prefer woody, moist areas and are active on beaches only at night. Spotted skunks live in dense dune and other scrubby areas.

DID YOU KNOW? Armadillos invaded the US from Mexico about 150 years ago. They are now extensive predators of reptile eggs, including those of sea turtles. Spotted skunks warn aggressors with foot-stomping and handstands that precede the spray of a foul, irritating musk. Their accuracy extends to 15 ft (4.5 m).

Beach Mice

1. Perdido Key
2. Santa Rosa
3. Choctawhatchee
4. St. Andrews
5. Southeastern
6. Anastasia Island

Santa Rosa beach mouse

RELATIVES: Beach mice are rodents in the family Cricetidae.

IDENTIFYING FEATURES:

Beach mice *(Peromyscus polionotus* sspp.), are plum-sized, distinctly pale-furred versions of the inland, oldfield mouse *(P. p. polionotus)*. There are remnant populations of six Florida subspecies named for their beach location:

Perdido Key *(P. p. trissyllepsis)*
Santa Rosa *(P. p. leucocephalus)*
Choctawhatchee *(P. p. allophrys)*
St. Andrews *(P. p. peninsularis)*
Southeastern *(P. p. niveiventris)*
Anastasia Island *(P. p. phasma)*

One subspecies that lived between Daytona Beach and St Augustine, the pallid beach mouse *(P. p. decoloratus)*, has been lost to extinction.

HABITAT: Beach mice rest, cache seeds, and bear pups within multiple burrows in the dune. Burrow openings are triangular and about two fingers wide.

DID YOU KNOW? Beach mouse burrows have an arm-length tunnel leading to a main chamber, and a backdoor tunnel ending just below the sand surface. This backdoor provides an escape route from front-door predators like snakes. All but the Santa Rosa beach mouse are listed as Threatened or Endangered. They are declining due to predation by suburban cats, and to an inability to live in condominium parking lots.

Choctawhatchee beach mouse

Anastasia Island beach mouse

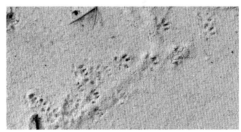

Tracks left from nocturnal foraging

A beach mouse burrow in the primary dune

197

A bandit caught on a nocturnal, sea turtle nest-raid

Raccoons are nervous in open daylight

Prints from forepaws (below) and hindpaws (above)

Northern Raccoon

RELATIVES: Raccoons share the family Procyonidae with coatis and kinkajous, and are distantly related to bears.

IDENTIFYING FEATURES:

Northern raccoons *(Procyon lotor),* 35 in (89 cm), are lumbering, heavy-bodied critters with a dark mask and a thick, ringed tail. Their coat color varies with habitat but most are grayish-red or buff. Raccoons have dexterous forepaws and a reputation for troublesome handiwork.

HABITAT: Adaptation to suburban life has made the raccoon one of the most common wild mammals found in human populated areas. It is likely that fresh water from mosquito impoundments and lawn irrigation, and food subsidies from garbage cans and fishing discards, have allowed raccoons to densely populate some beach areas.

DID YOU KNOW? The northern raccoon is one of seven raccoon species from Mexico and the Caribbean. Suburban raccoons are clever and coordinated enough to lift trashcan lids, climb bird feeders, and open simple latches. Purposefully feeding raccoons is illegal and encourages all sorts of delinquent behavior. Subsidized raccoons will happily move in with you, overpopulate the local habitat, and decimate nearby populations of birds and reptiles. This crafty mammal is responsible for the vast majority of depredated sea turtle nests in Florida (see page 154).

Bobcat and Eastern Mole

Bobcat   Eastern Mole

Bobcats are seen mostly at dawn and dusk

RELATIVES: Bobcats are in the family Felidae (cats) and moles are insectivores in the family Talpidae.

IDENTIFYING FEATURES:

Bobcats *(Lynx rufus),* 35 in (89 cm), resemble super-sized house cats with ear tufts and stubby tails (but longer than the bob-tails of their northern cousins). Their spotted coats are tawny-gray in winter and reddish-brown in summer. Tracks are as from a middleweight dog but without claw marks.

Eastern moles *(Scalopus aquaticus),* 7 in (17 cm), have gray fur, a naked snout, spadelike forelimbs, and tiny eyes covered by skin and fur. They are always underground and are best recognized by their ridge tunnels.

HABITAT: Bobcats are nocturnal and prefer to hunt small mammals and birds where dense growth meets open space. Eastern moles search for earthworms and insects hiding beneath grassy fields with sandy soils.

DID YOU KNOW? About 12 bobcat subspecies roam North America. They are solitary, territorial, and require hundreds of acres of living space. Moles dig deep nest-burrows with an array of tunnels that form the hub for shallow ridge tunnels used only for gathering groceries. Moles on the beach are either brave explorers or desperately lost.

Bobcat tracks   *Dog tracks*

Temporary tunnels (ridges) made by an eastern mole

199

Bottlenose dolphins

The V-shaped blow of a North Atlantic right whale

Cetaceans

Bottlenose Dolphin   *North Atlantic Right Whale*

RELATIVES: Cetaceans are divided between the toothed whales (Odontoceti, like dolphins) and baleen whales (Mysticeti, like the right whale).

IDENTIFYING FEATURES:

Bottlenose dolphins *(Tursiops truncatus),* 8 1/2 ft (2.6 m) are small, sleek, toothed whales that are gray above and white below. Their dorsal fin is rounded back and their head is melonlike with a distinct snout.

North Atlantic right whales *(Eubalaena glacialis),* 56 ft (17 m), are large black whales with no dorsal fin and a large head bearing pale, wartlike growths called callosities. They commonly swim in shallow water right off the beach. Right whales have two widely separated blowholes that create a V-shaped blow.

HABITAT: Bottlenose dolphins inhabit coastal and inshore waters and often swim and feed off beaches. North Atlantic right whales feed on plankton in subpolar waters and migrate to northeastern Florida to bear their calves January through March.

DID YOU KNOW? North Atlantic right whales are Endangered; only about 325 remain. Vessel strikes are their leading threat. To protect whales and people, it is illegal for boats to approach right whales within 500 yards. Report whale sightings to the US Coast Guard.

The tail fluke of a North Atlantic right whale

Manatee and
Marine Mammal Stranding

West Indian Manatee　　　*Strandings*

RELATIVES: Manatees (order Sirenia) are more closely related to elephants and aardvarks than to other marine mammals. Marine mammal strandings are mostly dolphins and other toothed whales.

IDENTIFYING FEATURES:

West Indian manatees *(Trichechus manatus),* 13.5 ft (4.1 m), are rotund, aquatic mammals with gray-brown skin, a round fluke, and no dorsal fin. They seldom show more than their flared nostrils and broad back, and may pass a beach observer unrevealed but for shadowy hints from their blimplike form.

Strandings occur when marine mammals are injured, disoriented, or become too ill to escape the surf. All beached marine mammals should be reported to 1-888-404-FWCC (3922). While waiting for help for live animals, drape a wet cloth over them and keep the blowhole clear.

HABITAT: Manatees munch on a variety of vegetables within coastal rivers, lagoons, and bays. They often migrate through inlets and along beaches. Most whale species that strand on beaches normally live in deep waters offshore.

DID YOU KNOW? Manatees are federally Endangered, and all marine mammals are protected by federal law. Most strandings other than boat strikes and entanglement remain a mystery to scientists.

A West Indian manatee in the surf

Two manatees showing nose and tail fluke

A stranded pygmy sperm whale (Kogia breviceps)

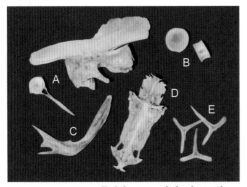

Fish bones and shark cartilage

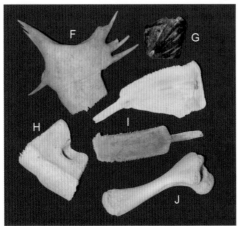

Sea turtle bones and scute

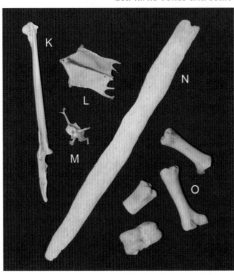

Bird and mammal bones

Verte-bits

Vertebrates are animals with backbones. These critters commonly leave bits of their bony skeletons on beaches.

Fish vertebrae (backbone segments) from both bony fishes (**A**) and sharks (**B**) are deeply cupped at each end. The girdle bones supporting their fins are thin, curved, and flattened (**C**). Fish skulls contain many small bones that don't stay together, although the cranium (**D**) is easily recognized by its spadelike shape and underlying crucifix. Spines from porcupine pufferfish (**E**) are but one of many strange fishparts.

Sea turtles have large thin scales and dense bones in occasionally strange shapes. Their flat, spiked plastron (lower-shell) bones (**F**); carapace (upper shell) scales or scutes (**G**); marginal shell-bones (**H**); ribs fused with shell-bone (**I**); and stout limb bones (**J**) are often found where strandings have occurred.

Birds have bones so light that some can float in water. Easily recognized bird bits include wing bones (**K**) and the breastbone or sternum (**L**), which have keels and other processes to anchor large flight muscles. Bird neck vertebrae (**M**) often have delicate projections.

Marine mammals have large, dense bones. Their vertebrae have long, flat processes and their ribs are gently curved (**N**). Whale ear bones are very persistent; there are fossilized examples of these in the *Beach Minerals* section.

Pigs have their feet used as bait in stone crab traps. Most of these remnants are fingerlike and stout (**O**). These pig's knuckles are common on many southwestern Florida beaches.

BEACH PLANTS

What are Beach Plants?

Plants use sunshine to turn carbon dioxide and water into sugar, starch, fiber, and wood. But pulling this off at the beach can be difficult. Sure, the beach has sunshine, but it also has toxic salt, desiccating sands, and earth-altering sea-storms to reckon with. These tough conditions cull the list of **dune plants** that can thrive at the beach, and the hardy few making the list share some exquisitely adaptive characteristics.

As you'll see, not all beach plants have their roots anchored in sand. Some of the plants commonly found on the beach live elsewhere, such as the **marine plants**— algae and seagrasses. These are what most folks would call "seaweed." At sea, these plants are fundamental pillars of marine food chains, and on the beach they are essential elements of the wrack. The energy gathered and food they make out at sea are put to good use within the beach community. Many beach plants and animals are dependent upon the regular arrival of this gift from the sea.

Some of the most intriguing beach plants are those we never see except for their ocean-drifting pieces and parts. These plants may live many hundreds of miles away in places far from a sandy beach. But because their parts persist and float, they are able to travel the globe and herald their presence by arriving on a beach. The seeds, nuts, fruits, and pods that make these journeys are collectively known as **seabeans**. Other drifting plant parts include stems, corky bark, and entire tree trunks—the seaborne stuff generically categorized as **driftwood**. Note that despite its woody origin, lumber is placed in the section called *Hand of Man*.

The waxy leaves and early-morning flowers of the railroad vine are adaptations for beach life

Sea Oats and Beach Panicum

Sea oats

RELATIVES: All of the following dune plants are angiosperms—flowering plants. Sea oats and beach panicum are grasses in the family Poaceae.

IDENTIFYING FEATURES:

Sea oats *(Uniola paniculata),* 2 ft (60 cm) high, dominate most Florida dune faces. It is a perennial grass with curl-edged blades growing from clumps that spread by underground stems (rhizomes). The gracefully flagging clusters (panicles) of golden oatlike seeds mature in summer and reach 6 ft (1.8 m).

Beach panicum *(Panicum amarum),* 2 ft (60 cm) high, is a perennial grass with waxy, bluish-green, broad blades in clumps that spread by rhizomes. Their pale panicles with small seeds mature in summer and reach 6 ft (1.8 m) tall.

Beach panicum clump

HABITAT: These grasses grow on the dune and out onto the open, upper beach. They are among the most important dune-creating and dune-stabilizing plants.

DID YOU KNOW? These grasses live in partnership with nitrogen-fixing bacteria and water-absorbing fungi that help them live in barren beach sands. Wild sea oats are protected from collection due to their critical role in maintaining dunes. Many native nurseries sell sea oats.

Beach panicum panicle

Coastal sandbur

Seashore dropseed

Seashore dropseed with narrow seed head

Coastal Sandbur and Seashore Dropseed

RELATIVES: These plants are grasses, family Poaceae.

IDENTIFYING FEATURES:

Coastal sandbur *(Cenchrus spinifex),* 6 in (15 cm) high and sprawling, is a perennial grass most conspicuous when its stickers penetrate tender feet. Winter through July, the plants may be without burs and look like lawn grass.

Seashore dropseed *(Sporobolus virginicus),* 18 in (46 cm) high, is a perennial grass with long runners above or below the sand. On the beach, this grass grows upright with long blades. In the dune it may spread densely and have shorter, spiky blades. The seed head is a single spike that is evident in summer and fall. The similar seashore saltgrass *(Distichlis spicata)* has a seedhead with several spikelets.

HABITAT: Sandburs grow throughout the dune and have the endearing habit of sprawling into foot-trails. Seashore dropseed inhabits the dune but may also spread out onto the open beach.

DID YOU KNOW? To unstick sandburs, spit on the fingers you use to pull them out and don't squeeze. This keeps the micro-barbs on the bur-spines from clinging anew. Seashore dropseed was an important forage grass for grazing cattle in dry coastal areas.

Crowsfoot Grass, Saltmeadow Cordgrass, and Beach Star

Crowsfoot Grass   Saltmeadow   Beach Star
Cordgrass

RELATIVES: Crowsfoot grass and cordgrass are in the family Poaceae. Beach star is a sedge, family Cyperaceae.

IDENTIFYING FEATURES:

Crowsfoot grass in dredged spoil on a beach

Crowsfoot grass *(Dactyloctenium aegyptium)*, 8 in (20 cm) and sprawling, is an annual grass with blades that are hairy at the margins and midrib. It has no runners, and almost immediately upon sprouting in spring it produces flower/seed spikes like bird's feet.

Saltmeadow cordgrass *(Spartina patens)*, 39 in (1 m) high, is a perennial grass with wiry blades in dense bunches.

Beach Star *(Cyperus pedunculatus)*, 6 in (15 cm) high, is a perennial, compact, spiky sedge, starlike in form due to its recurved leaf blades. Sedges differ from grasses in having blades of three around a triangular stem.

Saltmeadow cordgrass at the crest of the dune

HABITAT: Crowsfoot grass is an alien invader from northern Africa and grows best on artificial dunes/beaches with alkaline sands. Saltmeadow cordgrass grows throughout the dune including the crest. Beach star prefers open sands, including the upper beach.

DID YOU KNOW? Saltmeadow cordgrass has been used as hay for livestock. Beach star is Endangered due to the human alteration of beaches.

Beach star

207

Sisal hemp with old flower stalk

Sisal Hemp, Spanish Bayonet, and Mound-lily Yucca

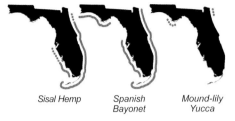

Sisal Hemp   Spanish   Mound-lily
               Bayonet   Yucca

RELATIVES: These plants are allied with other agaves and yuccas in the family Agavaceae. They are distantly related to lilies and asparagus.

IDENTIFYING FEATURES: These plants have swordlike leaves.

Sisal hemp (century plant) *(Agave sisalana)*, 6.5 ft (2 m) high, has broad, bluish leaves with smooth margins. Mature plants send up a flower stalk as tall as 30 ft (9 m), after which the main plant dies and tiny suckers live on.

Spanish bayonet *(Yucca aloifolia)*, 10 ft (3 m) high, has deep-green leaves with finely serrated edges and sharp, stiff tips. Stalks with white flowers appear in spring.

Spanish bayonet

Mound-lily yucca *(Yucca gloriosa)*, 6.5 ft (2 m) high, has bluish-green leaves with smooth margins and gently pointed tips. Stalks with white flowers appear in summer.

HABITAT: All grow on the dune crest and landward.

DID YOU KNOW? Sisal was introduced widely for hemp fiber and is now an invasive exotic in Florida. This "century plant" lives only 6–9 years. Spanish bayonet grows for decades to a precarious height, falls over, and keeps growing. Mound-lily yucca is Endangered.

Mound-lily yucca

Sabal Palm and Saw Palmetto

RELATIVES: These palms are together in the family Arecaceae.

IDENTIFYING FEATURES: These palms have fan-shaped leaves (fronds).

Sabal (cabbage) palm *(Sabal palmetto),* 16 ft (5 m) high, has a vertical trunk and fronds with an arcing midrib. It flowers and fruits in summer.

Cabbage palms take a beating from salt spray

Saw palmetto *(Serenoa repens),* 10 ft (3 m) high, has a sprawling, branching trunk. Its fronds have a serrated leafstalk and no obvious midrib. Most Atlantic-coast palmettos are silver-green. The palms flower and bear fruit spring through summer.

HABITAT: Both palms grow on the dune crest and landward; saw palmetto is the most tolerant of salt spray.

DID YOU KNOW? The sabal palm is Florida's state tree. Sabal palms inland can grow to 90 ft (27 m). Their other name, cabbage palm, generously describes the taste of their "heart" (frond bud). Such "swamp cabbage" ordered in Cracker restaurants is likely to have come from the palm-deforestation of Mexico (and from a different palm species). Saw palmetto berries have become popular with maturing male baby-boomers, who benefit from an extract that treats prostrate swelling. These may be Florida's oldest plants; estimates are that some of the largest specimens may be up to 700 years old.

A network of saw palmetto roots stabilizes a dune

Frond of sabal palm   *Frond of saw palmetto*

209

Coconut palm

Ripening coconut fruits

Coconut Palm

RELATIVES: Coconut palms share the family Arecaceae with sabal palms and saw palmetto.

IDENTIFYING FEATURES:

Coconut palm *(Cocos nucifera),* 40 ft (12 m) high, has a wide base, upward-bending trunk, and very long shredded fronds. Its fruits are the familiar coconuts, which are either green or yellow on the outside. Young palms have entire (not shredded) fronds and may accompany the old coconut husks from which they sprouted.

HABITAT: This palm grows on low dunes and in frost-free areas where landowners desire the Hollywood version of island ambiance.

DID YOU KNOW? The coconut palm is native to Southeast Asia and the islands of the eastern Pacific, but it has been transported all over the world's tropics. There are many varieties. In south Florida, most of the towering old "Jamaica Tall" coconuts have succumbed to a disease called lethal yellowing, which is caused by a plasmid (a piece of autonomous DNA) vectored by a leafhopper insect. Most Florida coconuts are now the less-stately Malayan varieties with straighter trunks. Many coconuts reach Florida beaches but few ever result in a palm.

210

Beach Spiderlily and Dune Greenbriar

Beach Spiderlily   *Dune Greenbriar*

RELATIVES: Spiderlilies are monocots in the family Amaryllidaceae (kin to dafodils and irises). Greenbriars are woody monocot vines in the family Smilacaceae.

IDENTIFYING FEATURES:

Beach spiderlily *(Hymenocallis latifolia),* 3 ft (90 cm) high, is a perennial herb with long, shiny leaves that grow from an underground bulb. Its large, white, frilly flowers appear in summer and fall.

Dune greenbriar *(Smilax auriculata),* 6.5 ft (2 m) in clumps, is a woody, climbing vine with prickles, tendrils, and dark-green ear-shaped leaves.

HABITAT: Beach spiderlily grows in the dune and may live on the seaward dune-face of low-energy beaches. Dune greenbriar lives throughout the dune and frequently covers shrubs on the salt-pruned dune face.

DID YOU KNOW? Many nurseries stock spiderlilies as beautiful, salt-tough plants for coastal gardens. Greenbriar is a thoroughly edible plant. Its shoots are tender and nutty-flavored, and its roots can be made into flour, soup thickener, and jelly. Related plants, referred to as sarsaparilla, provided the roots for the original root beer.

Beach spiderlily

Beach spiderlily flowers

Dune greenbriar

211

Crested saltbush with its wind-pollinated flowers

Saltwort thistle

Crested Saltbush and Saltwort Thistle

Crested Saltbush   Saltwort Thistle

RELATIVES: These plants share the family Amaranthaceae with ornamental amaranths and tumbleweeds, and are kin to beets and spinach.

IDENTIFYING FEATURES:

Crested saltbush *(Atriplex cristata),* 3.3 ft (1 m) high, is a bushy annual with scaly, silvery leaves that often curl and point upward.

Saltwort (Russian) thistle *(Salsola kali),* 3.3 ft (1 m) high, is a bushy annual with short, sharp-tipped, spiky leaves. Its lower stems and leaves may be bright red. Dried bushes in winter take on the familiar look of tumbleweeds (which they are).

HABITAT: Both of these annuals burst into growth during summer and die back by the winter dry season. Crested saltbush grows throughout the dune. Saltwort thistle grows at the dune base and out onto open beach.

DID YOU KNOW? Crested saltbush has edible, pre-salted leaves. Saltwort thistle is an invader from Russia's Ural Mountains. As its brown skeleton rolls about on the beach, it releases hundreds of thousands of tiny seeds. These tumbleweeds cause the largest problems out west where they happily take over what once was prairie.

Samphire, Seaside Joyweed, and Chaff-flower

Samphire   Seaside Joyweed   Chaff-flower

RELATIVES: These plants share the family Amaranthaceae with ornamental amaranths.

IDENTIFYING FEATURES:

Samphire (silverhead or saltweed) *(Blutaparon vermiculare),* 24 in (61 cm) high, is a sprawling, succulent perennial (or occasionally annual) with thick, shiny, elongate leaves. Its flower heads are white or light pink and dry to a silvery white. Blooms are seen all year.

Seaside joyweed *(Alternanthera maritima),* 6 in (15 cm) high and sprawling, is a perennial with oppositely arranged glossy leaves. Its long stems root at their nodes, which allows the plant to cascade down the dune face. The small, white flowers bloom spring through fall.

Chaff-flower (yellow joyweed) *(Alternanthera flavescens),* 2 ft (61 cm) high, is a vinelike perennial with opposite tapered leaves. Its year-round flower heads are yellow-white.

HABITAT: Samphire and seaside joyweed grow out on the dune face and open beach. Chaff-flower grows amidst taller plants on the dune.

DID YOU KNOW? Samphire and seaside joyweed have shiny leaves due to a water-conserving waxy coating. Chaff-flower has been introduced to Florida from South America.

Samphire

Seaside joyweed

Chaff-flower

213

Indian blanket flower

Dune sunflower

Indian Blanket Flower and Dune Sunflower

Indian Blanket Flower   Dune Sunflower

RELATIVES: These plants share the family Asteraceae with daisies and the tall flower of sunflower-seed fame.

IDENTIFYING FEATURES:

Indian blanket flower (fire-wheel) *(Gaillardia pulchella),* 18 in (46 cm) high, is an upright annual (north) or biennial (south) with alternating fuzzy leaves. Its long-stalked flowers come in yellow, orange, red, and two-tone combinations, and bloom in summer and fall.

Dune sunflower *(Helianthus debilis),* 2 ft (61 cm) high, is a sprawling perennial that shows long-stalked, yellow flowers with brown centers. The flower-base leaflets (bracts) are hairy, as are the alternating, stalked, triangular leaves. The plant flowers all year with some die-back in winter.

HABITAT: Each lives in sunny areas with sandy soils and throughout the dune. Dune sunflowers also grow on the dune face.

DID YOU KNOW? Indian blanket flower is the state flower of Oklahoma. Both flowers can be propagated by seed or by rooting small plants and watering a few weeks. After that, they do best when ignored. East-coast dune sunflower should not be used on the Gulf coast in order to avoid the genetic swamping of a unique southwest Florida variety.

Sea Oxeye Daisy and Camphorweed

Sea Oxeye Daisy   Camphorweed

RELATIVES: These plants share the family Asteraceae with Indian blanket flower and dune sunflower.

IDENTIFYING FEATURES:

Sea oxeye daisy *(Borrichia frutescens),* 3 ft (91 cm) high, is an upright, shrub-like perennial with fleshy leaves covered by dense, gray fuzz. Its flowers are yellow with brownish-yellow centers and can be seen all year.

Camphorweed *(Heterotheca subaxillaris),* 18 in (46 cm) high, is a biennial with thick, roughened, wavy-edged leaves and all-yellow flowers on long stems. Although most flowering is during summer and fall, flowers may be present all year.

HABITAT: Each lives in sunny areas with sandy soils on the dune. Sea oxeye daisy is also common near salt marshes. Camphorweed grows in many disturbed areas.

DID YOU KNOW? The fuzz (pubescence) covering leaves of the sea oxeye daisy traps humidity to conserve water. Both of these flowers are favored by butterflies. Camphorweed glands emit a pungent smell that dissuades grazers. This plant has been spreading south to north and is used as an example of how global warming is affecting distributions of plants and animals.

Sea oxeye daisy

Camphorweed

Coastal ambrosia

Beach elder

Beach elder flowers in late summer

Coastal Ambrosia and Beach Elder

Coastal Ambrosia

Beach Elder

RELATIVES: These plants share the family Asteraceae with Indian blanket flower, dune sunflower, and daisies.

IDENTIFYING FEATURES:

Coastal ambrosia *(Ambrosia hispida),* 12 in (30 cm) high and sprawling, is a perennial with crinkled, many-lobed leaves. Its reddish, hairy stems run along the sand and root at the nodes. It blooms in spring with inconspicuous green flowers.

Beach elder *(Iva imbricata),* 39 in (1 m) high, is a perennial, shrubby herb with fleshy, alternating leaves. Some lower leaves may be opposite. Late-summer plants are festooned at their tips with green, pealike flowers, whose fruits turn brown in the fall along with the outer tips of the branches.

HABITAT: Coastal ambrosia grows in sunny areas of the dune. Beach elder grows from the dune crest out onto the open beach.

DID YOU KNOW? Although coastal ambrosia is related to ragweed (same genus), it is not an important pollen source for those suffering from hay fever. Beach elder fosters many dunes and helps to stabilize them as they mature. The plants can be easily started from transplanted suckers and cuttings.

Pink Purslane and Sea Purslane

Pink Purslane   Sea Purslane

Pink purslane

RELATIVES: Pink purslane is related to succulent herbs in the family Portulacaceae. Sea purslane is in the carpetweed family, Aizoaceae.

IDENTIFYING FEATURES:

Pink purslane *(Portulaca pilosa),* 3 in (8 cm) high, is a fleshy-stemmed annual arranged with alternating, fingerlike leaves, many with hairs at their base. Its pink flowers have five petals and are slightly smaller than a dime. They bloom spring through fall.

Sea purslane *(Sesuvium portulacastrum),* 24 in (61 cm) high, is a sprawling, fleshy, perennial herb with inflated, green or red leaves arranged oppositely on the stem. Its starlike, purple-pink flowers are without petals and have five, colored sepals. They bloom all year.

HABITAT: Pink purslane grows on the dune crest and landward, including between the cracks in sidewalks. Sea purslane is a pioneer from the dune face out to the upper beach.

DID YOU KNOW? Sea purslane, also called sea pickle, has edible stems and leaves that taste like a salty green bean. In many parts of Asia this plant is sold in vegetable markets and is believed to treat kidney trouble and scurvy. Sea purslane can be propagated simply by poking a cut stem into moist soil.

Sea purslane

Sea purslane

217

Northern sea-rocket showing lavender flowers

Southern sea-rocket fruits (L), flowers (R)

The dried two-stage fruits of a southern sea-rocket

Northern Sea-rocket and Southern Sea-rocket

Northern Sea-rocket   *Southern Sea-rocket*

RELATIVES: Sea-rocket is in the mustard family, Brassicaceae.

IDENTIFYING FEATURES:

Northern sea-rocket *(Cakile edentula)*, 12 in (30 cm) high, is a small upright annual that has wide, blunt-tipped, succulent leaves with irregular margins. Its four-petal flowers are white or lavender, and its duel-segmented fruits go from green, to yellow, to brown, summer through fall.

Southern sea-rocket *(Cakile lanceolata)* is similar to the northern sea-rocket, except that it reaches bush size (3 ft, 90 cm) and has long, leggy branches and elongate, blunt-tipped leaves, which may have smooth or slightly irregular margins.

HABITAT: Both of these sea-rockets blast off with the first rains of spring and are among the first plants to reclaim the open beach that was swept by winter waves.

DID YOU KNOW? Sea-rocket greens taste like mild horseradish. The plant's succulent leaves plump after rains to store water for drier times. Each stage of the plant's rocketlike pods has seeds. The end stage is corky and breaks off to drift at sea, sprouting plants far away. The base stage stays attached, is buried by wind-blown sand, and starts local plants.

218

Sand Ground-cherry and Burrowing Four-o'clock

Sand Ground-cherry   *Burrowing Four-o'clock*

RELATIVES: Ground-cherries are in the tomato family (Solanaceae) and four-o'clocks are in the bougainvillea family (Nyctaginaceae).

IDENTIFYING FEATURES:

Sand ground-cherry *(Physalis walteri),* 12 in (30 cm) high, is a perennial herb with fuzzy leaves and stems. Its yellow flowers appear spring through fall and its drooping fruit is a berry within a papery sac. The coastal ground-cherry *(P. angustifolia)* has narrower leaves and is found only on Gulf-coast dunes.

Burrowing four-o'clock (beach peanut) *(Okenia hypogaea),* 6 in (15 cm) high and spreading, is an annual herb with running stems. The opposite leaves are fleshy and ribbed, have purplish margins, and are covered in tiny, stiff hairs. Its vivid fuchsia flowers bloom spring through fall.

HABITAT: Sand ground-cherry grows in sunny areas including the dune face. Burrowing four-o'clock is largely limited to the dune face and open beach.

DID YOU KNOW? Burrowing four-o'clock seems to do well when hurricanes and sea turtles shift upper-beach sands containing their seeds. The plant is Endangered in Florida and has disappeared from most of its thin range due to artificial rearrangement of dunes.

Sand ground-cherry on a dune face

Sand ground-cherry fruits and flower

Burrowing four-o'clock

Poorman's patch sticks to clothing like Velcro

Tread softly

Poorman's Patch and Tread Softly (Stinging Nettle)

Poorman's Patch

Tread Softly

RELATIVES: Poorman's patch is in the family Loasaceae with tropical, prickly herbs. Tread softly is related to the spurges, family Euphorbiaceae.

IDENTIFYING FEATURES:

Poorman's patch *(Mentzelia floridana),* 3 ft (91 cm) high, is a shrubby perennial with three-lobed Velcro-like leaves that, along with the brittle stems and fruits, aggressively cling to clothes, skin, and hair. Its flowers are yellow with five petals.

Tread softly *(Cnidoscolus stimulosus),* 12 in (30 cm) high, is an erect perennial with three- or five-lobed leaves. Nearly the entire plant is covered with stiff hairs that cause a burning rash when brushed against sensitive skin. On the bright side, the plant does have lovely pure-white flowers from spring through fall.

HABITAT: Poorman's patch often covers large areas of dune behind plants that are more tolerant of salt spray. Tread softly is often tucked between sea oats and other grasses on and behind the dune crest.

DID YOU KNOW? Poorman's patch sticks to almost everything due to its covering of tiny, barbed hairs. The clinging nature of this plant may help it spread by fragmentation. Tread softly fruit is a capsule with three large, edible seeds.

Coastal Beach Sandmat and Seaside Sandmat

Coastal Beach Sandmat   *Seaside Sandmat*

RELATIVES: These plants are spurges in the euphorb family, Euphorbiaceae.

IDENTIFYING FEATURES: Both of these spurges have a milky sap and have fruits that are three-lobed capsules.

Coastal beach sandmat *(Chamaesyce mesembrianthemifolia),* 2 ft (60 cm) high, is a leggy, upright, perennial herb with opposite, leathery leaves that fold up on the stem during dry conditions. Its yellow-green flowers appear in summer.

Seaside sandmat *(Chamaesyce polygonifolia),* 4 in (10 cm) and sprawling, is a matlike annual herb with opposite, supple leaves on many reddish branches. Its tiny flowers appear in summer.

HABITAT: Both plants grow throughout the dune and on the dune face.

DID YOU KNOW? The milky sap from these spurges contains a latex that can cause vomiting, nausea, and diarrhea if ingested, and severe inflammation upon contact with eyes or open cuts. In small doses, these euphorbs are well known for their medicinal utility. The family is named for Euphorbus, a Greek physician during the first century AD.

Coastal beach sandmat

Coastal beach sandmat with flowers and fruits

Seaside sandmat

221

Silver-leaf croton

Silver-leaf croton with fruits

Seaside evening primrose, flower inset

Silver-leaf Croton and Seaside Evening Primrose

Silver-leaf Croton

Seaside Evening Primrose

RELATIVES: Silver-leaf croton is a spurge in the family Euphorbiaceae. Seaside evening primrose is in the family Onagraceae.

IDENTIFYING FEATURES:

Silver-leaf croton (beach tea) *(Croton punctatus),* 3 ft, (90 cm) high, is a perennial shrubby herb with fuzzy, gray-green leaves on rusty branches. The fruit is a fuzzy, three-lobed capsule seen all year.

Seaside evening primrose *(Oenothera humifusa),* 12 in (30 cm) high, is an upright, woody, bushy, or sprawling biennial with thick, furry, smooth-edged leaves. Its flowers appear in summer and are yellow, turning orange-pink as they wilt. The fruit is an elongate, furry capsule. This plant tends to be shrublike in south Florida.

HABITAT: Both of these plants grow in sunny areas on the dune crest and upper beach.

DID YOU KNOW? Evening primrose flowers open at dusk to attract moths and other night-flying pollinators. The plant's genus is derived from the Greek *oinos* for wine; the herb is believed to treat hangovers from drinking too much. Evening primrose oil has been used to treat menopausal symptoms, asthma, and high cholesterol.

Golden Beach Creeper, Gopher Apple, and Beach Pennywort

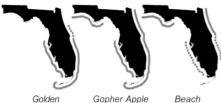

| Golden Beach Creeper | Gopher Apple | Beach Pennywort |

Golden beach creeper

RELATIVES: Beach creeper (family Rubiaceae, madders and coffee), gopher apple (Chrysobalanaceae, cocoplum family), and pennywort (Araliaceae, ginseng family) are only distantly related.

IDENTIFYING FEATURES:

Golden beach creeper *(Ernodea littoralis),* 2 ft (60 cm) high, is a reclining vinelike shrub with clusters of alternating, shiny, stiff, pointed leaves. It has tubular white flowers in fall followed by round, yellow fruit in spring.

Gopher apple *(Licania michauxii),* 18 in (45 cm) high, is a low shrub with shiny leaves and underground branches. It has white flower clusters in spring and a pale, round, single-pitted fruit.

Gopher apple

Beach (largeleaf) pennywort *(Hydrocotyle bonariensis),* 8 in (20 cm) high, is a perennial herb with creeping lateral stems buried in sand and circular, scallop-edged leaves. Its white flower clusters appear spring through summer.

HABITAT: Each of these plants grows in sunny dune areas. Gopher apple grows farthest from the beach, and beach pennywort spreads out onto the upper beach.

DID YOU KNOW? Like a gopher, the branches of the gopher apple remain underground, and its fruit is enjoyed by the tortoise of the same name.

Beach pennywort

223

Southern prickly-pear

Southern prickly-pear with fruit

Eastern prickly-pear

Prickly-pear Cacti

Southern
Prickly-pear Cactus

Eastern
Prickly-pear Cactus

RELATIVES: Prickly-pears are related to other cacti in the family Cactaceae.

IDENTIFYING FEATURES: Prickly-pears *(Opuntia* spp.) are perennial cacti with succulent, branching, oval pads (stems), and occasional sharp spines (modified leaves). The spines protrude from eyes (areoles) that also have tufts of tiny barbed bristles. Large, yellow flowers appear in spring.

Southern prickly-pear *(O. stricta)* has dull pads and yellow spines on mature plants.

Eastern prickly-pear *(O. humifusa)* has compressed, glossy pads and spines that are gray, white, or brown.

In northeastern Florida and the Panhandle, cacti on the dunefront may be the cockspur prickly-pear *(O. pusilla)* with less-compressed, barrel-shaped pads.

HABITAT: These cacti grow throughout the dune.

DID YOU KNOW? Gopher tortoises eat both the pads and fruits of the prickly-pear. The southern prickly-pear is in decline due to habitat loss and is Threatened in Florida. Prickly-pear cacti of several species are being lost to an alien cactus moth from Argentina *(Cactoblastis cactorum)* that was introduced into Florida and is spreading northward.

Railroad Vine, Beach Morning Glory, and Beach Pea

Railroad Vine   Beach   Beach Pea
Morning Glory

RELATIVES: Railroad vine is with other morning glory flowers in the family Convolvulaceae. Beach pea is a legume in the family Fabaceae.

IDENTIFYING FEATURES:

Railroad-vine (morning glory) *(Ipomoea pes-caprae),* 6 in (15 cm) high with beach-length stems, is a shiny-leaved perennial vine that tends to run more than climb. Its flowers are purple to pink and bloom spring through fall.

Beach morning glory *(Ipomoea imperati),* 6 in (15 cm) high, is similar to railroad vine but has shorter runners (often buried) and more leathery leaves, often with three lobes. Its flower is white with a yellow center.

Beach pea (bay bean) *(Canavalia rosea),* 12 in (30 cm) high or climbing, is a sprawling perennial vine with leathery leaves in compound threes, pink flowers, and hot-dog-sized seedpods (see page 259).

HABITAT: These vines grow among other plants on the dune crest and dune face. By late summer, railroad vine may have its "tracks" stretched to the tide line.

DID YOU KNOW? The nitrogen-fixing nodules on the roots of the beach pea, which allow it to grow quickly in nutrient-starved dune sands, also provide fertilizer for other plant species.

Railroad vine (morning glory)

Beach morning glory

Beach pea

Partridge pea

Coralbean leaves

Coralbean flowers

Partridge Pea and Coralbean

Partridge Pea   Coralbean

RELATIVES: These plants are in the family Fabaceae with other legumes such as soybeans.

IDENTIFYING FEATURES:

Partridge pea *(Chamaecrista fasciculata),* 24 in (60 cm) high, is an annual herb with alternate, compound leaves each with about a dozen leaflet pairs. Its yellow, five-part flowers bloom from summer to mid-fall.

Coralbean (Cherokee bean) *(Erythrina herbacea),* 10 ft (3 m) high, is a treelike herb that has compound leaves with three leaflets bearing midrib prickles. Most plants lose leaves in winter. The woody stems and trunk have occasional spines and a thick, greenish bark. The tubular, scarlet flowers protrude from an otherwise bare plant in early spring.

HABITAT: Partridge pea grows throughout the dune and onto the dune face. Coralbean intertwines with saw palmetto and other plants for salt-spray protection and is generally landward of the dune crest.

DID YOU KNOW? Partridge pea flowers are either right- or left-handed based on the direction that their stamens bend. During water stress, the plant's leaflets fold up tightly. Coralbean flowers are shaped to be pollinated almost exclusively by hummingbirds.

226

Mangroves

A mature red mangrove

RELATIVES: Red mangroves (family Rhizophoraceae) are only distantly related to black mangroves (family Avicenniaceae).

IDENTIFYING FEATURES:

Red mangrove *(Rhizophora mangle),* 15 ft (4.6 m) high, is a sprout, bush, or tree with oppositely arranged, smooth, thick, elliptical leaves. Larger plants develop arcing proproots and have a thick, scaly, gray and reddish bark. The pale-yellow flowers appear in spring. The fruit is a cone-shaped, leathery, brown berry that sprouts on the tree and later falls as a floating propagule.

Black mangrove *(Avicennia germinans),* 20 ft (6.1 m) high, is a tree with oppositely arranged, smooth-edged leaves that are shiny above and fuzzy below. White flowers in summer produce green capsules like a split lima bean. Roots "breathe" through vertical "snorkel roots" (pneumatophores).

Red mangrove with sprouting propagules

HABITAT: Red mangrove grows into the water only on the calmest beaches. Black mangrove grows at low elevations away from waves.

DID YOU KNOW? Red mangrove proproots supply air to submerged roots, brace the plant as it stands in water, and trap silt so as to create the tree's own island. Black mangrove leaves are coated with excreted salt. These plants do not need fresh water to grow.

Black mangrove with pneumatophores

Cocoplum

Cocoplum with fruit

Natal plum

Cocoplum and Natal Plum

Cocoplum   Natal Plum

RELATIVES: Cocoplum is in the family Chrysobalanaceae. Natal plum shares the family Apocynaceae with jasmines and oleanders.

IDENTIFYING FEATURES:

Cocoplum *(Chrysobalanus icaco),* 4 ft (1.2 m), is a sprawling shrub with alternating, oval, leathery leaves. Its clusters of small, white flowers appear in late spring, and by summer the plant has round plumlike fruits that are blushed yellow to purple.

Natal plum *(Carissa macrocarpa),* 6 ft (1.8 m), is a dense shrub with opposite, glossy, dark-green, oval, spine-tipped leaves on branches bearing pairs of forked spines. The white, waxy, five-pointed flowers bloom any time of year. Ensuing fruits look like reddish plums.

HABITAT: Both cocoplum, a Florida native, and Natal plum, an alien import, compete for space throughout the dune out to its crest.

DID YOU KNOW? Florida shares the cocoplum with much of tropical America and the Caribbean. The bush is commonly used as a hedge in southern Florida. Natal plum was brought to Florida from the Natal provence in South Africa. Fruits from both plants are tasty, although the remainder of the Natal plum plant, especially its sticky, white latex, is poisonous.

Inkberry and Beach Naupaka

Inkberry   Beach Naupaka

Inkberry with flowers

RELATIVES: These tropical plants are together in the family Goodeniaceae.

IDENTIFYING FEATURES: Both plants are shrubs with succulent stems, smooth, leathery, oval leaves, and white, frilly flowers that appear in summer and seem to be missing their upper half.

Inkberry *(Scaevola plumieri),* 3 ft (92 cm) high, has thick, medium-green leaves. Its fruit matures summer–fall and is an inky-black, grapelike berry.

Beach naupaka *(Scaevola taccada),* 6 ft (1.8 m) high, has elongate, curled, pale-green leaves. Its fruits appear as numerous, white berries in the summer and fall.

HABITAT: Both plants compete for space near the dune crest and dune face.

Inkberry fruit

DID YOU KNOW? Both plants are often called beach half-flower. Inkberry is a native Florida plant that has become rare and is threatened with extinction. Beach naupaka is an alien invader from the Indo-Pacific. It has been widely planted as a landscape plant on south-Florida dunes and is currently crowding out many of the native dune plants unique to Florida. Beach naupaka has a tough competitive edge over native plants, especially when irrigated. Both *Scaevola* species have flowers with a special structure that dabs pollen on the backs of visiting pollinators.

Beach naupaka flowers and fruits

Seagrape with fruits

Seagrape showing new, red leaves

White indigoberry with maturing green fruits

Seagrape and White Indigoberry

Seagrape

White Indigoberry

RELATIVES: Seagrape shares the family Polygonaceae with buckwheat and rhubarb. Indigoberry is in the family Rubiaceae with madders and coffee.

IDENTIFYING FEATURES:

Seagrape *(Coccoloba uvifera)*, 20 ft (6.1 m) high, is a woody tree with circular, hand-sized, cardboard-stiff leaves. New leaves are glossy red and old leaves turn brick-red before falling in winter. Lengths of small ivory flowers bloom in early summer and produce clusters of green grapes only on the female trees.

White indigoberry *(Randia aculeata)*, 5 ft (1.5 m) high, is a woody shrub with opposite, leathery leaves clustered at the ends of its branches. Its small, starlike, white flowers bloom all year and its green fruits turn white when ripe.

HABITAT: Both plants grow throughout the dune. Seagrape is the dominant woody plant on many south Florida dunes.

DID YOU KNOW? Seagrape fruits are a conspicuous grape-purple when they mature but are seldom seen because the ripe fruits are quickly eaten by a variety of birds. This sturdy, salt-resistant tree protects other plants and preserves the dune during hurricanes. Tourists used to send the tough, papery leaves of seagrape as postcards. The flowers of white indigoberry have a lavish fragrance for their small size.

Australian Pine and Brazilian Peppertree

Australian Pine   *Brazilian Peppertree*

RELATIVES: Australian pines are flowering trees (not pines) in the family Casuarinaceae. Brazilian pepper shares the family Anacardiaceae with poison ivy and poison sumac.

IDENTIFYING FEATURES:

Australian pine (beach she-oak) *(Casuarina equisetifolia)*, 50 ft (15 m) high, is a towering, shaggy tree with green, segmented branchlets that look like pine needles. Other similar *Casuarina* species are uncommon near beaches.

Brazilian peppertree *(Schinus terebinthifolius)*, 20 ft (6.1 m) high, is a woody tree that grows multiple, arcing trunks that form a tangled thicket. Their compound leaves typically have 7 or 9 leaflets. Its clusters of shiny red berries are obvious in winter. When its branches break they emit the pungent odor of peppery turpentine.

HABITAT: Both of these trees grow throughout the dune and have been known to exclude most other plants. Australian pine trunks are highly persistent on the beach.

DID YOU KNOW? Both are highly invasive plants from the places in their names. For some, Brazilian peppertree sap causes a rash similar to that of poison-ivy. Australian pine makes excellent, hot-burning, resin-free firewood.

Australian pines haunt a south Florida beach

Australian pines have shallow, spreading roots

Brazilian peppertree

231

Bay cedar

Sea lavender

Sea lavender flowers

Bay Cedar and Sea Lavender

Bay Cedar   *Sea Lavendar*

RELATIVES: Bay cedar (family Surianaceae) is not a cedar and may be distantly related to legumes. Sea lavender is in the family Boraginaceae with forget-me-nots.

IDENTIFYING FEATURES:

Bay cedar *(Suriana maritima),* 10 ft (3 m) high, is a shrubby tree with rugged, dark, flaky bark and fuzzy, fleshy, gray-green leaves. Its individual yellow flowers occur all year.

Sea lavender *(Argusia gnaphalodes),* 5 ft (1.5 m) high, is a shrub with elongate, succulent, silvery blue-green leaves covered by silky hairs. Its clusters of small white flowers with lavender centers are seen all year.

HABITAT: Both of these shrubs grow on the saltier parts of the dune and out onto the upper beach where wave overwash is infrequent.

DID YOU KNOW? These plants are built for beaches. Their fuzzy leaf-coverings keep leaves shrouded in humid air despite dry beach conditions, and their seeds can survive sea-travel to other beach locations. Both plants have become rare in crowded south Florida and are Endangered. Both are beautiful, ecologically intricate plants that thrive on neglect and are excellent choices for coastal gardens.

Hercules'-club and Yaupon Holly

Hercules'-club   *Yaupon Holly*

RELATIVES: Hercules'-club shares the family Rutaceae with oranges and other citrus. Yaupon is in the family Aquifoliaceae with the other hollies.

IDENTIFYING FEATURES:

Hercules'-club *(Zanthoxylum clava-herculis),* 10 ft (3 m) high, is a thorny tree with alternate, compound leaves of about 9 asymmetrical, waxy leaflets with wavy margins.

Yaupon holly *(Ilex vomitoria),* 10 ft (3 m) high, is a shrubby tree with small, alternating, elliptical, dark-green leaves with wavy-toothed margins. Female plants have pea-sized berries that mature from green to red in fall.

HABITAT: Hercules'-club grows among other salt-spray-shielding plants on the dune. Yaupon holly may form a low canopy on the dune and live in a severely salt-pruned form on the dune face (see page 7).

DID YOU KNOW? Hercules'-club leaves have a citrus smell from an aromatic bitter oil called xanthoxylin, which has a number of folk medicinal applications. Also known as the toothache tree, this plant's fruit and leaves are able to numb mouth pain. Young yaupon holly leaves are caffeinated and make a good tea despite the plant's scientific name. The fruits, however, are a purgative emetic.

Hercules'-club thorny branches

Hercules'-club compound leaves

Yaupon holly

233

Sand live oak with developing acorn

Tough buckthorn

Tough buckthorn with fruit

Sand Live Oak and Tough Buckthorn

Sand Live Oak   *Tough Buckthorn*

RELATIVES: Oaks are together with beech trees in the family Fagaceae. Tough buckthorn is related to the chicle (chewing gum) tree in the family Sapotaceae.

IDENTIFYING FEATURES:

Sand live oak *(Quercus geminata),* 20 ft (6.1 m) high, is a woody tree with tough, corky bark on its trunk. Most of its thick, older leaves have curled margins and are shaped like upturned canoes with a pale fuzz on their concave underside. New leaves may be asymmetrical and holly-like. This oak's acorns mature in fall and are generally in twins (hence the species name).

Tough (bully) buckthorn *(Sideroxylon tenax),* 10 ft (3 m) high, is a thorny tree with dense growth between dead, salt-pruned branches. Its new stems and leaves are covered by a coppery fuzz, which remains beneath the older leaves. Small white flowers appear in spring and dark berries mature in summer and fall.

HABITAT: Both grow throughout the dune to its crest.

DID YOU KNOW? Sand live oak is closely related to the more inland live oak *(Q. virginiana).* Tough buckthorn is tough because of its finger-length thorns formed by old sharp-tipped branches.

Green Algae *(Sea Lettuce, Hollow Green Weed, and Hair Algae)*

RELATIVES: Green algae (Chlorophyta) are closer to land plants than to the brown and red algae. Sea lettuce and hollow green weed are in the family Ulvaceae, and hair algae are within the Cladophoraceae.

IDENTIFYING FEATURES:

Sea lettuce *(Ulva* spp.), 2 in (5 cm) wide straps, is a bright, apple-green alga with wavy edges. Its slick, translucent sheets begin attached but are easily torn free.

Hollow green weed *(Enteromorpha* spp.) is hairlike when short and forms strands of narrow, limp cylinders when up to 6 in (15 cm) long.

Hair algae *(Cladaphora* spp.) beach as tough, compact, cottonlike balls to 2 in (5 cm) and may be sun-bleached white.

HABITAT: Sea lettuce grows on jetty rocks and nearshore reefs during calmer summer months and is common in fresh wrack after the first rough warm-season weather. Hollow green weed covers hard surfaces in the wavewash. Puffy hair-algae balls grow in shallow waters.

DID YOU KNOW? Sea lettuce is yummy either raw or boiled in soup. Hollow green weed often grows where it is only submerged at high tide. The beached balls formed by hair algae are tough enough to stay cottony for many years, although they quickly bleach.

Sea lettuce revealed on jetty rocks at low tide

Sea lettuce that has been torn free

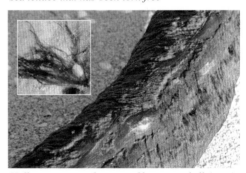

Hollow green weed on a surf log, on a shell (inset)

The green, cottony balls of hair algae

Grape caulerpa

Common caulerpa

Sailor's eye

Green Algae *(Grape Caulerpa, Common Caulerpa, and Sailor's Eye)*

Grape and Common
Caulerpa

Sailor's Eye

RELATIVES: All are green algae. Caulerpa species are in the family Caulerpaceae, and sailor's eye is in the family Valoniaceae.

IDENTIFYING FEATURES:

Grape caulerpa *(Caulerpa racemosa),* 6 in (15 cm) long, has pale yellow rhizomes with green branches bearing stubby branchlets that end in swollen tips.

Common caulerpa *(Caulerpa prolifera),* 4 in (10 cm) long, has slightly twisted, dark-green straps with slender stalks attached to rhizomes.

Sailor's eye *(Ventricaria ventricosa),* 2 in (5 cm) spheres, looks like a smooth, turgid, dark-green, miniature water-balloon. Its surface is occasionally covered with encrusting algae of other types.

HABITAT: Both caulerpa species grow on reefs and seagrass pastures. Sailor's eye attaches with hairlike threads to hard substrates in waters more than 5 ft (1.5 m) deep.

DID YOU KNOW? A toxic, alien species of caulerpa *(C. taxifolia)* from the Tropics has invaded the Mediterranean Sea and is causing big ecological troubles. The invaders may be clones of a single released aquarium plant. Sailor's eye is a single, enormous cell, one of the largest known to science.

Green Algae *(Green Fleece, Cactus, and Shaving Brush Algae)*

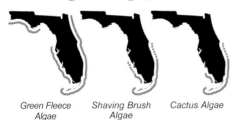

Green Fleece Algae   Shaving Brush Algae   Cactus Algae

Green fleece

RELATIVES: All are green algae. Green fleece is in the family Codiaceae. Cactus algae and shaving brush algae are together with other calcareous algae in the family Udoteaceae.

IDENTIFYING FEATURES:

Green fleece *(Codium* spp.), 12 in (30 cm) long, looks like forked, spongy, dirty-green fingers attached at a single holdfast. In the water it forms a domed clump.

Cactus algae *(Halimeda* spp.), 6 in (15 cm) long, grow as chains of calcareous segments attached to a stiff base and rhizoids (rootlike structures). They are drab green when alive and brilliant white when bleached.

Cactus algae rapidly bleach from green to white

Shaving brush algae *(Penicillus* spp.), 4 in (10 cm) long, look like a thin broccoli floret, or something that could efficiently apply shaving cream. The growing algae are firmly anchored by their stiff stalk to a mass of rhizoids.

HABITAT: Green fleece algae grow on nearshore reef out to 50 ft (15 m). Cactus algae and shaving brush algae live on shallow seagrass beds and sand flats.

DID YOU KNOW? Much of the coarse, white beach in the Keys is made of pulverized cactus algae.

A shaving brush alga

237

Balloon seaweed

Iridescent-banded alga

A three-cornered hat alga

Yellow-green Algae

(Balloon Seaweed, Iridescent-banded Alga, and Three-cornered Hat Algae)

Balloon Seaweed and   Three-cornered
Iridescent-banded Alga   Hat Algae

RELATIVES: These are yellow-green algae (Ochrophyta), unrelated to green algae. Balloon seaweed (family Scytosiphonaceae), iridescent-banded algae (family Dictyotaceae), and three-cornered hat algae (family Sargassaceae) are all distantly related.

IDENTIFYING FEATURES:

Balloon seaweed *(Colpomenia* spp.), 1.5 in (3.8 cm), beaches as individual or clustered, green-brown bubble-balls that appear partially flattened.

Iridescent-banded alga *(Stypopodium zonale),* 12 in (30 cm), is formed of flat, splitting, green-brown blades with concentric bands and a common holdfast. Outer margins are not curled as in *Padina* spp.

Three-cornered hat algae *(Turbinaria* spp.), 6 in (15 cm), beach as golden bouquets of pyramid-shaped fronds. The algae live attached and float when free due to air in their fronds.

HABITAT: All live attached to hardbottom in shallow water. Detached frond clusters of three-cornered hats float for months.

DID YOU KNOW? Iridescent-banded algae have bitter chemicals to discourage grazing by fish.

Yellow-green Algae
(Sargassum Weed)

RELATIVES: These yellow-green algae are allied with three-cornered hat algae in the family Sargassaceae.

IDENTIFYING FEATURES:

Pelagic sargassum (sargasso) *(Sargassum* spp.), 16 in (40 cm) clumps, forms golden bunches with tooth-edged leaves, air-filled bladders, and no central holdfast. *Sargassum fluitans* has smooth bladders and *Sargassum natans* has spur-tipped bladders. Both turn dark brown on the beach. Its dark, BB-sized bladders are common within the tide line.

Attached sargassum *(Sargassum hystrix),* 16 in (40 cm) long, has smooth, brown, elongate, leathery leaves covered by tiny, faint dots. Branches connect to a tough holdfast. The longest plants have air bladders.

HABITAT: Pelagic sargassum drifts on Gulf and Atlantic currents. Attached sargassum grows anchored to hardbottom in waters out to 50 ft (15 m).

DID YOU KNOW? The mid-Atlantic Sargasso Sea is an end-point for pelagic sargassum, rather than an origin. Currents circling the North Atlantic bring the floating algae to the center of an ocean-spanning gyre. As it drifts, sargassum provides a habitat life-raft for hundreds of species of animals. Many that can't swim away end up stranded when the algae reach the beach.

Pelagic sargassum beaches in abundance

Pelagic sargassum (Sargassum fluitans)

Attached sargassum

Red spineweed

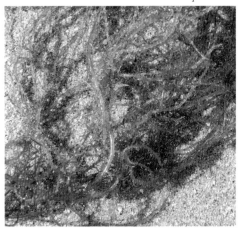
Spiny seaweed

Graceful redweed

Red Algae *(Red Spineweed, Spiny Seaweed, and Graceful Redweed)*

RELATIVES: These are red algae (Rhodophyta), unrelated to yellow-green algae and somewhat related to green algae.

IDENTIFYING FEATURES:

Red spineweed *(Bryothamnion triquetrum),* 8 in (20 cm), has brown-red branches with tiny, stiff, pointed branchlets in whorls of three.

Spiny seaweed *(Acanthophora spicifera),* 8 in (20 cm), has fragile, pale-pink branches with stubby branchlets. Colors also may be yellowish or pale green.

Graceful redweed *(Gracilaria tikvahiae),* 12 in (30 cm), has greenish to bright-red, forked branches like sinuous clumps of spaghetti. This alga quickly bleaches clear.

HABITAT: All grow in shallow water. Spiny seaweed can stand moderate wave-surge and attaches to anything, including pebbles, snails, rope, and turtles. Graceful redweed grows in calm lagoons and often lives as unattached drift algae.

DID YOU KNOW? Red algae have a photosynthetic pigment that reflects red light and absorbs blue light, which allows these plants to live at greater depths than green plants.

Red Algae *(Red Grapes, Thicket Algae, and Branching Coralline Alga)*

Red Grapes   Thicket Algae   Branching Coralline Alga

RELATIVES: Red grapes algae (family Rhodymeniaceae), thicket algae (family Galaxauraceae), and coralline algae (Corallinaceae) are distantly related.

IDENTIFYING FEATURES:

Red grapes *(Botryocladia occidentalis)*, 12 in (30 cm) long, have numerous, small, bubbly branchlets. Several lengths with individual holdfasts may grow in clumps attached to a shell or pebble.

Thicket algae *(Galaxaura* spp.), 6 in (15 cm), have reddish, flat, evenly forked branches rooted at a single holdfast.

Branching coralline alga (sturdy needleweed) *(Amphiroa rigida)*, 4 in (10 cm), is found on the beach as bushes of stiff, brittle, cylindrical, forked branches not swollen at their joints. The alga is pale lavender in life.

HABITAT: Red grapes and thicket algae grow on shallow hardbottom. Branching coralline algae grow in shallow seagrass beds.

DID YOU KNOW? The bubble-branchlets of red grapes contain sugars and protein for buoyancy so that strands remain upright in water. The crushed skeletons of thicket algae and branching coralline algae are sources of beach sand.

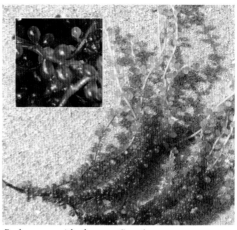

Red grapes with close-up (inset)

A thicket alga

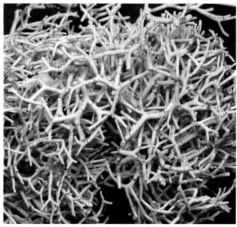

Sun-bleached branching coralline alga

241

Freshly beached turtle grass

Blades, fresh and sun-bleached, with rhizomes

Sprouting turtle grass seeds

Turtle Grass

RELATIVES: Turtle grass, like all seagrasses, is a vascular, flowering plant, not an alga. Turtle grass is in the family Hydrocharitaceae along with tape grasses and frogs bit.

IDENTIFYING FEATURES:

Turtle grass *(Thalassia testudinum),* 2 ft (60 cm) long, has ribbonlike blades with about a dozen parallel veins. Their shoots connect to tough, tubular rhizomes with wiry root-tufts. Blades may be sun-bleached pure white, and rhizomes may strand in tangled masses. Its fruits (0.5 in, 1.3 cm) are green and fleshy with a rough, brown covering, and sprouted seeds are like button-sized mushrooms with a tiny protruding blade.

HABITAT: Turtle grass lives in relatively calm waters out to 30 ft (9 m). After storms, their blades and rhizomes are a major part of the wrack in southern Florida.

DID YOU KNOW? Turtle grass plants are either male or female, with different-looking tiny, underwater flowers. The pollen from male flowers disperses in negatively buoyant slimy strings. Turtle grass is the most common Caribbean seagrass and is food or habitat for thousands of marine creatures.

242

Manatee Grass and Cuban Shoal Grass

Fresh manatee grass blades

RELATIVES: Manatee grass and Cuban shoal grass share the family Cymodoceaceae.

IDENTIFYING FEATURES:

Manatee grass *(Syringodium filiforme)*, 12 in (30 cm) long, has thin, arcing, tubular leaves that are slightly stiffer than cooked spaghetti. Its pale rhizomes are tougher than the fragile leaves, which often beach in broken segments. Leaf segments float and often drift until they are white from sun-bleaching.

Cuban shoal grass *(Halodule wrightii)* has leaves of similar width to manatee grass, but has flat blades.

HABITAT: Manatee grass and Cuban shoal grass live in calm waters out to 20 ft (6 m). Manatee grass is most common in the wrack line because is grows in pastures open to the ocean and Gulf. Shoal grass colonizes areas where turtle grass and manatee grass can't grow because it can tolerate a wide range of light, temperature, and salinity.

DID YOU KNOW? Very long leaves of manatee grass probably came from deep waters. This grass grows most commonly interspersed with turtle grass and other species. Its fragile leaves mean that it is the first to strand on beaches when the weather gets rough.

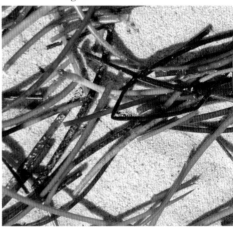

Tubular manatee grass with flat-bladed shoal grass

Sun-bleached segments of manatee grass

243

Plant Drifters—Seabeans and Driftwood

A **seabean** is a fruit or seed that has made a sea voyage. Some drift to disperse their genes, and others are lost, having floated far from where they could hope to grow. By design or by luck, these drifters end up on particular beaches during selective times. Florida's seabean season is roughly September–March, when tropical storms and winter weather give persistent winds that blow drifters out of sea-currents and onto beaches. Seabean season minus travel time may also correspond to the period when tropical seeds enter the world during the annual Amazonian flurry of flood-season fruiting. One seabean hotspot is the Atlantic coast where the Florida current is closest to shore, but tropical cyclones can drop bounties of seabeans on any beach. **Driftwood** describes stems, trunks, and other plant parts that reach many of the beaches where seabeans are found.

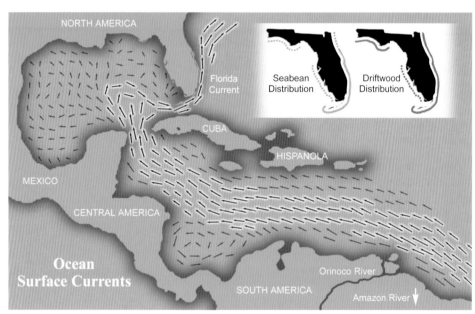

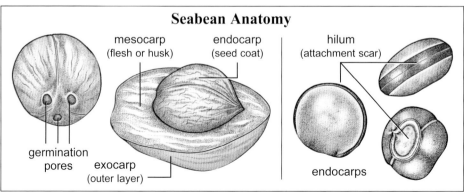

Prickly Palm and Starnut Palm

RELATIVES: These nuts come from palms (family Arecaceae) that are in the cocoid palm group, allied with coconut and cohune palms.

IDENTIFYING FEATURES:

Prickly palms (*Acrocomia* spp.) produce fruits with roundish, black, stony nuts. When weathered they may be gray or powdery brown. The outer, hard part of the nut (the endocarp) is unique in having three equally spaced pores around its middle.

Prickly palm endocarp, max 1.25 in (3.2 cm)

Starnut palms (*Astrocaryum* spp.) have nuts with hard, black, tear-shaped endocarps. The nut's rounded end has 3 pores that may be obscured by part of the original fibrous husk. Lengthwise ridges are typically easy to see, but the tear-shape may vary from sharply pointed to spherical. Young nuts have an oily feel and old nuts are weathered brown.

ORIGIN: Starnut palms grow in the lowland rainforests of Central America and the basins of the Amazon and Orinoco Rivers. A likely source for Florida's prickly palm drift seeds is the macaw palm *(A. aculeata),* endemic to Martinique and Dominica, but common as a landscape palm throughout the wider Caribbean.

Starnut palm endocarp, max 2 in (5 cm)

DID YOU KNOW? Prickly palms are named for their wickedly long trunk spines. Starnut palms are named for the auras around their nut pores. Neither palm nut strands as a viable seed, and many are empty. The stony endocarps of each nut can be polished to a high gloss. These brilliant seeds are often used in jewelry.

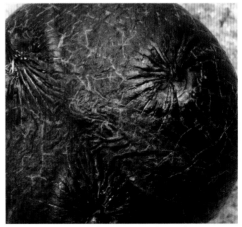

The starlike pores of a starnut palm endocarp

245

Coconut endocarp, max 15 in (38 cm)

Immature coconuts

Cohune palm

Rabbitface seed

Coconut, Cohune Palm, and Rabbitface

RELATIVES: These nuts come from palms (family Arecaceae) that are in the cocoid palm group (tribe Cocoeae), allied with starnut and prickly palms.

IDENTIFYING FEATURES:

Coconuts *(Cocos nucifera)* strand on beaches as mature football-sized fruit, immature fruit, endocarp, and husk. Some shriveled immature forms may look unfamiliar. The three-pored mature endocarp contains a layer of fleshy white meat and is partially filled with liquid.

Cohune palms *(Attalea cohune)* bear clusters of egg-sized fruits. Their time at sea leaves only a blackish nut (2 in, 5 cm) worn through to tan, woody endocarp. Its three cocoid pores are often replaced by a ragged hole.

Rabbitface seeds (1.3 in, 3.2 cm) appear on beaches as nonviable drifters from a cocoid palm yet to be identified. The hard, black, three-pore seed has a rabbitlike face with eyes, nose, and mouth.

ORIGIN: Coconuts grow on warm beaches all over the world. Cohune palms grow in the rainforests of Central America. Rabbitface seeds come from some mysterious corner of the Tropics.

DID YOU KNOW? In the coconut, the Portuguese recognized the surprised face and fibrous hair of a coco (monkey) staring back at them, which is how the fruit got its name. The three germination pores are where the developing root exits in cocoid palms. A coconut takes a year to mature on the parent tree. Recognizable parts may drift for 30 years or more.

246

Sea Coconut and Polynesian Screw Pine

RELATIVES: Sea coconuts are in the family Arecaceae and are related to the betel nut palm. Screw pines are distantly related to palms, not pines, and are in the family Pandanaceae.

IDENTIFYING FEATURES:

Sea coconuts *(Manicaria saccifera)* grow on the bussu palm in singles, twos, or threes within a brown, lumpy husk. The sea often erodes free the spherical seeds, which have a single scar like a bellybutton and are covered by brownish, glossy, endocarp occasionally obscured by flaky layers of fruit. They may be weathered to a tan or gray.

Polynesian screw pines *(Pandanus tectorius)* produce fruit masses like a round pineapple composed of dozens of fruitlets. These fruit segments reach distant beaches as brown cones with a fibrous narrow end.

ORIGIN: Sea coconuts drop from bussu palms growing near the rivers of the American tropics. Screw pines are native to the tropical Indo-Pacific but they have been introduced as landscape plants throughout the wider Caribbean, including southern Florida.

DID YOU KNOW? Bussu palm seeds roll downhill, float, and are dispersed by tropical floodwaters. The palm grows in swampy areas as a slender-trunked palm with enormous fronds to 26 ft (8 m) long. Locals use the giant leaves as sails for small boats and as the preferred thatching for their huts. Polynesian screw pines have stalkless, grasslike leaves that leave screw-thread scars on the old stem.

Sea coconut, max 3 in (7.6 cm)

Sea coconuts with husk

Polynesian screw pine, max 2 in (5 cm)

247

Mango endocarp, max 4 in (10 cm)

Hog plum mesocarp, max 3/4 in (2 cm)

Pond apple seed, max 1/2 in (1.3 cm)

Mango, Hog Plum, and Pond Apple

RELATIVES: All are flowering plants in the family Anacardiaceae.

IDENTIFYING FEATURES:

Mangos (*Mangifera indica*) contain large, thin, fibrous seeds that weather at sea to become tan and fuzzy with conspicuous radiating veins.

Hog plums *(Spondias mombin)* arrive on beaches as tannish, oblong fruits with only the fibrous mesocarp showing.

Pond apples *(Annona glabra)* are yellow, pungent fruits that release small, oval seeds. Seeds making a sea voyage may be shiny brown, or tan if more weathered.

ORIGIN: Mangos are native to India, have been introduced all over the Tropics, and are sold at produce stands worldwide. Hog plum is found throughout tropical America and the Caribbean. Pond apple drops its fruit in wet coastal areas of southern Florida, the American tropics, and western Africa.

DID YOU KNOW? Weathered mango seeds on Florida beaches likely come from the galleys of passing ships. Mangoes from India indirectly inspired the paisley motif, Europe's oldest weaving pattern, which was copied from Kashmiri shawls designed in the 1400s. The hog plum falls from the tree as a long yellow fruit with a juicy, clear, acidic pulp that is in fact relished by hogs. Pond apple trees often grow with mangroves. The plant is native to Florida but is currently a highly invasive pest in the coastal swamps of tropical Australia.

Mangroves

RELATIVES: Red mangroves (family Rhizophoraceae), black mangroves (family Avicenniaceae), and white mangroves (family Combretaceae), despite their common names, are not closely related (see page 227).

IDENTIFYING FEATURES:

Red mangroves *(Rhizophora mangle)* produce seeds that sprout on the parent tree and eventually drop as variously curved propagules that look like flamboyantly long, green writing pens. The root-end is brownish and may have begun sending out rootlets before reaching the beach.

Red mangrove, max 12 in (30 cm)

Black mangroves *(Avicennia germinans)* have yellow-green fruits like plump, pointed lima beans that have split and sprouted. Their velvety root sprouts may be lengthy or withered.

White mangroves *(Laguncularia racemosa)* have ribbed fruits shaped like spearpoints. New fruits are dark brown and the most weathered fruits are pale tan.

ORIGIN: All of these mangroves live in coastal areas of the American tropics north to the Florida peninsula. White mangroves grow the farthest from water but still inhabit swamps flooded by the highest tides.

Black mangrove, max 1 1/4 in (3 cm)

DID YOU KNOW? Black mangrove seeds can survive an ocean drift for four months. Red mangrove propagules float vertically, root-end down, and can survive a year before arriving home. White mangroves live in hypersaline conditions by excreting salt from glands at the base of their leaves.

White mangrove, max 3/4 in (2 cm)

249

Tropical almond, max 2.75 in (7 cm)

Worn tropical almonds without outer skin

Tropical almonds in various weathered stages

Tropical Almond

RELATIVES: Tropical almonds are allied with white mangrove in the family Combretaceae and are not related to commercial almonds.

IDENTIFYING FEATURES:

Tropical almonds *(Terminalia catappa)* beach as corky fruits in various stages of disintegration. Black or brown fruits with the familiar almond shape may not have drifted very long. More weathered fruits are bleached and fibrous, and the oldest drifters are deeply pitted. Many of the most disintegrated seeds are recognizable only by their deep lateral grooves that seem to separate what might be propulsion pods on a wrecked, Flash Gordon–style spaceship.

ORIGIN: Tropical almonds fall from a large-leaved tree that grows with vertically separated branches in a pagoda form. The tree is a native of tropical Asia but has been introduced throughout the Tropics and has become invasive in some areas, including southern Florida. New-looking seeds may have come from Florida, although the tree is most numerous around tropical America and the Caribbean.

DID YOU KNOW? The kernel within a tropical almond tastes like a commercially grown almond and is generally eaten raw. It has been shown to have a sedative or aphrodisiac effect on rats and nut extracts have promise in treatments for diabetes. Because the tree is beginning to invade wetland habitat in southern Florida, landscapers should avoid the temptation to plant these alien seeds.

Box Fruit, Anchovy Pear, and Calabash

RELATIVES: Box fruits and anchovy pears (family Lecythidaceae) are related to the Brazil nut tree. Beached calabash fruits are from trees in the family Bignoniaceae, which includes the sausage tree, and are not true gourds (which are related to cucumbers).

IDENTIFYING FEATURES:

Box fruits (sea putat) *(Barringtonia asiatica)* are brownish, lantern-shaped fruits with 4 (rarely 5) keels. Weathered fruits become tan and fibrous.

Box fruit, max 6 in (15 cm)

Anchovy pears *(Grias cauliflora)* beach as dried, tan, football-shaped fruits with 8 veiny ribs and contain a single large seed.

Calabashes *(Crescentia cujete)* from the calabash tree are hard, light, rattling, baseball- to football-sized brownish-gray fruits with a protruding scar.

ORIGIN: Box fruit trees are native to Southeast Asia but have been introduced throughout the Tropics. Anchovy pear trees are native to the West Indies and grow in groves near rivers and marshes. Calabash fruits drift from Central America and the Caribbean.

Anchovy pear, max 4 in (10 cm)

DID YOU KNOW? The box fruit tree, aka the sea poison tree, has many parts that are pulverized to release a poison that stuns fish. Its buoyant fruits can be viable after two years at sea and were recorded as being among the first living things to reach the new beaches of Krakatau after the former island went kaboom. The hard shell of the calabash fruit is used for containers, scoops, and crafts. A fresh anchovy pear has the appearance and taste of a mango.

Calabash, max 9 in (23 cm)

251

Smooth porcupineseed, max 2 in (5 cm)

Prickly porcupineseed, max 1.5 in (4 cm)

Beach-worn porcupineseeds, possibly C. glabrum

Australian pine, max 3/4 in (2 cm)

Porcupineseeds and Australian Pine

RELATIVES: Porcupineseeds come from sawari nut trees in the exclusively neotropical family Caryocaraceae. Australian pines (family Casuarinaceae) are flowering trees, not pines.

IDENTIFYING FEATURES:

Smooth porcupineseeds *(Caryocar glabrum)* have brownish-black, oval or kidney-shaped endocarps that are typically split on one side. Their surface is covered by dull, woody spines.

Prickly porcupineseeds *(Caryocar microcarpum)* are black or brown, kidney-shaped, split, hollow endocarps with clusters of sharp spines.

Other porcupineseed forms *(Caryocar* spp.) have a dense covering of thin spines or a covering worn down to the texture of dull, coarse sandpaper.

Australian pines *(Casuarina equisetifolia)* drop dime-sized, gray-brown cones that look like tiny, spiny pineapples.

ORIGIN: Porcupineseeds come from sawari trees that grow in frequently flooded areas of the Amazon and Orinoco River basins. Australian pines are native to Australia and the western Pacific but have made a facilitated invasion of the world's tropical coasts, including southern Florida beaches (see page 231).

DID YOU KNOW? Sawari nut trees are one of the largest trees in the Amazon rainforest canopy, growing to 160 ft (50 m) tall with a trunk 8 ft (2.5 m) in diameter. Their porcupineseeds protect a kernel that is pleasantly sweet and widely eaten.

Cocoplum, Laurelwood, and Deerhoof

RELATIVES: Cocoplums (family Chrysobalanaceae), laurelwood fruits (family Clusiaceae, not a laurel), and deerhoof seeds (family Apocynaceae) come from distantly related trees and bushes.

IDENTIFYING FEATURES:

Cocoplums *(Chrysobalanus icaco)* have fleshy fruits with hard, light brown, tear-shaped seeds covered with netlike ridges.

Laurelwoods (Santa-maria) *(Calophyllum* spp.) bear spherical, green fruits that weather into a brown or tan, eyeball-like sphere. Most beached fruits are smooth with a small nub surrounded by short fibers. Less worn specimens may have a fibrous covering. Of two similar fruit forms, *C. inophyllum* is slightly larger than *C. calaba* (aka *C. antillanum)*.

Deerhoof *(Ochrosia elliptica)* seeds come from elliptic yellowwood shrubs. Their poisonous, paired fruits are red and fleshy, and have a unique, cloven, fibrous, tan seed.

ORIGIN: Cocoplums are native to the American tropics, including Florida (see page 228). *Calophyllum calaba* is native to the West Indies and *C. inophyllum* is native to Indian Ocean islands. Both are exotics in Florida. Elliptic yellowwood is native to Australia, but is widely planted in Florida.

DID YOU KNOW? Cocoplums are important tropical dune plants in south Florida and the Caribbean. Laurelwood trees are cut for a light, hardwood timber used in boat-making.

Cocoplum seeds, max 3/4 in (2 cm)

Laurelwood, max 1.5 in (3.8 cm)

Deerhoof seeds, max 2 in (5 cm)

253

Mary's-bean, max 1 in (2.5 cm)

Railroad vine seeds, max 3/16 in (5 mm), with split pod

Moonflower (top), railroad vine (bottom)

Mary's-Bean, Railroad Vine, and Moonflower

RELATIVES: Mary's-beans, railroad vine, and moonflowers are all morning-glory flowers in the family Convolvulaceae.

IDENTIFYING FEATURES:

Mary's-beans *(Merremia discoidesperma)* look like a scorched hot-cross bun. They are black or brown, stony seeds with an oval hilum (attachment scar) and a distinct, indented cross.

Railroad vine seeds *(Ipomoea pescaprae)* mature within a papery pod that splits to liberate fuzzy, brown, angular seeds with a circular hilum. Those surf-washed enough to lose their fuzz are glossy and hard (see page 225).

Moonflower seeds *(Ipomoea alba)*, 5/16 in (8 mm), are similar to railroad vine seeds but are larger and occasionally lighter.

ORIGIN: A Mary's-bean reaching Florida likely dropped from a single-seed pod festooning a winding vine growing on the coast of Central America. Most railroad vine and moonflower seeds may come from Florida, although these plants grow all over the wider Caribbean. Each of these seeds may drift for many years and thousands of miles.

DID YOU KNOW? Mary's-bean, named after the Virgin Mary, gets its cross from the impression of a narrow strap that secures it in its pod. Mary's-beans provide believers with good luck in avoiding evil, in recovery from snakebite and hemorrhoids, and in the easy delivery of a baby.

Antidote Vine, Candlenut, and Rubber Tree

RELATIVES: Antidote vine is a member of the melon family Cucurbitacae. Candlenuts and rubber trees share the family Euphorbiaceae with about 6,000 species of flowering plants.

IDENTIFYING FEATURES:

Antidote vines *(Fevillea cordifolia)* produce fruits that are brownish, warped disks containing about 10 seeds that do not rattle within.

Antidote vine, max 2.25 in (5.7 cm)

Candlenuts (kukui) *(Aleurites moluccanus)* have a walnut shape and are typically black with a waxy sheen. Some may be powdery brown or tan but all nuts are stone-hard.

Rubber tree seeds *(Hevea brasiliensis)* have a glossy-black to flat-brown endocarp and an elliptical shape with angular sides from sharing a three-seed capsule.

ORIGIN: Antidote vines grow throughout tropical America and the Greater Antilles. Candlenut trees are native to the Indo-Pacific but are now widely cultivated in the Tropics. Some grow in southeastern Florida. Rubber trees are native to the Amazon region where they are cultivated and tapped for their latex.

Candlenut, max 1.25 in (3.2 cm)

DID YOU KNOW? Antidote vine seeds are rich in an oil used as a purgative and antidote for many kinds of poisoning. Both fruits and seeds float to disperse the plant after freshwater floods. Candlenuts (kukui in Hawaii, where the Polynesian transplant is the state tree) are polished into black gleaming nuggets suitable for jewelry. Rubber trees ooze latex originally used by the Mayan people for rubber balls in court games played about 3600 years ago.

Rubber tree, max 1.2 in (3 cm)

255

Manchineel, max 1.2 in (3 cm)

Monkey pistol pod segments, max 1.5 in (3.8 cm)

Jamaican naval-spurge, max 2 in (5 cm)

Manchineel, Monkey Pistol, and Jamaican Naval-Spurge

RELATIVES: These fruits, seeds, and seed pods come from plants in the family Euphorbiaceae.

IDENTIFYING FEATURES:

Manchineel (poison apple) fruits *(Hippomane mancinella)* drop from trees as yellow, fleshy, flattened globes. They arrive on Florida beaches as corky, tan fruits in various stages of disintegration, ranging from slightly wrinkled to a skeletal endocarp of radiating ribs.

Monkey pistol (sandbox) trees *(Hura crepitans)* have pods with woody segments in torqued earlike shapes. Pod segments float, but seeds do not.

Jamaican (cobnut) naval-spurge seeds *(Omphalea diandra)* are blackish-brown with a fine, knobby surface and are angled on one side. The brittle endocarp is occasionally cracked, allowing an unforgettable experience with the putrid decay of the oily kernel.

ORIGIN: Manchineel trees are native to Central America and the wider Caribbean, including Florida (although rare). Monkey pistol trees are native to tropical America and some have been introduced in the Keys. Jamaican naval-spurge comes from tidal swamps and rivers of the American tropics.

DID YOU KNOW? Manchineel fruits are poisonous when fresh but harmless after drifting. The tree is Endangered in Florida. Monkey pistol seeds develop within a woody, pumpkinlike pod that explodes like a shot when ripe. The seeds flutter down from one of the tallest trees in Central America. The tree has a spiny trunk and poisonous juice.

Cabbagebark and Nickernuts

RELATIVES: These seeds come from legumes, family Fabaceae. Well-known relatives include the garden pea.

IDENTIFYING FEATURES:

Cabbagebark seeds *(Andira inermis)* beach within a hard, fibrous, round mesocarp encircled by a ridge connected to faint veins. The surface is generally brownish and pitted.

Gray nickernuts *(Caesalpinia bonduc)* are hard, grayish beans that look like swollen ticks. The endocarp typically has faint fracture lines encircling the seed. Yellow seeds may be yellow nickernuts *(C. ciliata)* from the Caribbean.

Brown nickernuts *(C. major)* are similar to gray nickernuts, including having the faint fracture lines, but are larger, less spherical, and brown.

ORIGIN: Cabbagebark trees grow throughout the American tropics and the West Indies. Gray nickernuts grow along the world's tropical coastlines and occur throughout the southern US. Brown nickernuts are more rare and more tropical than gray nickernuts.

DID YOU KNOW? Cabbagebark gets its name from the smell of its bark, which has effects as a narcotic, laxative, and de-wormer. The tree often grows on the banks of rivers, which carry away the floating fruit not scattered by bats and rodents. All nickernuts can be polished to a lustrous shine. They are amazingly hard and have floated for more than 30 years in experimental trials. Nickernut beans develop in pods that are bristling with sharp spines that match the recurved prickles covering the rest of the plant.

Cabbagebark, max 2 in (5 cm)

Gray nickernut, max 3/4 in (2 cm)

Brown nickernut, max 1 in (2.5 cm)

257

Bloodwood, max 2 in (5 cm)

Coin vine, max 1.5 in (3.8 cm) (A), moneybush (B)

Cat's eye, max 1.75 in (4.5 cm)

Flame of the forest, max 1.5 in (4cm)

Bloodwood, Coin Vine, Cat's Eye, and **Flame of the Forest**

RELATIVES: These beans and fruits are legumes in the family Fabaceae.

IDENTIFYING FEATURES:

Bloodwood pods *(Pterocarpus officinalis)* are a little larger than a quarter and a few times as thick. Most are brownish or gray with a veined texture and a roundish, irregular, winglike shape.

Coin vine pods *(Dalbergia ecastophyllum)* are thin, papery, leaflike fruits about the size of a nickel. Pods larger than 1.5 in (3.8 cm) may be from the **moneybush**, *D. monetaria,* a rarer find on Florida beaches.

Cat's eye pods *(Pongamia pinnata)* drop from the poonga oil tree. The pods are glossy tan, uniformly thick, and have a persistent stem.

Flame of the forest *(Butea monosperma)* seeds are kidney-shaped and beach in various stages of decay.

ORIGIN: Bloodwood trees grow in coastal swamps of tropical America and the West Indies. Coin vine is a leggy bush common in coastal habitats around the wider Caribbean, including southern Florida. Moneybush grows in freshwater marches of northern South America. Poonga oil trees are native to Malaysia but have been introduced to Florida. Flame of the forest grows as an ornamental all over the Tropics and is native to India.

DID YOU KNOW? Roots and bark of coin vines are crushed for use as a fish poison. Oil from the poonga oil tree is being tried as a source of biodeisel fuel.

Bay Bean, Yellow Flamboyant, and **Little Marble**

RELATIVES: These beans and fruits are legumes in the family Fabaceae.

IDENTIFYING FEATURES:

Bay beans (beach peas) *(Canavalia rosea)* are hard seeds in the classic bean shape and have an elongate, oval hilum. They have a slightly dark mottling to a background of tan, brown, or red. Local beans tumble from hotdog-shaped pods growing on dune vines and are dull when fresh. Older beans are shinier.

Bay bean, max 3/4 in (2 cm)

Yellow flamboyant (poinciana) fruits *(Peltophorum pterocarpum)* have a flat-tened flame shape with thin edges and a texture of tiny parallel grooves.

Little marbles *(Oxyrhynchus trinervius)* are black, round, glossy, stone-hard beans almost completely encircled by a hilum with a light groove and lipped margins.

Bay beans and pod

ORIGIN: Most bay beans on Florida beaches probably come from local beach-pea vines growing on the dune, but some may have drifted from anywhere in its wide range: the Gulf states through the Caribbean. Yellow flamboyant trees are native to Southeast Asia through tropical Australia, but have been planted as shade trees all over the Tropics. They are common in the Florida Keys. Little marbles drop from pods grown on a vine from the canopy of Central American rainforests.

Yellow flamboyant, max 3 in (7.6 cm)

DID YOU KNOW? Bay beans are eaten by few insects because they have an imposter amino acid (protein build-ing block) that interferes with an insect's protein metabolism. Little mar-bles are rare seabeans that take on a bril-liant shine when polished.

Little marble, max 1/2 in (1.3 cm)

259

Coralbean, max 1/2 in (1.5 cm)

Mora excelsa (A) and M. oleifera *(B), 7 in (18 cm)*

West Indian locust, 7 in (15 cm)

Coralbean, Mora, and West Indian Locust

RELATIVES: All are true beans (legumes) in the family Fabaceae.

IDENTIFYING FEATURES:

Coralbeans *(Erythrina* spp.) are scarlet, orange, or (rarely) yellow. Their oval hilum is slightly offset from center. Most are glossy and all are stone-hard.

Mora seeds *(Mora* spp.) look like shriveled kidneys. They are brownish, rubbery cotyledons either together as a pair or divided. Wrinkled seeds are *Mora excelsa* and smoother seeds are *Mora oleifera.*

West Indian locust pods *(Hymenaea courbaril)* are compressed but rounded, jumbo bean pods with a tough stem and a rough, thick, brown exocarp (covering). The 2–6 seeds within are the size of a dime and reddish-brown.

ORIGIN: Coralbeans fall from an herbaceous tree that grows along the southern US coastline. Mora trees grow in flooded tidal areas of the southwestern *(Mora oleifera)* and southeastern *(Mora excelsa)* Caribbean. As the name suggests, West Indian locust is native to the West Indies, although isolated trees have been planted in south Florida.

DID YOU KNOW? Seabean expert Ed Perry has combed Florida beaches and found coralbean seeds from plants other than our local species *(E. herbacea).* He suspects that thumbnail-sized beans of brown or purple are from more tropical *Erythrina* species, and that some red seeds also may be tropical coralbeans. Mora seeds have the largest plant embryo known (the part that drifts and beaches is all embryo).

Sea Purse and Sea Heart

RELATIVES: Sea purses and sea hearts are true beans (legumes) in the family Fabaceae.

IDENTIFYING FEATURES:

Sea purse beans *(Dioclea reflexa)* are stone-hard, glossy seeds that are purse-shaped due to a flattened side. They are orange-brown and darkly mottled with a thin, dark hilum outlined in orange wrapping all but the flattened side. Similar beans that are plain dark or orange may be *Mucuna* species.

Sea heart beans *(Entada gigas)* are hard, compressed, circular or heart-shaped seeds with an inconspicuous hilum in their indentation. Although they may have some crusty sea-growth, beneath they are a glossy purple-brown or dark mahogany. The smallest sea hearts tend to be rounder and may have come from the smallest end of the pod.

ORIGIN: Sea purse beans develop with 2–4 sibling seeds in short, plump sausagelike pods on tropical rainforest vines. The vine is thought to be native to all of the world's tropics, in part due to its impressive survival at sea. Sea hearts tumble from the long, twisting pods of the monkey ladder vine, a woody canopy-climber from the rainforests of the Central and South American tropics.

DID YOU KNOW? The sea heart's monkey ladder vine has the longest bean pod in the world. These seabeans are famous as beach finds as far from their tropical origin as northern Europe. The discovery of a sea heart floating in the eastern Atlantic helped inspire Columbus' search for land to the west.

Sea purse, max 1.5 in (4 cm)

Unidentified, sea purse–like beans (see page 263)

Sea heart, max 2.25 in (5.7 cm)

261

Brown hamburger bean, max 1 in (2.5 cm)

Red hamburger bean, max 1.2 in (3 cm)

Colors of brown (A) and red (B,C) hamburger beans

True Seabeans

RELATIVES: True seabeans are in the family Fabaceae.

IDENTIFYING FEATURES:

Brown hamburger (horse-eye) beans *(Mucuna sloanei)* are circular, stone-hard seeds with a thick, black hilum encircling about 3/4 of their circumference. Their texture is slightly roughened away from the hilum. Shapes range from a plump disk to a sphere. Colors are generally on the gray side of brown, and the light border of the hilum is more gray than yellow.

Red hamburger (ox-eye) beans *(Mucuna urens)* are difficult to separate from brown hamburgers but for subtle difference in shape and color. Red hamburger beans tend to be flatter (seldom spherical) and redder (on the red side of brown). Their hilum border is more yellow than gray and they often show dark mottling over a red-brown background.

ORIGIN: These hamburger beans develop within spiny pods hanging on long stems from tropical rainforest vines native to the American tropics and the West Indies. Brown hamburger beans are also known from Western Africa.

DID YOU KNOW? These beans are rich in an alkaloid called L-Dopa, which is used in treating the tremors from Parkinson's disease. L-Dopa is toxic in high doses and is known to cause hallucinations, delirium, and other ills. This chemical defense, along with the seed pod's irritating spines, apparently ensures that few critters eat these beans. Their high survival in the rainforest helps explain why so many hamburger beans end up on distant beaches.

Thick-banded Mucuna and Black Mucuna

RELATIVES: These species are in the family Fabaceae with true seabeans.

IDENTIFYING FEATURES:

Thick-banded mucunas *(Mucuna* spp.) are similar to red and brown hamburger beans except for size and hilum thickness. They are fattened disks larger than a quarter and have a wide, black hilum band for most of their thickness. These beans look like the seeds of *M. fawcettii,* but their identification is uncertain.

Thick-banded mucuna, max 1.25 in (3.2 cm)

Black mucunas *(M. holtonii)* are black, roughened, hard, disk-shaped, nickel-to quarter-sized seeds with a thin, protruding hilum. Many have a deflated appearance.

ORIGIN: Thick-banded mucunas are a mystery. If *M. fawcettii,* then they may come from Caribbean islands. Black mucunas drop from velvety pods on vines native to Central America.

DID YOU KNOW? Black mucunas come to us thanks to Commissaris's long-tongued bat. The seabean's flower has a unique echo-reflector that advertises it to the bat's sonar. Bats landing on the flower are rewarded with an explosion of nectar and the plant is rewarded with pollen from another flower. *Mucuna* species are enigmatic beans for beachcombers because only the seeds of the plant are seen. Beans with a roughened endocarp and a wide hilum band are likely *Mucuna* species. But two forms of seabeans that look a bit like sea purses *(Dioclea)* may also be *Mucuna.* Seabean sleuths working to get flowers from sprouted beach beans are hoping to solve this mystery.

Black mucuna, max 1.25 (3.2 cm)

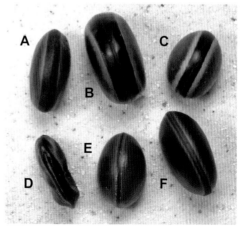

Mucuna *(A-D), and* Mucuna *or* Dioclea *(E,F) species*

263

Lantern tree, max 1/2 in (1.5 cm)

Blisterpod, max 2 in (5 cm)

Calatola, max 1.5 in (3.8 cm)

Lantern Tree, Blisterpod, and Calatola

RELATIVES: The lantern tree (family Hernandiaceae), blisterpod (Humiriaceae), and calatola tree (Icacinaceae) are distantly related, tropical, flowering plants.

IDENTIFYING FEATURES:

Lantern tree seeds *(Hernandia sonora)* come from a round, fleshy fruit. Most beached seeds are hard, mahogany, marble-sized globes with faint longitudinal indentations. Many have tan ribs adhering from remnant, dried fruit-flesh.

Blisterpods *(Sacoglottis amazonica)* look like WWII-era hand grenades because of their woody, air-filled, bulging blisters. Worn pods have open blisters, but internal air pockets surrounding the single, inch-long seed remain to keep the pod floating.

Calatola seeds *(Calatola costaricensis)* are a wrinkled, rugby-ball shape with an encircling, longitudinal ridge and many lower, connecting ridges. The rough-coated endocarp is typically light, hollow, and without a viable seed.

ORIGIN: Lantern trees grow in wet forests and along river banks in tropical America and the West Indies and may be found throughout the world's tropics. Blisterpods fall from small trees native to the Amazon and Orinoco Basins. Calatola trees are from Central America.

DID YOU KNOW? The bubble-wrapped seed of the blisterpod is exquisitely adapted to flotation dispersal within the periodically flooded forests of the Amazon, but the seed does not remain viable after ocean voyages.

Water Hickory, Pignut Hickory, and **Bitternut Hickory**

RELATIVES: These nut trees are allied with pecan and walnut trees within the family Juglandaceae.

IDENTIFYING FEATURES:

Water hickory nuts *(Carya aquatica)* beach as brownish, lumpy, slightly compressed shells with encircling ridges and variably pointed apexes.

Pignut hickory nuts *(Carya glabra)* often come ashore with their charcoal, tear-shaped, 4-part husk intact. The nut within is similar to the water hickory.

Bitternut hickory nuts *(Carya cordiformis)* look like the hickory nuts above but are smoother, without encircling ridges, and have pronounced apex-points if not worn.

ORIGIN: These nuts fall from trees distributed over the southeastern US. Their upstream source is likely to be the major rivers emptying into the Gulf of Mexico, especially the Mississippi. Beached bitternuts have probably traveled the farthest because their trees are most common north of Florida.

DID YOU KNOW? These are true nuts: a dry fruit with a hardened ovary wall not attached to the seed within. All nuts are seeds, but not all seeds are nuts. Edible, oil-rich hickory nuts have been used by Americans for about 9000 years. The Powhatan people of Virginia believed that spirits traveling to the rising sun could only complete their afterlife journey after a drink of *pokahichary* served by a goddess. The drink, made from hickory nuts pounded with water, gives us the name for the tree and its fruit.

Water hickory, max 1 in (2.5 cm)

Pignut hickory, max 1.5 in (3.8 cm)

Bitternut hickory, max 1 in (2.5 cm)

265

Pecan, max 1.5 in (3.8 cm)

Mockernut, max 1.25 in (3.2 cm)

Tropical walnut, max 1.75 in (4.5 cm)

Pecan, Mockernut, and Tropical Walnut

RELATIVES: These nut trees are allied with hickory trees within the family Juglandaceae.

IDENTIFYING FEATURES:

Pecans *(Carya illinoensis)* are similar in shape to the store-bought variety but tend to have a wider range of size and color. Runts may be as small as 1 in (2.5 cm) and color ranges from mahogany to tan.

Mockernuts *(Carya tomentosa)* have rounded ridges and a thick shell, often split at the pointed apex.

Tropical walnuts *(Juglans jamaicensis)* have a smooth but wrinkled surface and are depressed at one end, bluntly pointed at the other. Their color varies between black and light gray.

ORIGIN: Pecan and mockernut trees grow around the southeastern US, but not into southern Florida. Tropical walnut trees do not grow in Jamaica, despite their species name. They do grow on the Caribbean islands of Cuba, Hispanola, and Puerto Rico. There they have been cut down to make room for houses and agriculture and are now Endangered.

DID YOU KNOW? Few of these nuts are viable or even contain seeds following a lengthy drift at sea. Tropical walnuts were reported by drift-seed experts Charles Gunn and John Dennis to float for nearly two years.

Black Walnut, Tallownut, and Madagascar Olive

RELATIVES: Black walnuts are with pecan and hickory trees in the family Juglandaceae. Tallownut (tallow wood) trees (Olacaceae) and Madagascar olive (Oleaceae) are not closely related.

IDENTIFYING FEATURES:

Black walnuts *(Juglans nigra)* are brownish-gray with a roughly wrinkled surface. They are bluntly pointed at one end and rounded at the other, and are occasionally heart-shaped.

Black walnut, max 1.5 in (3.8 cm)

Tallownuts (hog plums) fall from the tallow wood tree *(Ximenia americana)* and are light, hard fruits the size of a quail egg or smaller. Weathered fruits are tan and have four bumps separated by a cross (+) at their roundest end. Some fruits have a brown crust from the formerly yellow fruit flesh.

Madagascar olive *(Noronhia emarginata)* fruits are woody and tan with an olive size and shape. Fresh off the bush they are yellow or purple, but none of this color remains on most beached fruits. Some fruits have a rattling pit.

Tallownut, max 1 in (2.5 cm)

ORIGIN: Black walnut trees are most common north of Florida from Texas to New York. Beached nuts are likely to have washed down the Mississippi River into the Gulf. Tallow wood is native to southern Florida. Madagascar olive is in fact native to Madagascar but has been introduced as an ornamental plant to south Florida.

DID YOU KNOW? The salt-tolerant Madagascar olive may lend its fruits to drift because it is often planted near beaches.

Madagascar olive, max 1 in (2.5 cm)

267

Oak species

Oak, Crabwood, and West Indian Mahogany

RELATIVES: Oaks are together with beech trees in the family Fagaceae. Crabwood and mahogany are allied within the family Meliaceae.

IDENTIFYING FEATURES:

Oak acorns *(Quercus* spp.) are glossy nuts that may or may not have the familiar scaly cap. Some may have a cap completely enclosing the nut. Shapes vary between species from spherical to elongate. Naked nuts show the scar where the cap was attached.

Crabwood seeds *(Carapa guianensis)* are dull gray-brown and flattened on two sides and rounded on the other. An elongate, distorted hilum scar is opposite the rounded side.

West Indian mahogany fruits *(Swietenia mahogani)* are brownish, woody, and round or faintly 5-sided in cross-section. A stem or stem-scar is opposite their narrow end.

Crabwood, max 1.75 in (4.5 cm)

ORIGIN: Acorns come from oaks all over North America, but most beached nuts likely made their way down rivers into the Gulf of Mexico. Crabwood is a type of mangrove tree living on coastlines from Central America through the Caribbean to Brazil. West Indian mahogany grows in the West Indies, the Bahamas, and southernmost Florida.

DID YOU KNOW? Mahogany fruits split on the tree to release fluttering, papery seeds. The tree is now rare in Florida due to the value of its wood and occurs mostly in a few parks. Beached pods may come from the Caribbean where the tree is also disappearing.

West Indian mahogany, max 3.5 in (9 cm)

Nutmeg, Seagrape, and Black Pearl

RELATIVES: Nutmeg (family Myristicaceae), seagrape (family Polygonaceae), and black pearl trees (family Sapindaceae) are not closely related.

IDENTIFYING FEATURES:

Nutmeg seeds *(Myristica* spp.*)* come from the center of an apricotlike fruit and are black, textured, and egglike when they strand on beaches. Larger seeds are probably the commercially grown species, *M. fragrans.*

Seagrape seeds *(Coccoloba uvifera)* are hard, brownish, fiber-shrouded pits with a rounded end and a pointed end.

Black pearl (soapberry) seeds *(Sapindus saponaria),* as their name suggests, are dark, glossy, stone-hard, little spheres. Fruits grow in clusters and fall from trees as orange-brown, fleshy berries. Black pearls strand as fruits with a glossy, brown skin or a fibrous net surrounding a papery sac (probably from Florida trees) or as naked seeds.

ORIGIN: Kitchen-variety nutmeg is native to eastern Indonesia (the Moluccas) but is grown extensively in Grenada (southeastern Caribbean). Small nutmeg seeds may be from tropical American species. Seagrape is common on the coast from southern Florida through the American tropics. Black pearls come from southern Florida through South America.

DID YOU KNOW? Black pearl fruits make a sudsy lather in water. Mexican Indians preferred this soap for washing hair and delicates even after commercial soaps were introduced.

Nutmeg, max 1 in (2.5 cm)

Seagrape, max 3/4 in (20 mm)

Black pearl, max 1/2 in (13 mm)

269

Sapote eggfruit, max 3.5 in (9 cm)

Eggfruit, unknown species, max 1.2 in (3 cm)

False mastic, max 3/4 in (2 cm)

Eggfruit and False Mastic

RELATIVES: These seeds are from trees in the family Sapotaceae.

IDENTIFYING FEATURES:

Eggfruit (sapote) seeds *(Pouteria sapota)* are shaped like small, compressed footballs. They are brownish and smooth except for a wide, roughened hilum over their entire length. Rounder seeds smaller than 2 in (5 cm) are likely to be other eggfruit species sharing the genus *Pouteria.* All sizes of eggfruit seeds tend to rattle.

False mastic seeds *(Sideroxylon foetidissimum)* are glossy red-brown to dull gray with an indented, light, oval hilum just shy of its least rounded end. Seeds larger than 5/8 in (1.6 cm) and elongate may be from the more tropical tempisque tree *(S. capiri).*

ORIGIN: Sapote trees are native to Central America and the West Indies but are cultivated for their fruit from tropical South America to south Florida. Other types of eggfruit seeds may come from anywhere in tropical America. False mastic has a native range from Mexico and the West Indies to southern Florida. The loss of coastal hammocks has made the tree scarce in Florida.

DID YOU KNOW? Trees in this family make up about a quarter of the Amazon Basin's tall trees. Although the sapote is named for the Aztec word, *tzapotl,* for soft, sweet fruits, most other eggfruits have pulp like dry hard-boiled egg yolk. False mastic seeds fall to the ground as part of a yellow-orange fruit with gummy pulp loved by raccoons and other hammock critters.

Bamboo and Reeds

RELATIVES: Bamboos are really big grasses in the family Poaceae, shared with their smaller cousins, the reeds.

IDENTIFYING FEATURES:

Bamboo (tribe Bambuseae, many species) beaches as sections of hollow, compartmentalized cane (the grass's culm), often with its associated rhizome, and commonly with cut marks or other signs that it has been used by people. Bamboo canes put to structural use are commonly introduced Asiatic species of

Bamboo cane revealing hollow compartments

Bambusa, although hundreds of species are native to tropical America. Canes are often 6 in (15 cm) in diameter and 30 ft (9 m) or longer.

Common reeds *(Phragmites australis)* beach as large bundles of finger-thick rhizomes bound by dense roots. The bundles stay together after lengthy sea travel even when the mass has sun-bleached to a light gray. Fresher bundles are brownish and may have remnants of the thinner reeds bending at right angles to the rhizomes.

ORIGIN: Bamboo has a wide range between North and South America, and

Bamboo rhizome and base of culm

introduced species are ubiquitous. Common reeds are native to the Americas, although they were uncommon in Florida until recently. They grow in marshes and on river banks and are abundant where waters drain into the western Caribbean and Gulf of Mexico from Central America to Florida.

DID YOU KNOW? Bamboo is used to make houses, furniture, boats, bicycles, bridges, music, and dinner, among thousands of other useful and artistic things.

Common reed rhizome bundle

271

Beach tangleballs, max 10 in (25 cm)

Tangleballs involve many plant parts

Turtle grass rhizomes with fibrous root tufts

Beach Tangleballs and Turtle Grass Rhizomes

RELATIVES: Tangleballs may involve many parts of many kinds of plants. Turtle grass is a seagrass in the waterweed family Hydrocharitaceae.

IDENTIFYING FEATURES:

Tangleballs are spherical clumps of intertwined plant parts. These parts vary but commonly include stiff roots, rhizomes, pine needles, and thin twigs. These sea-woven balls keep their shape long after being beached.

Turtle grass rhizomes *(Thalassia testudinum)* are hollow, coarse, fibrous tatters generally 3/16 in (5 mm) in diameter. They may be brown, tan, or sunbleached gray. Most have visible nodes and yarnlike tufts of roots. These rhizomes often beach in large numbers and persist for many weeks in the upper beach wrack.

ORIGIN: Beach tangleballs are woven from coarse fibers dense enough to collect on the seabottom, which is where these balls are formed. Storms erode plant roots from the dune and wash other plant parts down rivers to the sea. The material that reaches the surf is snowballed together by the rolling action of breaking waves. Turtle grass rhizomes are eroded from seagrass pastures following severe storms.

DID YOU KNOW? Tangleballs form in large lakes and seas all over the world, wherever erosion and waves occur. They are unique conversation pieces and are occasionally sold to tourists as "whale burps." This term also describes the events that produce tangled masses of beached sea stuff.

Saw Palmetto, Greenbriar, Cypress, and Cordgrass

RELATIVES: Saw palmetto (Arecaceae), greenbriar (Smilacaceae), and cordgrass (Poaceae) are distantly related monocots. Cypress trees are conifers in the family Cupressaceae.

IDENTIFYING FEATURES:

Saw palmetto *(Serenoa repens)* trunks are fuzzy, curved, and composed of densely packed fibers. Some may retain roots and frond boots that give them the appearance of a giant shrimp.

Saw palmetto trunk, max 12 ft (3.7 m)

Greenbriar *(Smilax* spp.) tubers are dark, multilobed masses with occasional remaining roots.

Cypress *(Taxodium* spp.) logs are typically straight with a wide buttress at their base. Other trees growing on river banks have a similar shape, but cypress is unique in being a pale softwood (no vessels in cross-section) with high resistance to decay.

Cordgrass *(Spartina* spp.) has long (3 ft, 90 cm) strawlike stems that arrive on the beach like piles of broken hay bales.

ORIGIN: Saw palmetto trunks and greenbriar tubers are eroded from the dune during severe storms. Cypress logs float down rivers to the sea. Cordgrass comes from tidal marshes behind barrier islands. Much of this material may be from Florida, although all the states from Texas to Georgia may contribute.

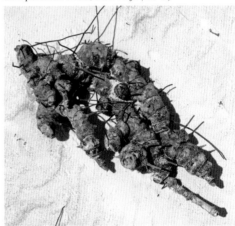

Greenbriar tuber, max 24 in (61 cm)

DID YOU KNOW? The Big Bend region and northeast Florida have the most extensive cordgrass-dominated saltmarsh, which is replaced by mangrove in southern Florida.

A cypress log and pile of cordgrass stems

273

Driftwood takes on beautiful, weathered shapes

A hand-cut tropical hardwood log

A reddish tropical hardwood with marine boreholes

Driftwoods

RELATIVES: Florida receives driftwood from hundreds, perhaps thousands, of tree species, from both conifers (gymnosperms) such as pines and cedars, and broad-leaved flowering trees (angiosperms) such as oaks and tropical hardwoods.

IDENTIFYING FEATURES:

Wood identification is tricky even when its origin is known. Determining wood species drifting from unknown sources requires laboratory detective work. On the beach, moderately educated guesses can be made after looking at the wood in cross-section (a smoothly cut sample) end-on. Pines often have soft wide rings with conspicuous resin canals and no vessels. Oaks have numerous vessels in their rings and have conspicuous rays. Most tropical hardwoods have a tight grain and many are dark or reddish under their sun-bleached exterior. Folks who are haunted by persistent driftwood mysteries can send a 1x3x6-inch sample to the USDA Forest Service, Center for Wood Anatomy Research, Forest Products Laboratory, One Gifford Pinchot Drive, Madison, WI 53726-2398.

ORIGIN: Much of this wood probably comes from rivers, either by bank erosion or from loss of felled timber. Many tropical species are resistant to rot and may drift at sea for years.

DID YOU KNOW? Much of the tropical driftwood reaching Florida beaches is usable for woodworking. Beached species include beautiful woods such as mahogany and purpleheart.

Surfwood and Peat

RELATIVES: Surfwood may be from one of hundreds of tree species, including palms, conifers, and hardwoods.

IDENTIFYING FEATURES:

Surfwood is found as smooth, rounded wood pieces, generally hand-sized or smaller. Like driftwood, surfwood is difficult to identify to its tree species. Many pieces are too soft to reveal their grain. Occasionally, conspicuous clues can be seen, such as the uniform fibrous wood of a palm tree.

Beach-worn surfwood

Peat lumps are fist- to boulder-sized masses of dark vegetable matter. Most lumps eroded from the dune have been smoothed by the surf's sanding action. Occasionally, flat, tablelike formations many yards across become exposed on eroding beaches.

ORIGIN: Surfwood may be the last remnants of surf-sanded driftwood or the smoothed pieces of logs pounded into chunks by the sea. Peat is a composite of very old but only partially decayed vegetation. It forms in swampy areas like mangrove forests. Most Florida peat found on beaches is probably from mangrove matter. Peat is a clear indication that a beach is advancing on a former mangrove swamp behind the former dune.

Palm surfwood showing its fibrous grain

DID YOU KNOW? Peat within old red mangrove swamps can reach a depth of dozens of feet (several meters). It forms where there is little or no oxygen and it is acidic enough to dissolve the limestone bedrock beneath it. The acidity comes from organic acids produced by anaerobic decomposition.

Peat lumps from an eroded dune after a storm

Kapok tree thorns

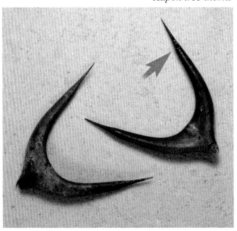

Bull's horn acacia thorns with ant entrance hole

Trumpet-tree trunks

Kapok Thorns, Bull's Horn Thorns, and Trumpet-Tree

RELATIVES: Kapok trees (Bombacaceae, the baobab-tree family), bull's horn trees (Fabaceae, the legume family), and trumpet-trees (Moraceae, the mulberry family) are distantly related.

IDENTIFYING FEATURES:

Kapok trees *(Ceiba pentandra)* are studded with numerous cone-shaped, corky thorns (technically, bark prickles) crowding their bulbous trunk and branches. The thorns are a perfect cone or may have a spiny tip and remnants of the tree's thin, formerly green bark.

Bull's horn trees *(Acacia cornigera)* grow dual thorns that look just like the tree's name. The hollow thorns begin growing at the base of the tree's compound leaves. Older thorns occupy woody branches.

Trumpet-trees *(Cecropia* spp.) have tall, thin trunks, with centers formed of hollow compartments. Beached portions include entire trunk sections or the papery compartments only.

ORIGIN: Kapok trees and trumpet-trees are native to Mexico, Central America, northern South America, and the Caribbean. Bull's horn is a native of Central and South America.

DID YOU KNOW? Kapok pods have seeds surrounded by fluffy fibers that were once commonly used in mattresses, pillows, and life jackets. Bull's horn trees and trumpet-trees are both protected by aggressive ants that live in the hollow thorns or trunk compartments and receive "bribes" of food from special leaf structures.

BEACH MINERALS

What are Beach Minerals?

Beach minerals are loosely defined here as the natural, nonliving, solid parts of the beach. Most of the beach's framework is mineral—its **sands** and underlying **rock**. Other minerals scattered throughout the beach include **stones** that have broken from the beach's rocky foundation and **fossils** (mineralized animal parts) that likewise have been uncovered by erosion.

True minerals have a homogeneous crystalline structure with a particular chemical composition and set of characteristics like color and hardness. Quartz, which makes up most beach sands, is a true mineral. So too are the various forms of calcium carbonate that make up limestone, the most common Florida beach rock. Beach limestone varies greatly and includes rocks that are essentially a sand-and-seashell granola glued together with calcite (the most common and stable form of calcium carbonate). As you'll see, a wide variety of animal parts can become rock. It is evidence of the living nature of beaches that even their inanimate parts are intertwined with the remnants of former lives.

Perhaps the most important aspect of beach minerals is how they reveal a beach's geological history. Sands, rocks, and fossils describe what beaches were like hundreds, thousands, even millions of years ago. The descriptions tell of how beaches were assembled, what forces have kept them in their constant state of change, and what their future is likely to hold.

Coquina limestone is a composite "rock" formed from cemented seashells

Florida Beach Sands

WHAT ARE THEY? Sand is pulverized rock (mostly quartz), shell, and other skeletons of plants and animals. The **Florida beach-sand sampler** to the right shows some of the variety in color, grain-size, and composition.

SIZE: Technically speaking, sand is finer than gravel and coarser than silt, with grains between 0.06 and 2.0 mm. Florida's beach sands average about 0.3 mm, but there is much variation among and within beaches. Finer sands are found on Gulf beaches, in northeastern Florida, during summer, in the dune, and in the offshore bar. Coarser sands occur on mid-Atlantic beaches, during winter, and on the lower beach.

ORIGIN: Most of the quartz in Florida's beach sands washed down rivers from the Appalachians beginning roughly 25 million years ago. This sand has moved north to south on each coast while being eroded and deposited over millions of years of sea-level changes. Carbonates from shell and other skeletal bits came from the ocean and may be just as old, although the sea is still making this material. Shells are broken to bits by the surf, and by the shell-munching actions of sponges, mollusks, crabs, and fishes.

DID YOU KNOW? The whitest sands are nearly 100% quartz. Amber sands have aged seashell bits. Orange sands are rusty from iron oxides. Dark, coarse grains are often fossilized bone or teeth. Dark peppering among paler grains is often ilmenite, an iron titanium oxide. Many Keys beaches are made from crunched coral bits and coralline algae.

Crooked Is., NW

Little Talbot Is., NE

Casey Key, SW

Guana River Beach, NE

Sanibel Is., SW

Smyrna Dunes, NE

Long Key, Keys

Archie Carr Refuge, SE

Wilma Key, Keys

Cape Florida, SE

279

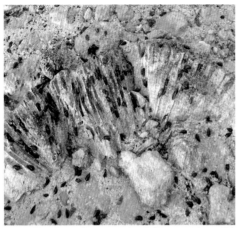
Key Largo limestone (with false cerith snails)

High tide at Blowing Rocks, Jupiter Island

Coquina limestone of Washington Oaks State Park

Rocky Beaches

WHAT ARE THEY? Rocky beaches have their underlying limestone exposed to the ocean. These are natural rocks that are covered by sand on most beaches. Outcroppings on Keys beaches are mostly **Key Largo limestone**. Atlantic outcroppings north of the Keys are mostly worn layers of **coquina limestone** composed of cemented shell and sand.

SIZE: Approaching a mile (1.6 km) long and as high as 8 ft (2.5 m) above the surrounding sand.

ORIGIN: Most exposed rocks along the central Atlantic coast are part of the Anastasia Formation, which formed roughly 500,000 to 100,000 years ago during the Late Pleistocene Epoch. Outcroppings of the Key Largo Limestone Formation are from a relict coral reef that stopped growing about 120,000 years ago.

DID YOU KNOW? At Blowing Rocks Preserve, Jupiter Island, waves crashing into the ventilated rocky caves can force vertical plumes of spray as high as a two-story building. Rocky ledges of the Anastasia Formation make up a series of reefs that run parallel to the beach in southeastern Florida. The troughs between these reefs are an important source of beach sands. Reef depth greatly influences incident wave energy and helps determine many aspects of Florida's Atlantic beaches.

Beach Stone, Worm Rock, and **Pumice**

Beach Stone   Worm Rock   Pumice

WHAT ARE THEY? Beach stones are smooth limestone pebbles or cobbles formed from fine, cemented sands. They vary in color from dark gray to tan and often have bulges and pits. **Honeycomb worm rocks** are worn pieces of reef formed by polychaete worms in the family Sabellariidae (see page 124). The rocks are made of sand and shell bits cemented with a sticky protein. **Pumice** is a floating rock formed during explosive volcanic eruptions. These are rocks of frozen foam, infused with gas bubbles held by fragile volcanic glass and other minerals.

SIZE: All are generally less than 1 ft (30 cm) in diameter.

ORIGIN: Atlantic beach stones were formed during the Pleistocene Epoch, roughly 120,000 years ago and were part of the Anastasia Formation. Gulf-coast beach stones are older, between 120,000 and 20 million years, and are from Ft. Thompson, Bermont, Caloosa-hatchee, or Hawthorn Group formations. Honeycomb worm rock is from the recent reef-building of worms in the surf zone. Pumice is likely to have drifted from the eastern Caribbean.

DID YOU KNOW? Some beached pumice has been cut into blocks and bears the mortar from its use as a building material.

Beach stones

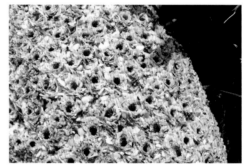

Honeycomb worm rock

Pumice, with brick mortar (A) and surf-worn (B)

Color variations of pumice

281

Storm erosion uncovers broken coquina slabs

Coquina limestone

Flat coquina from thin layers of dark mineral sands

Coquina

WHAT ARE THEY? Coquina is limestone made of cemented shell and sand. It is named for the coquina clam (see page 109), which is one of the rock's most common shelly elements. Some coquina is mostly shell and some is mostly sand. **Flat dark coquina** is composed of layers of mineral sand that is largely ilmenite, an iron-titanium oxide (see page 11). This thin, dark coquina is much heavier than coquina formed of shell and quartz. Coquina limestone is part of the Anastasia Formation.

SIZE: The largest coquina rocks are flattened, reaching the size of a driveway.

ORIGIN: Coquina began to form when waves swept together layers of sand and shell hash (see page 11). As the shells partially dissolved, they became bathed in water saturated with calcium carbonate. In this saturated water, calcite formed, cementing the sand-shell mix together in layers. Most coquina formed about 120,000 years ago when sea level was 7-20 ft (2-6 m) higher than it is today.

DID YOU KNOW? The Anastasia Formation of coquina is named for Anastasia Island, the site where the Spanish quarried this limestone to construct the massive Castillo de San Marcos in St. Augustine. Many Atlantic-coast beaches have layers of coquina limestone several feet beneath their sands.

Fossils

Crab Stones   Other Fossils

Crab stones

WHAT ARE THEY? Fossils are parts of living things that have been dug up (the Latin *fossus* means a hole in the ground). On beaches, the surf does the digging. Although there is no age requirement, most fossils are pretty old and have been buried long enough to become mineralized or surrounded by rock.

Arrow shows the claw of a crab that got stoned

Crab stones are ghost crabs (see page 132) that were trapped in their burrows by ancient storm-wash and gradually turned to limestone. They are found among other beach stones and coquina rock. Occasionally, the persistent, heavy remnants of **whale earbones** tumble free in the surf. Those pictured are from baleen whales. Fossil shells like the scallops *Nodipecten* (**A**) and *Lyropecten* (**B**), along with **urchin-test stones** (**C**), erode from coastal deposits. Like crab stones, urchin-test stones are buried animals (sea urchins, see page 142) that were turned into limestone. Some of the most familiar **vertebrate fossils** from coastal deposits are **shark's teeth**.

Whale earbones

SIZE: Most beach fossils are hand-sized or smaller and collect with similar-sized stones and shell on the lower beach. Whale earbones may be the size of cobbles and the smallest shark's teeth fragments may be the size of coarse sand grains. On beaches like Casey Key (see page 279), dark fossil grains make up a significant fraction of beach sand.

Scallop species (A,B) and urchin-test stone (C)

283

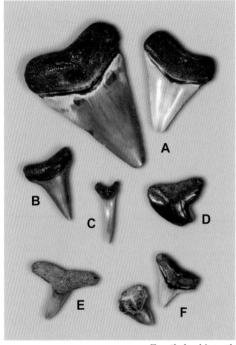

Fossil shark's teeth

A fossil mix of animals, both aquatic and terrestrial

ORIGIN: Because beach dynamics mix many ages of material together, beach fossils may span ages from recent times to more than 25 million years. Most beach fossils are from the Pleistocene Epoch (10,000 to 1.8 million years ago). During this epoch, Florida's coastline advanced and retreated with four major changes in sea level, each corresponding to an ice age.

DID YOU KNOW? Florida has no dinosaur fossils. The state is too young. The peninsula's highest ridge has been above water only for the last 25 million years or so. The most prized of Florida fossils may be teeth of the extinct, giant white shark *(Carcharocles megalodon)*. The robust, triangular teeth can be as large as an outstretched hand. The shark itself was as long as a bus.

Vertebrate beach fossils:

A. **Great white shark teeth** *(Carcharodon carcharias)*

B. **Mako shark tooth** *(Isurus)*

C. **Sand shark tooth** *(Odontaspis)*

D. **Tiger shark tooth** *(Galeocerdo cuvier)*

E. **Lemon shark tooth** *(Negaprion brevirostris)*

F. **Requiem shark teeth** *(Carcharhinus)*

G. **Pufferfish teeth** *(Diodon)*

H. **Alligator skin-bone (osteoderm)** *(Alligator mississippiensis)*

I. **Deer leg bone** *(Odocoileus)*

J. **Horse molar** *(Equus)*

K. **Garfish scale** *(Lepisosteus)*

L. **Pond-turtle carapace bone** (family Emydidae)

M. **Shark's teeth fragments**

HAND OF MAN

What Have We Had a Hand In?

A lot. Humans are arguably one of the most important elements of a living beach. We contribute to, consume, manage, and shape many of the other elements of the beach. Even on remote beaches, the synthetic crumbs of our existence are ubiquitous. Just as beaches record connections between the "natural" components of continents and seas, coastal sands also receive our own well-traveled discards.

The acquaintance we have with many of the items that follow (after all, we made them) makes this section different from the others in this book. But even recognizable things can have unfamiliar stories. Questions about these beach-finds abound: Who made it? Where did it come from? Why are there so many of such an odd item? How did it get here?

In some ways, the human influence on beaches can be heavy-handed. One of our most profound effects seems to arise from our desire for a permanent presence on the beaches we love. Living persistently on beaches has required battle against the perpetual forces that shape the shore. These skirmishes have brought about both drastic measures and unintended consequences.

And yet, it is the peaceful beauty of beaches that beguiles us. Visitors taken by the joy of the beach often feel compelled to leave testament of their spiritual experience. And further, many actively respond to a sense of obligation to conserve what pleases us.

A chert-stone arrow point made by the Ais (5000–300 years B.P.), found in the surf near Sebastian Inlet

Beach Shrines and Sand Castles

WHAT ARE THEY? Beach shrines are human constructions using local beach debris as ephemeral art. **Sand castles** may include sand sculptures of all shapes, using either the bucket-mold, hand-smoothed, or wet-drip methods. Each ranges in size from small to large. Although most are limited by day-length, work ethic, and location relative to the tide, some are added to by subsequent beach visits and may become several yards in diameter.

HOW COME? Why did the Druids construct Stonehenge? Perhaps, because they could . . . or perhaps because they had time to kill? Like Stonehenge, the cultural significance of many beach shrines may remain a mystery. One hypothesis is that a trip to the beach can bring about a sense of whimsy in just about anyone.

DID YOU KNOW? Shrines we've seen have included the creative use of pig bones, underwear, sponges, doll heads, fish heads, mismatched flip-flops, mummified stingrays, and a plethora of colorful plastic drift-toys—all common beach-finds. Sand castles formed of moist sand are typically on the lower beach. This makes their average lifespan in the Panhandle about twice as long as on the Atlantic (see tides, page 18).

Emotive expression in a flotsam collage

A driftwood dragon

Pyramids bejeweled with bittersweet shells

287

One Spanish coin can start a lifetime search

Cob coins of gold (A) and silver (B,C)

Discarded dunnage snapped by heavy cargo

Treasure and Dunnage

Treasure   Dunnage

WHAT ARE THEY? Some beach treasures are of silver or gold. Finds are from roughly 2,000 colonial-era shipwrecks within Florida waters. Prominent wrecks include Spanish galleons from the "treasure fleets" of 1715 and 1733 that beached during hurricanes, scattering jewelry, personal items, and **cob coins**. Silver cobs are found as greenish or blackish, rough-margined disks (**B**). Cleaning reveals their stamps and dates (**C**). Unlike treasure, **dunnage** lumber is jetsam (jettisoned) cargo. These packaging boards serve as skids, braces, or chocks for heavy shipping freight and are generally rough, North American or tropical hardwoods of high compression strength.

HOW COME? Florida beaches are at an intersection between former Spanish fleet routes and hurricane paths. Dunnage is tossed from the many international cargo ships plying the Atlantic and Gulf.

DID YOU KNOW? Florida's Treasure Coast (Indian River to Martin Counties) was named following numerous treasure finds beginning in the 1960s. Cob coins were struck from the end (cabo) of a bar of silver or gold and hand-trimmed. Famed silver pieces-of-eight (8 Reales de Plata) and gold doubloons are among recent treasure-finds. Tropical dunnage can provide beautifully figured wood for small woodworking projects.

Ships and Boats

WHAT ARE THEY? Beaches punctuate the final sea voyages of many vessels and their parts. Primitive boats and rafts from Cuban **balseros** (rafters) are part of an informal sea-exodus from Cuba to Florida that has involved thousands of fragile vessels made from dunnage lumber, Styrofoam, innertubes, and auto parts. Other boat parts include **yacht fenders** and **teakwood**. Atlantic-coast erosion often reveals parts of boats abandoned during Prohibition-era rum-running from the Bahamas. **Foam polyurethane** is used as floatation in boats and has a long life at sea.

This balsero craft had an old Russian car engine

HOW COME? Balsero-fashioned craft are testaments to the difficulty, desperation, and ingenuity in a land just upstream. Rumrunning was the drug-running of the 1920s and 1930s, when illicit cargo was more valuable than boats. A teak rudder from a rumrunner is shown (right). Foam is one of the most common floating remnants of foundered vessels.

1920s teak rudder *Present-day yacht fender*

DID YOU KNOW? The ingenuity of balseros is an answer to scarcity and the covert nature of raft-building in Cuba. Boat-construction materials are evidence of intent to leave the country and are illegal. Between 1959 and 1994, more than 63,000 people left Cuba by rafting and reached the U.S. alive. At least 16,000 additional balseros did not survive the passage.

Foam polyurethane is used as flotation in boats

Man-overboard radio beacons

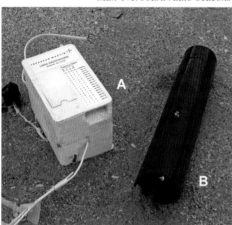

Balloon radiosonde (A) and dropsonde (B)

An expended graphite-epoxy motor

Sondes and Rocket Parts

Sondes and Beacons   *Rocket Parts*

WHAT ARE THEY? Man-overboard radio beacons are used to mark the last-known points of people in the water. **Balloon radiosondes** measure and broadcast atmospheric data on their way up to 100,000 ft (31,000 m), and often have shreds of the balloon that carried them. **Dropsondes** are GPS and atmospheric computers that broadcast data during their fall from hurricane-hunter aircraft. **Graphite-epoxy motors** (GEMs) are solid-fuel boosters that fall from the sky after helping to launch Boeing Delta II and IV rockets, as well as Lockheed Martin's Atlas 5.

HOW COME? Man-overboard beacons are on most vessels and occasionally wash overboard even when there is no distress. Radiosondes and dropsondes are disposable instruments extensively deployed to forecast hurricanes and other weather. Cape Canaveral rockets launch over the Atlantic so that expended boosters don't fall on our terrestrial interests.

DID YOU KNOW? Although beacons and sondes contain relatively expensive electronics, they are not worth much on eBay. GEMs helped launch most of the GPS satellites used by hurricane-measuring dropsondes. The GEM boosters formerly contained grains of rubber or aluminum mixed with an oxidizer such as ammonium perchlorate.

Sea Heroes (Drift Toys) and Seaglass (Beach Glass)

Sea Heroes

Seaglass

WHAT ARE THEY? Sea heroes are plastic, once-cherished, childhood friends set adrift on the open seas. These little synthetic figures often bear evidence of their lengthy voyage—sun-fading, lost limbs, and accumulations of fuzz, crust, and barnacles. **Seaglass** pieces are broken bottle shards that have been rounded, smoothed, and etched by sand and surf.

HOW COME? Sea heroes may be either lost or discarded. Seaglass shows the sea's way of making common and disdained items into interesting and beautiful objects. Although seaglass has human origins, it ends up on beaches the same way seashells do—by tumbling within waves and currents. A piece of seaglass may move on and off the beach for many decades.

DID YOU KNOW? Variations on the classic plastic army man and baby-doll arms and legs seem to be the most common sea heroes. We've collected nearly a hundred plastic figures and no two are the same. Many figures may be from developing countries upstream, having long ago fallen out of favor with sophisticated American kids. For those in search of an eccentric hobby, look no further. Seaglass colors from most to least common are (generally) brown, green, clear, light green, dark green, light blue, dark blue, yellow, and red.

A sampling of sea heroes and drift toys

Seaglass arrives along with shell hash

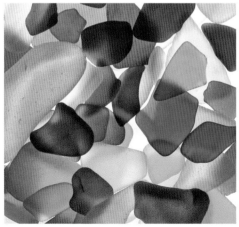

Brown seaglass is common, blue is rare

291

Foil balls, 2 in (5 cm), tell of human foibles

Sponge balls (A), clay pebbles (B), 1/2 in (1.2 cm)

Roll-on balls, typically 0.4-1.4 in (1.0-3.6 cm)

Nurdles, max 3/16 in (5 mm)

Balls and Nurdles

Foil Balls, Roll-on Balls, and Nurdles   *Sponge and Clay Balls*

WHAT ARE THEY? Aluminum **foil balls** are buoyant elements of galley waste. Taprogge **sponge balls** are little scrubbers used by electrical power plants, desalination plants, and other industries to clean fouling organisms from filter tubes. Liapor **expanded clay pebbles** are construction materials used to make lightweight concrete block. **Roll-on balls** are hollow plastic spheres that top the common underarm deodorant applicator. **Nurdles** is the colloquial name entirely too cute for industrial resin pellets of HDPE (high-density polyethylene). The pellets are precursors for plastic products.

HOW COME? Foil balls are symptoms of two common habits—wadding up used cooking foil and tossing trash overboard. Coastal industries using sponge balls make attempts to recapture them after their use, but many end up escaping into the wild. Roll-on deodorant containers are part of the worldwide circulation of discarded plastic. The balls are the most persistent part of the deodorant package and may float for decades. Clay pebbles and nurdles are spilled during mass transport at sea.

DID YOU KNOW? Little turtles eat nurdles, although the plastics are bad for them. About 85% of small loggerhead sea turtles washed ashore in Florida have ingested plastics.

Container Seals and Packaging

Plastic container seals

WHAT ARE THEY? Container seals record that shipboard containers have not been opened. Containers (isotainers) are the international, semi-trailer-sized boxes that haul just about every product on the planet. On a smaller scale, these products have their own individual **packaging**, most often plastic.

HOW COME? Plastic floats, and it persists for decades. Beached container seals reveal the maritime tradition of overboard discard, as well as the astronomical volume of goods shipped in containers. Plastic packaging is multinational, which may indicate its most common source: international shipping. Plastics also enter the sea after washing down rivers.

An international array of beached trash

DID YOU KNOW? Worldwide, over 18 million shipping containers made more than 200 million trips in 2005. Household (and shipboard) plastic packaging enters the ocean at an estimated rate of 6.4 million tons per year, reports the National Academy of Sciences. This is roughly ten times what gets recycled. In an unscientific sampling of languages that label packaging found on Florida beaches, English and Spanish were most common, followed by Chinese, Greek, Korean, Arabic, Portuguese, and Japanese. Most household plastics become brittle in sunlight after several years and break into tiny shards. These remnants are ingested by many sea animals.

Possible component of an overboard survival kit

293

Stone crab (A) and lobster (B) floats, 8 in (20 cm)

Deep-water floats, 6 in (15 cm)

A longline "bullet" buoy, 18 in (46 cm)

Hand-made floats from old foam and flipflops (inset)

Fishing Discards *(Floats)*

WHAT ARE THEY? Almost every fishing activity involves some sort of float. **Stone crab trap floats (A)** bear an X-number, **spiny lobster trap floats (B)** bear a C-number, and blue crab floats have a V-number identification. Most of these are foam polystyrene and painted colors unique to the fishers who used them. Hollow, hard-plastic spheres are **deep-water floats** used for deep longlines (thousands of fish hooks on a long, heavy monofilament line) and trawl (vessel-towed) nets. PVC-foam **bullet buoys** are used for surface long-lines. Primitive, **hand-made floats** are often fashioned from reused flotsam such as polystyrene blocks, plastic jugs, and even used flipflops.

HOW COME? Many floats that reach beaches may be casualties of broken lines and stormy seas. But most floats and other fishing gear at the end of its useful life get disposed of at sea. Because floats float, they are among the most common types of fishing gear on beaches. Hand-made floats are probably from developing countries where various kinds of beach flotsam are welcome raw materials for fishing supplies.

DID YOU KNOW? The most traditional artisanal floats are club-shaped logs. Glass fishing floats formerly used by the Portuguese are rare now. Most sold in curio shops are reproductions.

Fishing Discards
(Floats and Traps)

Compressed Floats

Traps

Depth-compressed foam fishing floats

WHAT ARE THEY? Compressed fishing floats are small, hardened versions of can-shaped, football-shaped, and other floats. Beached **traps** (pots) are constructed of wood, plastic, or wire mesh and are designed to catch stone crabs, blue crabs, or spiny lobster. Each trap has (or had) a funnel entrance, latchable lid, marker float, and rope.

HOW COME? Some floats attached to lost nets sink to great depths where they are crushed by the tremendous pressure. Still buoyant, they are presumably freed when the line holding them disintegrates. Traps probably end up on beaches by accident and are evidence of the power of storms to move even deep objects over long distances. Some old traps have become miniature reefs with a wide variety of bottom creatures growing on them. But modern traps are often treated with copper oxides that are toxic to encrusting critters. Although stone crab and spiny lobster traps come from offshore waters, most blue crab traps come from coastal estuaries.

A partially buried spiny lobster trap

DID YOU KNOW? Depth-compressed floats often have seabottom animals growing on them, indicating that they were once sunken. A typical four-inch (10-cm) diameter can-float dragged to 100 ft (31 m) has about 1,600 lbs (730 kg) of pressure on it.

A blue crab trap in the swash zone

A crab trap showing the lid latch (lath) in use

Spiny lobster and stone crab lid latches

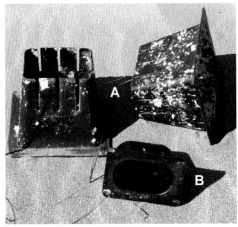

Spiny lobster (A) and stone crab (B) trap funnels

Fishing Discards *(Trap Parts)*

Lid Latches and Funnels

WHAT ARE THEY? These black-plastic trap parts are some of the most common fishing debris on Florida beaches. **Lid latches** (laths) hold the lids closed on both plastic and wooden traps for lobster and stone crabs. **Trap funnels** are entrances to traps that allow crustaceans to enter but not escape. Spiny lobster funnels end in a rectangle, and stone crab funnels end in an oval.

HOW COME? Lid latches are required to be fastened with a corrodible nail that eventually releases the lid after the trap is long abandoned. This design is an attempt to reduce the time that lost traps continue to collect their target crustaceans. Lost and abandoned traps are common. Wood traps slowly disintegrate, freeing their floating parts, including latches, bait cups, and funnels. These peculiar plastic pieces are persistent enough to puzzle our beachcombing progeny for hundreds of years.

DID YOU KNOW? The commercial season for trapping spiny lobster in Florida waters is early August through March. Stone crab season is open October 15 through May 15. Trappers in 2004 harvested about 3 million pounds (1360 metric tons) of stone crab claws and about 4.5 million pounds (2040 metric tons) of spiny lobster.

Fishing Discards *(Trap Parts)*

Trap Tags and Bait Cups   Octopus Pot

WHAT ARE THEY? In Florida waters, stone crab traps are required to have **tags** and floats bearing an X-number, and spiny lobster traps require a C-number. The tags are plastic and bear information about the owner's permit. Older tags were clasped on, but newer tags are nailed or stapled. **Stone crab bait cups** hold the bait (usually fish heads or pigs' feet) within traps (pots) set for stone crabs. **Octopus pots** are open plastic jugs set to catch octopi.

HOW COME? The C-number for lobster-trap identification stands for "crawfish," and the X-number for stone-crab gear stands for the crab's family, Xanthidae. Numbers identify trap owners to fish and wildlife officers. Bait cups are one of many trap parts freed when traps break apart. The octopus pots that beach are without the concrete or stone that originally lined their flattened side. Unbaited and lidless, they attract octopi only as a hiding place. The pots may come from Mexico where nearly 40 thousand pounds (18 metric tons) of octopi are caught for food each year.

DID YOU KNOW? Trap tags similar to ones from Florida fisheries occasionally come from traps set for American lobster *(Homarus americanus)* off New England and Canada. Plastic fishing gear is black because of the color's resistance to degradation in sunlight.

Styles of annual trap tags 1998–2006

Stone crab trap bait cups

Octopus pots are usually found battered and worn

297

Shrimp trawl netting

Beached gill net showing float line

Trap line

Fishing Discards *(Nets and Line)*

WHAT ARE THEY? Fishing nets are made of synthetic twine or nylon monofilament and are designed either to strain things from the water or to tangle them up. **Shrimp trawl nets** are of the straining variety, are made of stiff twine, and have meshes generally too small to get a fist through. Fish trawl nets are similar but may have larger meshes. **Gill nets** are either thin twine or monofilament and typically have a distinct float line (with floats) and a lead-cored line called a leadline. Most of these nets are not legally used within Florida's state waters, extending out 3 nautical miles into the Atlantic and 9 nautical miles into the Gulf. **Trap line** attaches buoys to traps and is nearly always black.

HOW COME? Shrimp and fish trawls are heavy nets dragged along the bottom by steel cables. Although the nets are strong enough to scrape up corals, sponges, and relatively large chunks of encrusted hardbottom, they occasionally encounter items too heavy to tear away from the sea floor, such as shipwrecks. Nets torn free of their tow vessels are subsequently moved by storms. Gill nets generally float at the surface and are either lost or discarded at sea. Trap line (rope) is made of braided polypropylene, chosen because it floats.

DID YOU KNOW? These nets often entangle interesting sea life.

Fishing Discards *(Miscellaneous)*

Baskets, Gloves, and
Glowsticks

Lobster Caller

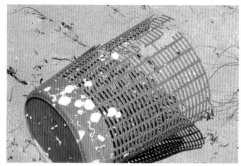

Seafood basket, 2 ft (60 cm)

WHAT ARE THEY? Seafood baskets are used on fishing and shrimping vessels to temporarily hold the catch. Latex **shrimp-heading gloves** are used by shrimpers as they pick shrimp from their trawl catch. **Fishing glowsticks** (lightsticks) are transparent plastic tubes containing cylume chemicals and fluorescent dyes. The sticks glow for several hours after an internal vial of hydrogen peroxide is broken. They have various attachment clips and rings. **Lobster callers** may be among the oddest of lost fishing gear. They are electronic emitters of an audible, periodic click believed to attract spiny lobsters into traps.

Shrimp-heading gloves

HOW COME? Most seafood baskets are damaged, indicating that they were discarded rather than lost. Shrimp-heading gloves and glowsticks are disposable items with a limited life. Glowsticks mark fishing buoys at night and are used as fish attractors on commercial longline hooks set to catch swordfish. Because they last only one night of fishing and the Atlantic longline fleet uses millions of hooks, glowsticks are one of the most common fishery items on the beach. Lobster callers are rare and presumably come from broken traps.

Fishing glowsticks, 3–6 in (8–15 cm)

DID YOU KNOW? During their brief use, glowsticks glow blue, green, yellow, white or pink.

Electronic lobster callers, 5 in (13 cm)

299

A Mylar balloon tells of inland festivities

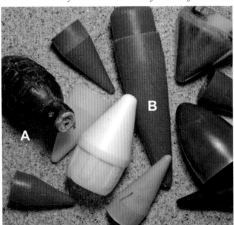

Hand grenade smoke bomb (A), firework tips (B)

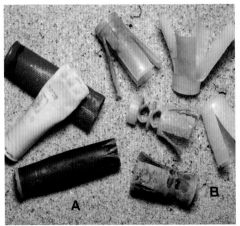

Shotgun shells (A) and plastic wadding (B)

Balloons, Fireworks, and Shotgun Discards

WHAT ARE THEY? Balloons that reach the beach were formerly filled with enough helium to keep them aloft. Latex balloons are often shredded, but **Mylar plastic balloons** are generally intact. Both balloon types typically have ribbons or strings attached. Tips from launched **fireworks** are common as plastic cones of many colors. Frequently found black-plastic hand grenades are spent **smoke bombs**. Plastic **shotgun shells** are generally missing their brass head and are merely a plastic casing. The shells fire a **plastic wadding** along with the lead shot.

HOW COME? Balloons illustrate the axiom that everything going up must come down. Balloons burst or leak their helium in the thin upper atmosphere and then fall to earth (or to sea). In this way, the joy of an inland birthday party can be transmitted for hundreds of miles. Fireworks end up in the ocean due to the common belief that water provides a safe location for ballistic revelry. The most common hunting on the ocean is probably of clay pigeons (skeet targets) launched from cruise ships. Both the shot wadding and the ejected casings float for many years.

DID YOU KNOW? Environmental concerns and passenger casualties have begun to curtail the use of shotguns on cruise ships.

Wax, Tar, and Oil

Surf-wax   Carnauba Wax   Tar

WHAT ARE THEY? Surf-wax is soft, pale, and often smells like coconut. When rubbed in lumpy layers, the wax gives surfers foot-traction on an otherwise slippery board. **Carnauba wax** is beached as hard, grayish or brownish chunks. The wax is harvested from fronds of the wax palm *(Copernicia cerifera)*, a native fan palm of Brazil, and transported by ship in commercial quantities. It is used in making varnishes, polishes, car wax, and candy. **Tarballs** are the sticky, semi-solid leftovers from weathered petroleum.

HOW COME? Surf-wax is rubbed onto boards at the beach, where Murphy's law dictates it will get dropped in the sand. The wax is not much good after that. Carnauba wax may fall from ships all over the Atlantic. The US Minerals Management Service reports that tanker-transported heavy fuel oils and tanker sludge discharges are the principal sources of oceanic tarballs. Sludge discharges result from illegal tank-washing at sea. Known spills have only a small annual contribution to beach tar.

DID YOU KNOW? Gulf tarballs "fingerprinted" for their chemical signatures were found to have originated as petroleum from Middle Eastern and Alaskan North-slope crudes, Florida's most commonly transported oil. Sunscreen assists a good first effort in removing tar from feet.

Surf-wax (A) and carnauba wax (B)

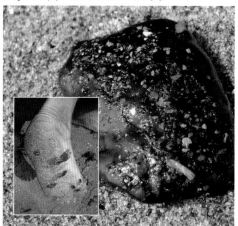

Tarballs come from many sources

Pinellas beaches after a heating oil spill, 1993

301

A groomed beach, Marco Island

A driving beach, St. Johns County

Dune crossover and steps

Sand fencing behind a sandy sea-rocket mound

Beach Grooming, Driving, Crossovers, and Sand Fences

Beach Grooming   Beach Driving   Crossovers and Sand Fences

WHAT ARE THEY? Grooming flattens the beach and mechanically removes the wrack. **Beach driving** is the use of beaches by private vehicles. **Dune crossovers** are decks, steps, and ramps on the dune and beach. **Sand fences** are posted lengths of plastic mesh or wired wooden slats.

HOW COME? The beach-grooming debate outlines divergent expectations. One is that beaches should be clean surfaces free of litter and biological material, even if their removal means the loss of shorebirds, beachcombing finds, and other aesthetics. An alternative expectation is that true litter can be plucked by hand, leaving beaches as functioning habitats where beachhoppers, seabeans, bird life, and natural sand sculpturing are well worth the inconvenience they cause. Public beach driving (legal in parts of Duval, St. Johns, Volusia, Gulf, and Walton Counties) stems from the expectation that beaches should be more convenient. Although crossovers can be obtrusive, expensive, and vulnerable to storms, the structures are seldom shared between properties. Sand fences function to prevent human access, to defend beach property lines, and to keep wind-driven sand on the beach and out of the dune. They seem only slightly poorer at attracting sand than beach plants.

Armoring, Groynes, and Jetties

Armoring and Groynes   Jetties

WHAT ARE THEY? Coastal **armoring** includes walls, rockpiles, and sandbags placed so that they reduce the movement of sand on the upper beach and dune. Walls are steel, aluminum, concrete, or wood, and may be vertical or inclined. **Groynes** are constructed perpendicular to the shore so that they interrupt the longshore drift of moving surf sand. **Jetties** are typically piles of rock lining channels into inlets.

HOW COME? Armoring is constructed to retain the existing sand beneath beachfront yards and buildings. Unintended consequences of armoring include an acceleration of erosion in front of and beside the structure, often leaving a hardened promontory in place of sandy beach and dune. Armoring is legally built in Florida following permits issued during frequent emergencies. Groynes promote accretion on their up-drift side, cause net erosion on their down-drift side, and have fallen out of favor for beach-sand management. Jetties have sand-starvation drawbacks similar to groynes, but remain a popular option for keeping sand out of deep inlet channels.

DID YOU KNOW? The proportion of Florida beaches with hard armoring is roughly 20% and increasing. Rising sea level is likely to accelerate the use of creative engineering in attempts to stop beaches from moving.

A steel sheetpile seawall performing as armoring

Groynes attached to a concrete seawall

The longest jetty is on an inlet's up-drift side

A short, down-drift jetty

303

Projects involve heavy equipment on land and sea

Pipes move offshore sand in a seawater slurry

Water drains into the surf and the sand is spread

A newly engineered beach

Artificial Nourishment

WHAT IS IT? **Artificial beach nourishment** is the accretion of beaches by artificial means. Most commonly this involves trucking sand from inland quarries or pumping sand from offshore sources. This process is also known as "beach renourishment," "beach restoration," and "dredge and fill."

HOW COME? Most projects take place where there is an unsatisfactory sand buffer between the sea and valuable structures built on the dune crest. Where seawalls, revetments, or buildings occupy the beach, artificial nourishment provides a beach that would otherwise only be possible if the structures were moved. Benefits to tourism and natural resources are also cited as justifications for nourishment projects, with the debatable assumption that there is a correlation between beach-width and use by tourists and wildlife.

DID YOU KNOW? Creating a living beach is difficult. Artificial beach projects smother existing swash-zone animals, beach plants, and their seeds with sterile sand, and tend to create berms that are wider, flatter, and harder than natural beaches. After about two years of surf action and colonization by plants and animals, many artificial beaches can be as alive as natural beaches. Federal, state, and local government funding for artificial nourishment in Florida ranges from 10 to 70 million dollars per year.

Lighthouses and Houses of Refuge

Cape St. George Lighthouse, 1852–2005

WHAT ARE THEY? Lighthouses are towers of wood, brick, or steel topped with a rotating light-source typically focused with a fresnel lens. Of Florida's 35 lighthouses, at least 26 are still lit each night. Only a few of these are close to beaches. **Houses of refuge** (HOR) were operated by the US Life-Saving Service, a predecessor of the US Coast Guard. Ten stations were built on the Atlantic and one near Pensacola. The house at Gilbert's Bar, Hutchinson Island, is the most unchanged of these structures.

HOW COME? Lighthouses were built to aid navigation around reefs and capes and into inlets. The 153-year-old tower at Cape St. George crumbled into the sea in 2005. The lighthouse was originally constructed hundreds of yards from the moving beach. HORs were conceived as refuge stations for shipwrecked sailors. Many added towers during the World Wars and were used as watch stations for enemy ships and submarines.

DID YOU KNOW? The Gilbert's Bar HOR (1876–present) has survived many hurricanes due to the Anastasia rock formation surrounding it. One of the last remaining HOR watch-towers at Cape Malabar (Floridana Beach) was toppled by Hurricane Frances in 2004. Other historic beach structures include forts at Amelia Island, Egmont Key, and Key West.

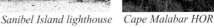

Sanibel Island lighthouse   *Cape Malabar HOR*

Gilbert's Bar HOR, Hutchinson Island

305

A loggerhead sea turtle bearing a metal flipper-tag

Morning nest-counts take place spring through fall

Nests are marked to measure their hatching success

Conservation *(Sea Turtles)*

WHAT IS IT? Because sea turtles are endangered, live coastally, and depend on sandy shorelines for their reproduction, many sea turtle **conservation** activities take place on beaches. Some turtles found nesting or stranded on the beach may have been identified with a numbered, stainless-steel **flipper-tag**. **Morning nest-counts** occur on about 800 miles (1300 km) of Florida beaches each nesting season (spring–summer).

HOW COME? Sea turtle tags help researchers monitor the travels and fates of sea turtles. Morning nest-counts serve to keep track of sea turtle reproduction and population trends. Nest surveyors often use small all-terrain motorcycles with low-pressure balloon tires to do this work. Their careful use leaves minimal ruts and does not harm advancing beach plants. Some researchers identify nests with cordons or simple stakes. The conspicuous markers protect nests from human activity and facilitate finding hatched and unhatched eggs for hatch-success inventories following the incubation period (about two months). The majority of nests on most beaches are not marked and do not suffer from just a few human footprints. Where major construction projects take place, such as beach nourishment, as many nests as possible are moved out of the way.

DID YOU KNOW? About 90% of sea turtle nesting in the US occurs in Florida.

Conservation
(Shorebirds and Beach Clean-ups)

American oystercatcher with bands and radio

WHAT ARE THEY? Researchers apply numbered and colored **bands** to birds in order to track their movements and fates. Some larger bands can be read with binoculars. Birds are also tracked with tiny **radio transmitters** and a trailing antenna. **Posted shorebird nesting areas** are sections of beach where entry by humans or dogs could cause birds to abandon their eggs and chicks. Only a few nesting areas are posted. Circling or agitated birds on the upper beach should be a sign that one's presence is unappreciated. **Beach clean-ups** are organized efforts to pick up trash from the beach.

HOW COME? Birds that are banded or tracked by radio reveal important information to resource managers trying to reduce threats to bird populations. Posted shorebird nesting areas protect birds from foot traffic and disturbance, as long as the signs are heeded. The most extensive beach clean-ups are sponsored by nonprofit conservation groups. Smaller scale efforts take place when individuals fill a small trash bag during casual beach walks. It is rumored that the experience gives one a unique satisfaction.

DID YOU KNOW? Careful behavior allowing birds their space brings about successful shorebird nesting even near highly developed areas.

Sign posting a shorebird nesting area

Clean-ups are a great excuse to beachcomb

307

Beach Quests

Although many beachcombers delight in the beach itself, others are driven by quests. These are the searches for uncommon finds whose prospects reinforce the beachcombing addiction. The rarest items can prompt legendary pursuits and become the symbolic excuse for a lifetime of beach adventures.

The facing page briefly outlines tactics for **where**, **when**, and **how** to target some of the many potential quests on Florida beaches. These tactics are the most likely times and places among many opportunities that are more fully described in the referenced pages. Even more research may be helpful. Knowing "habits" and having a complete "search image" are critical to recognizing rare opportunities. But the most important element in fulfilling a quest is persistence. Beaches are places where every footstep and every tide brings something different. An adequately persistent and prepared beachcomber will be able to fulfill all of these Florida beach quests, and even casual combers will find a few. Good luck!

The Green Flash

Gulf coast and western Keys, winter following a cold front, stare just before sundown, see **page 24**

By-the-wind Sailors

Central Atlantic coast, winter following east winds, search the recent tide line, see **page 41**

Junonia

Cape Romano, spring tide low or on a calm day following a storm, search high and low, see **page 81**

Lion's Paw

All coasts, on a calm day following a storm, search high and low, see **page 96**

Spirula

Atlantic coast, fall season following strong east winds, search the recent tide line, see **page 121**

Nesting Sea Turtles

Brevard to Palm Beach Counties, June & July, attend a guided turtle walk, see **pages 150–153**

Sea Turtle Hatchling Emergence

Brevard to Palm Beach Counties, August, following a dry evening, stroll just before dawn, see **page 150**

Snowy Plover

St. Joe Peninsula to Santa Rosa Island, April, bring binoculars and admire from a distance, see **page 171**

North Atlantic Right Whale

Northeast coast, December–March, ask state park rangers about previous sightings, see **page 200**

Burrowing Four O'clock

Palm Beach County beach parks, summer, look for fuchsia flowers on eroded dunes, see **page 219**

Mary's Bean

Central Atlantic coast and Keys, October–December after strong east winds, turn the wrack, see **page 254**

Crab Stone

South Brevard County, spring tide low or on a calm day following a storm, see **page 283**

Shark's Tooth

Casey Key and Manasota Key, spring tide low or on a calm day following a storm, see **page 284**

Blue Seaglass

Palm Beach County, summer during low tide, search areas with shell hash, see **page 291**

The Future of Florida's Living Beaches

The future of changing things is continuing change. So might we paraphrase Greek philosopher Heraclitus of Ephesus, who about 2500 years ago noted, "the only constant is change."

He must have been a beachcomber.

There may be no clearer example of perpetual change than the lives and forms of living beaches. In predicting that change, it's a safe bet that the future will be as dramatic as the past. Some of this drama will involve a rising sea level, barrier islands rolling toward the mainland, and the sinking and budding-off of sandy shorelines, all with gradual changes punctuated by sudden shifts caused by tumultuous storms. Although the geological record assures us that these events will occur, only sea-level rise approaches predictability in its timing. Sea level is currently rising a little over an inch (about 3 cm) every ten years and is predicted to accelerate with global climate change.

Other beach changes have fuzzy forecasts based on socioeconomics and will occur at the whim of our own choices and compulsions. Buildings installed onto dunes are likely to continue fomenting our war with beach-change. Some of these battles will leave dunes of concrete and steel (see page 303) and other battles will involve engineering attempts to make beaches stay put (see page 304). But as we struggle to pile sand back between our construction and the sea, suffer unintended consequences of armored shores, and incur scattered losses of our bold handiwork, both private and public interests are likely to adapt. We will probably debate, decide, and change our decisions about beaches many times—where lines belong between beautifully dangerous and persistently safe, between private living space and public visitation, and between private rights and public resources.

Wilma Key, west of Key West. The island formed in 2005 as the storm surge from Hurricane Wilma retreated. Almost immediately upon its exposure, plovers, sandpipers, gulls, terns, cormorants, and pelicans landed to rest. In the island's first year, nesting roseate terns (see page 192) entrusted their eggs to Wilma's isolated, brilliant, coralline-algal sands. People also visited, with their spiritual experiences ranging from shell collecting to a wedding and a funeral.

Both because of us and in spite of us, beaches will change. Changes forecast over millennia are difficult to fathom or care about, but many beach changes will take place before our very eyes. In the span of our short lives, hurricanes will overwash tree growth, piling sand into prominent ridges, and in this process, entire island strands will creep landward. We will also bear witness as dunes build and melt into the surf, as inlets form and fill, as sandbars trade places with sand spits, and as our buildings crumble and are rebuilt.

On Crooked Island in the Florida Panhandle, the Gulf of Mexico returns to reclaim former beach from the existing pine forest.

Our relationship with living beaches is also changing. When we were introduced, Florida's beaches were a sparsely trodden wilderness and we were few. There were abundant resources, wildlife, and space to accommodate activities from turtle hunting to auto racing. But in a flash, Florida's living beaches have become thin islands of rarity, with facets of their life threatened with extinction.

Like each of the prominent forces that shape beaches, we help determine the course of change. We have no small role, having inserted ourselves into both geological and biological processes—the very lives of beaches. What we cause, and what we allow to pass, will determine the fates of the lively beaches we love. Perhaps, to have beaches live we must accept their fickle nature. Living beaches do not merely change; they are born of change. Without change, or with different changes, beaches would be something else entirely. More phenomena than place, defined by time as well as space, beaches intertwine processes and cycles of life like few other aspects of our world.

So it may be unimpressive to predict that recurring phenomena will recur, and that Heraclitus was right. Beaches will change. Seas will rise, sands will shift, islands will move, and our children will mature to both question and appreciate our wisdom. And every moment of life will be different.

Resources and Suggested Reading

Beach Features

Pilkey, Orrin H., Tracy Monegan Rice, and William J. Neal. *How to Read a North Carolina Beach.* Chapel Hill, NC: University of North Carolina Press, 2004.

Whitney, Ellie D., D. Bruce Means, and Anne Rudloe. *Priceless Florida.* Sarasota, FL: Pineapple Press, Inc., 2004.

Beach Animals

Andrews, Jean. *A Field Guide to Shells of the Florida Coast.* Houston, TX: Gulf Publishing Company, 1994.

Farrand, John Jr., editor. *The Audubon Society Master Guide to Birding: 1 Loons to Sandpipers, 2 Gulls to Dippers.* New York, NY: Alfred A. Knopf, Inc. 1983

Kaplan, Eugene H. *Southeastern and Caribbean Seashores.* Boston, MA and New York, NY: Houghton Mifflin Company, 1988.

Morris, Percy A. *A Field Guide to Shells of the Atlantic and Gulf Coasts and the West Indies.* Boston, MA and New York, NY: Houghton Mifflin Company, 1973.

Rehder, Harald A. *National Audubon Society® Field Guide to North American Seashells.* New York, NY: Alphred A. Knopf, Inc., 1981.

Ruppert, Edward E., and Richard S. Fox. *Seashore Animals of the Southeast.* Columbia, SC: University of South Carolina Press, 1988.

Stevenson, Henry M. *Vertebrates of Florida.* Gainesville, FL: University Press of Florida, 1976.

Voss, Gilbert L. *Seashore Life of Florida and the Caribbean.* Miami, FL: Banyan Books, Inc., 1976.

Witherington, Blair. *Sea Turtles.* St. Paul, MN: Voyageur Press, 2006.

research.myfwc.com

www.jaxshells.org

Beach Plants

Duncan, Wilbur H., and Marion B. Duncan. *Seaside Plants of the Gulf and Atlantic Coasts.* Washington, D.C. and London: Smithsonian Institution, 1987.

Littler, Diane Scullion, Mark M. Littler, Katina E. Bucher, and James N. Norris. *Marine Plants of the Caribbean.* England: Airlife Publishing Ltd, 1989.

Nellis, David W. *Seashore Plants of South Florida and the Caribbean.* Sarasota, FL: Pineapple Press, Inc., 1994.

Nelson, Gil. *The Shrubs and Woody Vines of Florida.* Sarasota, FL: Pineapple Press, Inc., 1996.

Perry, Ed, IV, and John V. Dennis. *Sea-Beans from the Tropics.* Malabar, FL: Krieger Publishing Company, 2003.

www.plantatlas.usf.edu

www.seabean.com

Beach Minerals

Brown, Robin C. *Florida's Fossils.* Sarasota, FL: Pineapple Press, Inc., 1988.

Hand of Man

Bush, David M., William J. Neal, Norma J. Longo, Kenyon C. Lindeman, Deborah F. Pilkey, Luciana Slomp Esteves, John D. Congleton and Orrin H. Pilkey. *Living with Florida's Atlantic Beaches.* Durham and London: Duke University Press, 2004.

www.beachcombers.org

www.dep.state.fl.us/beaches

Entries in **bold** indicate photos and illustrations.